discovering JERSEY

30 Circular Walks

with fascinating historical insights of Island life through the ages

John Mallett

Drawings by Sarah Williams
Maps by Colin Smith

This book is dedicated to my late wife Norma
who, sadly, was not able to share the pleasure of the
fruition of the seeds of Island walking she had sown.

Norma was a very special and wonderful person
and an inspiration and support without whom my life
would not have been so rich and fulfilled.

Proceeds raised by the sale of this book
will be donated to
Jersey Hospice Care.

Acknowledgements

My heartfelt thanks to Selwyn and Lizzie Haas for their substantial and generous donation that has been a tremendous help in ensuring that Norma's name will be widely and more enduringly remembered.

This book would not have been possible without the help of a number of people.

First and foremost to all those, previously mentioned, who helped me in a myriad of ways with the first book - again thank you. Together we have not only benefited Jersey Hospice Care to date, but also set the platform for this second book.

To all of you subscribers and walkers who responded so well to the first book and have requested more challenges from within a new book.

A really big thank you to Dave and Jackie Edwards for their path walking 'audit' work, well beyond the call of duty, and also to others who played their part, including David and Denise Rigby.

A thank you too to Colin Smith for the new maps and the embryo of the St. Helier Walk.

Thanks also to Lizzie Haas and Geraldine Hunt for editing, proof reading and general support.

The Core Visual Communication for again turning up trumps - a big thank you to Sarah Le Marquand, Creative Director and Kate Warren, Art Director for turning words, maps and drawings, into such a professional book, with both aplomb and expertise.

And to all those people and organisations, too many to list individually, who gave valuable time and information so readily - a big thank you.

John Mallett

Contents

Contents

Introduction

It all began with a small walking group of friends inspired by my late wife Norma. As the idea of a walking book in her memory developed, help, inspiration and enthusiasm blossomed in abundance from a wide range of people, but particularly from those who had known her.

This second book has been born out of insistent and persistent requests after an incredibly successful first book published seven years ago and re-printed three times. The aim remains as strong today as it did then - to help those who want to explore the Island, by pointing them directly, explicitly and simply to some of the best circular walks within Jersey.

Jersey is a wonderful, beautiful and picturesque island, full of charm, surprisingly rustic and unspoiled. It is best explored by path, track, lane and byway, where sweeping landscapes and vistas of beach, headland and countryside seem to appear around every corner. This new book unlocks, indeed encapsulates, more than a hint of that variety, particularly now lanes and byways make a more balanced inclusion and St. Helier is included for the first time.

A vibrant history is always close to hand. The first nomadic inhabitants arrived over 250,000 years ago and Jersey became an island some 8,000 years ago. The Island always has had interestingly different and often stormy relationships with various neighbours and countries. Thus to titillate and increase the overall pleasure the book again flavours the walks with historical appetisers and insights.

The format of this book may mirror the previous in design, but it is so much more than a simple update. Although still primarily for the more novice walker, there has been a strengthening to cater for both the exercise of walking and for the depth of historical interest. So, yes, the best of the previous walks have been retained and updated, but with a number of those walks extended, new walks introduced and St. Helier included - it is more a completely new book.

The order of the walks fundamentally follows a clockwise direction around the Island. In Walk 1, The Ultimate St. Martin, you have two hours plus in which to taste virtually every aspect that is good about island walking. If initially you did not wish to be so adventurous then Walk 9, Fern Valley and Walk 14, Portelet Nature Reserve and Common, give you inland valley features and seascape respectively, both in under the hour.

Schedules present the walks in order of both time and difficulty. Additionally, each walk is headed by a page of helpful information including terrain, time and distance. Not forgotten too is how to get to the start - so no excuses!

Over to you. Enjoy!

Rules, Codes and Cautions

In essence, rules, codes and cautions surround being considerate, careful and understanding. In a phrase 'sympathetic to and in harmony with the environment'.

Jersey Country Code

Guard against all risk of fire.

Keep to footpaths, particularly on cliffs.

Keep dogs under control and remove waste.

Take your litter home. Plastic and glass is dangerous to wildlife.

Do not pick wild plants. Leave them so others can enjoy them.

Do not disturb birds' nests or remove eggs.

Trees take years to grow, do not damage them by climbing those too small to take your weight or by breaking off branches.

Keep all ponds, streams and reservoirs clear of pollution.

Respect the peace and quiet of the natural habitats and avoid disturbing others.

Shut all gates.

Leave livestock, crops and machinery alone.

Take special care on country roads.

Do not ride bicycles on footpaths.

Take great care when walking along the foreshore at low water. Always check tide tables prior to exploration.

After searching under rocks, replace them as you found them.

Wear appropriate boots and clothing.

Above all, enjoy Jersey's unique environment and try to learn more about the many different habitats and species.

Rules, Codes and Cautions

continued ...

Dogs - probably the most numerous of offences - to be under complete control at all times and **dog waste picked-up and properly binned or taken home.**

Re-emphasis of **no fires**, matches, cigarette ends, etc.

Keep to any local and temporary notices e.g. relating to path closures.

Take **full and serious notice** of the individual walk cautions e.g. tide conditions, path conditions, covering your legs.

Accept that the walks shown do not necessarily mean or infer an automatic right of way.

While every care has been taken in the compilation of this book **no responsibility** can be accepted for inaccuracies or future changes in and around the walks.

Throughout the text, road names are shown as detailed on the local road-name plates and/or road signs. Accordingly some of the prefixes, e.g. Le, La, Les, shown within the map books may be omitted, and other small differences may occur.

Summary Map of Walks

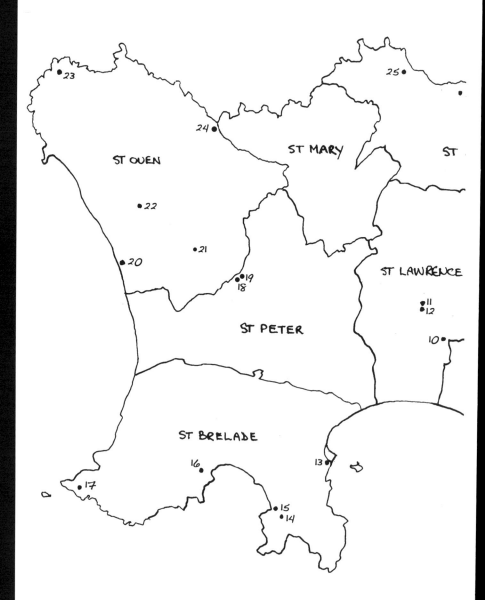

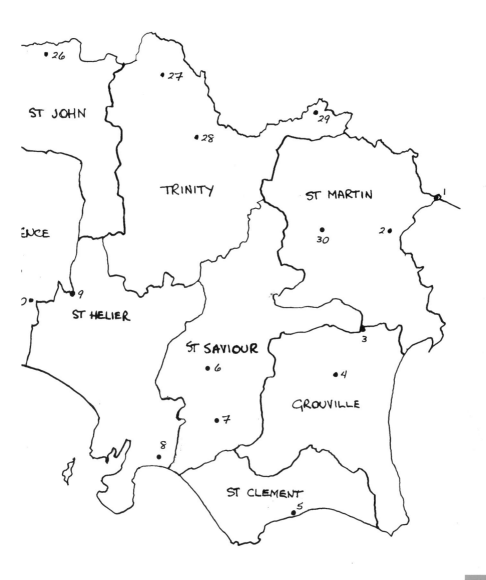

• 26

• 27

ST JOHN

• 29

• 28

TRINITY

ST MARTIN

1

ENCE

•
30

2 •

) •

• 9

ST HELIER

ST SAVIOUR

• 6

3

• 4

GROUVILLE

• 7

8
•

ST CLEMENT

• 5

The Ultimate St. Martin's

Parish	St. Martin
Special Features	Lovely sea views and superb coastal paths. A wonderful mix of woodland paths, countryside lanes and tracks. Excellent and wide ranging historical interest.
Start	Car park, St. Catherine's Breakwater. Follow the B29 (from Gorey, or via the B62 La Mont de la Mare Ste. Catherine from the St. Martin's direction) to the one–way system at the end of the road and park in the car park on the seaward side of the café.
Map Reference	**Jersey Telephone Directory** Map 5 H4 **Official Leisure Map** 71.4/52.9 **Jersey Street Guide** Map 17 F9
Terrain	Country roads, lanes, tracks and hillside, coastal and woodland paths. The walk starts with a steep path and a long uphill road.
Level of Difficulty	●● ○ **SOME DIFFICULTY**
Time (approx)	2 hours 10 minutes
Distance (approx)	6¼ kilometres (4 miles)

Amenities	**Start and Finish**
	     Public toilets
	     Public telephone
	     Café (all year round)
	
	En Route - (Archirondel)
	     Public toilets
	     Café (closed winter)

The Ultimate St. Martin's
Map Guide

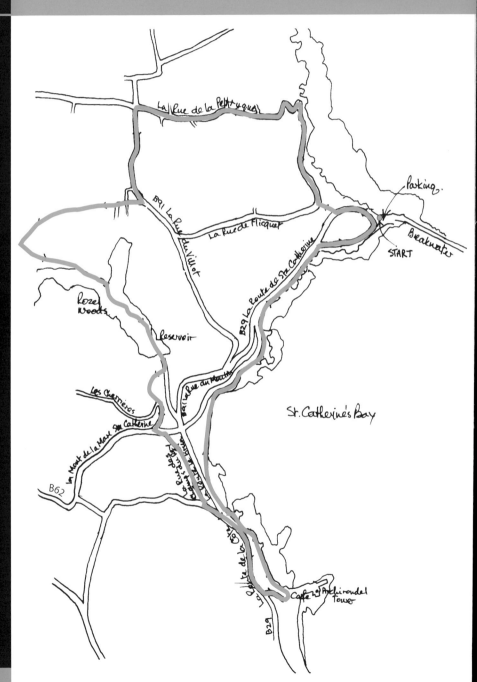

La Rue de la Petite yque)

Parking.

B91 La Rue du Villot

La Rue de Flicquet

Breakwater

START

B29 La Route de Ste Catherine

Rozel
Woods

Reservoir

St. Catherine's Bay

Les Charrieres

La Mont de la Mare Ste Catherine

La Rue du Moulin

B62

Café de Archirondel
Tower

La Route de la Côte

B29

The Ultimate St. Martin's
Walk Directions

St. Catherine's. *The area above the breakwater is known as Verclut Point or Le Fort de Verclut – wild and inaccessible until the British Government decided to create a harbour of refuge and build the associated road. It was here that the stone used in the construction of the breakwater was quarried. In the past, quarries opened up where and when stone happened to be required. This is a classic example and we can speculate that the remaining headland (known by the locals as Gibraltar or Gibraltar Rock) would have disappeared had the whole harbour project been completed.*

The St. Catherine's Breakwater is over 700 metres long and was completed in 1855, having taken over seven years to build, using thousands of tons of granite. It was commissioned by the British Government and 800 workmen had been brought in from England (although many were Irish) to work on this huge Victorian engineering project. It is noted for its splendid and indeed massive masonry. But it was to prove a folly.

The breakwater was originally planned to be the northern arm of a harbour of refuge – a deterrent to the French, with the planned other arm to be built from Archirondel. The second, southern arm was abandoned after very little work – the reason for the halt was never made public. One story was that the French had objected, another that it was made immediately obsolete by the advent of steamships but the real reason was that the northern arm had encouraged silting up – something warned of by an eminent hydrographer but ignored by the Admiralty.

With the project abandoned, and after 20 years of fruitless negotiation, due mainly to the stonewalling by The States of Jersey, the breakwater was finally handed over to the States in 1876 as a gift.

Now it is used mainly by walkers and anglers.

Turn back into the now 'No Entry' road that brought you into the car park and follow passing the public toilets on your left-hand side.

Once past the white railings on your right-hand side take the footpath to your right and then immediately ensure that you take the higher footpath - signposted 'La Ruette du Verclut – Footpath to Fliquet'.

Climb up and pass through two sets of upright iron posts.

The uprights are railway lines planted by the Germans during the Occupation as an obstacle to invasion – the railway lines being a relic of Jersey's long defunct railways.

Take the next footpath right (signposted 'Footpath').

Follow that path to the end and join the road, turning right downhill.

As you descend, notice along the first long granite wall the ormer shells emplaced in the older middle section.

The Ultimate St. Martin's
Walk Directions

At Fliquet (the bottom) carry on up the road leaving the tower to your right.

The Jersey Round Tower is called Fliquet Tower or Telegraph Tower and was built pre 1787.

Such towers are usually known by the inaccurate name 'martello'. Martello arises from Cape Mortella in Corsica where a round coastal tower caused the defeat of the British warships in 1794. The name has become very much generic for all Jersey's round towers.

In fact, Jersey round towers began to appear some fifteen years earlier based upon a plan to erect thirty-two. Twenty-two were built during the period 1780 – 1800, a number of which can still be seen around the coast. The plan called for beaches that were deemed vulnerable to attack from Napoleonic France to be protected by towers with corresponding batteries in all accessible parts of the coast. The round towers were of local design and quite different to the English martello – taller, tapering, more elegant and of granite with machicolations.

Several types of English martello were added in the early 19th century.

The adjacent World War II German bunker was a reinforced field type machine gun and mortar emplacement. The 10.5cm gun stood in an open position on a concrete platform just over the granite wall opposite. The platform was removed in 1999.

Fliquet Tower was also used by the Germans during The Occupation, linked to the bunker.

In more recent times the Tower was also known as Telegraph Tower because it served as an outlet for the telephone link with France.

Climb the road as it bends and twists.

Making the corner on the left-hand side is 'Fliquet Castle', a private residence, perhaps a folly. It was built over a long period of time, very much as a labour of love, from granite recovered from demolished old buildings.

Continue up and follow the road to the crossroads at the top.

As the road climbs less steeply and straightens into the distance note the renovated property on the left-hand side. As a design feature within its modern-style bespoke renovation, instead of the more usual Jersey granite and mortar, note the use of smaller pieces of South of England mud stone in a dry-stone wall. The stone has a real chalky feel, breaks very easily and is time consuming and difficult to use - but what a different and great finish in context!

At the crossroads turn left crossing over to the right-hand side. Follow past La Haie Fleurie.

Originally a thatched cottage (the front part of the house) believed to have dated from the 17th century. Undoubtedly it is one of the oldest properties in Jersey still owned by the descendants of the original owner. The original owner was named Whitley. He came to Jersey as a swordsman with Admiral Blake's fleet in 1651 and married a local girl from St. Martin.

In the yard there is an old pump and a salting trough carved out of solid granite that has a date of 1790 and the initials EW.

On the chimney at the far end is an excellent example of a dripstone – a protruding flat stone. Such stones are sometimes referred to as 'witches' seats' – in Jersey folklore they had to rest somewhere! Originally the property would have been thatched and such stones were so placed to deflect the rainwater at the vulnerable place where the thatch met the chimney.

At one time Haie Fleurie was an internationally recognised equestrian centre – international shows ceased in 1992 and it is now simply a local riding school. As a point of interest it is estimated that there are over 900 horses in the Island.

After another 400 metres turn right signposted 'La Rue des Mares Footpath to St. Catherine and St. Martin'. Shortly the road becomes an unmade track.

Keep on this track.

In the 19th century this path was very much a parish road created initially by the Seigneur of Rozel Manor to ease the journey of some of his tenants to their compulsory attendance at church, for what otherwise would have been a very circuitous and time consuming route.

Soon Rozel Manor will be in sight on the right-hand side.

Rozel Manor is one of Jersey's oldest manors and one of the Island's five major fiefs. Jersey's fiefs and their seigneurs were the fabric of Island life for more than 600 years.

In the Middle Ages the Channel Islands were annexed into the Duchy by the Duke of Normandy. Feudalism and the seigneurial system flourished in Jersey. All land was claimed by the Duke, which he granted to his favourites in return for services and rentes (a type of mortgage). Such grants were fiefs and their being may pre-date even the existence of the parishes.

In 1204 Normandy was lost to the French and land owners had to choose between remaining Norman or switching allegiance to the King of England. Those who returned to France lost their land to the Crown, whereupon the King re-granted their land to his favourites.

The Ultimate St. Martin's
Walk Directions

In essence the seigneurs enjoyed the benefits and duties (taxes) from the people who lived within the fief's boundaries. Tenants paid rent, gave 10% of their crop to the church and also had to work for the seigneur – they barely eked out an existence.

However, with the last of the seigneurial feudal dues abolished in 1966 - the title is now very much nominal.

Two of the conditions attached to this tenure are interesting. On the visit of his king by sea, the seigneur of Rozel had to ride his horse out to sea until the waves reached the girth of the saddle and likewise see him off on departure. Also for as long as the king may tarry in the Isle, he to act as his butler (earning the usual fee). The last time a seigneur had to play his part as butler was in 1922 when King George V visited Gorey.

In a similar way, on an earlier visit by H.M. The Queen, the seigneur of Trinity Manor presented her Majesty with two mallards (wild ducks) on a silver salver (their dead heads upright with the help of lollipop sticks). It is believed that H.M. The Queen was somewhat taken aback. Certainly by the time of a later visit in 2005 she had dispensed with this historic 'quaint' feudal obligation.

The original manor was demolished in 1770. Only one large old arch remains together with the original colombier (see below) and the 14th century manorial chapel. The current manor was built nearby as a Georgian granite house. Much enlarged in 1820, the interior is noble but the exterior is disappointing as it is covered in, the then fashionable, Roman cement. Also gothic-style turrets were added.

The manor is still owned by the Lemprière family, which traces its ancestry and ownership of the manor back to the 1360s.

The colombiers (dovecotes) were large, usually round, noisy places with up to 1000 pairs of birds. Only seigneurs were allowed such a luxury, ensuring that there would always be a meat pie during the winter months when meat was scarce.

The manor also had the dubious distinction of being allowed its own manorial gallows - these were certainly used for Thomas Le Seelleur (see later).

Pause at the gateway at the start of the wall on the right-hand side and observe the parkland of the manor.

Adjacent to the retaining wall on the right-hand side of the parkland is a sunken boundary (albeit currently somewhat overgrown). It is known as a 'ha-ha' and was created to keep in the deer that grazed in the park.

The track now becomes a path between two walls. Follow it down.

The area is known as Rozel Woods or St Catherine's Valley. It runs roughly east to west and comprises 18 hectares of mixed woodland – the largest such area in Jersey.

The area is a proposed ecological Site of Special Interest, hoping to gain all the protection that such a designation offers.

Sections of the valley path form part of the route of an ancient perquage from St. Martin's Church to the sea. In part, perquages were safe-conduct paths allowing criminals to escape arrest. Perquages ran from a sanctuary – the parish church – to the sea and a waiting boat.

'The Sanctuary of the Church' dates from the earliest medieval times and was abolished at the Reformation. A criminal was allowed refuge in the church. He had then to either stand trial or sell everything and leave the Island taking an oath never to return. In the latter case the criminal was led by the priests to the sea along 'un perquage'. Each parish had a perquage and it always followed streams.

It says much for the fear of trial and imprisonment, and the rough and ready legal system, that a criminal would voluntarily emigrate promising never to return.

This path was last used in 1546 by a habitual criminal Thomas Le Seelleur, but he did not escape the gallows. Caught again, having been in trouble previously and despite being guarded, he escaped from the church using the path. Later he gave himself up and surrendered his right to sanctuary. A wayward character he was in trouble again in 1553 and falsely accused others. As both a warning and an example to others he was hanged with his body left to rot.

Where the wall on your left-hand side stops turn left and follow this valley path.

Listen to the water as you turn.

Keep following the path, ignoring all opportunities to turn right or indeed left, passing first a wet-meadow and then a stream on your left-hand side.

Continue and cross over two streams by stepping-stones and then follow the path alongside the reservoir to your left.

Le Maseline is a small reservoir built by the Germans during the World War II Occupation. Now it is somewhat of a fisherman's retreat, being stocked with some 40/50 carp. You may be as lucky as I was (only once) to see a catch – a 13lb carp (and it was that big!) - it was put back as they have to be.

On a sunny day you can see them basking below the surface.

As you reach the car park's green locked gate absorb the information given on the St Catherine's Woods Information Board on your right-hand side.

Pass through two car parks. At the far right-hand corner of the second car park take the path via the wooden-posted exit and climb up.

Rozel Woods feature as a lovely walk in themselves - Walk 2.

Where the path meets the road turn left and proceed down the hill.

On your right-hand side in the wall, as you approach the main road, is a likely relic of desecration that took place during the Reformation. Serving no apparent purpose, it was probably used in the wall predominately on a 'waste not want not' basis.

At the 'T'-junction with the main road, turn left. Immediately cross over and turn right into Rue du Champ du Rey.

Keep to the right-hand side and follow the road to the end.

On your left-hand side is the property La Vielle Chapelle. It is built on what is believed to be the site of a building, perhaps a priest's house that was connected to the 14th century Sainte Catherine's Chapel. This chapel existed somewhere between the house and the beach but was in ruins in the 1850s when it was finally demolished (see later). It was this chapel that gave the name St. Catherine's Bay.

At the main (coast) road turn right. Immediately cross over to join the roadside path on the other side.

On your left-hand side is the St. Martin Parish Millennium Cross.

The States of Jersey presented each parish with a round section granite cross 2.475 metres high on a simple stepped plinth. The cross symbolises, and is in recognition and celebration of, the second millennium of the Christian faith.

This Cross was erected adjacent to the sites of two 14th century chapels- Sainte Catherine and St. Agatha which, although in ruins, were finally demolished in the 1850s to make way for a steam tramway.

This tramway was to be used to carry stone from the Verclut quarry for the building of the second arm of the proposed Harbour of Refuge, of which only the northern arm – St. Catherine's Breakwater – was ever finished.

The chapel ruins are presumably now under the road. Five skeletons were found near the chapel ruins - believed to be the remains of brothers of the fraternity who lived in this, then very lonely, spot.

Keep with the path across the front of the car park and continue as it becomes tarmac.

After another 60 metres turn left into Archirondel and proceed down towards the bay.

Turn left just before the car park (at the side of the toilets) and proceed up the short incline to the top of the slipway on your left-hand side.

The Ultimate St. Martin's
Walk Directions

Slipways (or slips) are a common feature along the coastline. They act as a link between the coast road and the beach and were used mainly by farmers to collect seaweed (vraic - pronounced 'rack' or 'wrack') for use as fertiliser – the best natural replacement for the lack of chalk and lime in the local soil. (It is said that the vraic helped to give the Jersey Royal potato its unique flavour thereby helping to establish it as the king of potatoes.) Vraic was also dried to act as both fuel and bedding.

The importance of vraic can scarcely be comprehended today. After the spring tides the beaches swarmed with carts. So popular was this free resource that collection had to be strongly controlled both as to timing and amount collected and was policed by vraic officers.

To your right is Archirondel Tower, a Jersey Round Tower built in 1793/4. It was built on L'Archirondel rock, then an islet 200 metres offshore at high tide. Facing Napoleonic France, this part of the coast was heavily fortified at that time with two towers and six batteries.

In the mid 19th century it was decided to use the tower as part of the southern arm of the harbour of refuge at St Catherine's. Work commenced joining this tower to the shore and then switched to Verclut and the breakwater. When the breakwater was completed no further work was done at this end as the project was then abandoned.

During The Occupation the Germans used the tower. Modifications included some concreting of the top to enable the mounting of machine guns, linking to the nearby bunker.

Of more latter times the tower has been painted red and white to act as a navigational aid.

See the adjacent Information Board for more information.

Walk down the slipway.

To your left is a German bunker. It was known as 'Resistance Nest Archirondel' and held a standard 7.5 cm anti-tank gun.

Join the coastal path to your left. Follow round **with care** (slippery underfoot in places and no protective railings on the high sea wall). Proceed to the next slipway.

In 1969 the Royal National Lifeboat Institution stationed an inflatable (in-shore) lifeboat at St. Catherine's. The original station (nearer the breakwater) became too small. This new station was built with the help of charitable donations and came into service in 1990. Local volunteers form the crew.

There is more information on the side of the building including details of the boat stationed here.

The Ultimate St. Martin's
Walk Directions

At the slipway cross over and pass seaward of the tower.

The tower is called St. Catherine's Tower. It is the second tower referred to earlier and was built pre 1787.

Proceed seaward of the car park to the next slipway.

Ship building was a huge Island industry in the mid 19th century. This beach housed the shipyard of J and T Huquet - 43 vessels were built in this shipyard alone between 1850 and 1879.

Adjacent to the tower on the sea wall read the Information Board for more information.

The slipway was built in 1892. Note the excellent workmanship in the masonry and in particular that the paving stones are set at an angle - which helped horses' hooves to grip when pulling up the wet heavily laden vraic carts.

Above the path in front of you is a white house. For good reason it is was called L'Hopital. The building was the hospital used during the harbour of refuge project. Most accidents, and there were many, were caused by blasting or the fall of large blocks of granite.

Follow the coastal path as it rises up on the other side of the slipway.

Carry on along the path ignoring the road. When the path comes up to the road (protected by a granite pillar in the middle of the path) bear right with the path and descend 9 steps.

Proceed along the path to reach an apparent fork in the path. Keep to the left - the right is a dead end - and climb the twenty steps to the road.

However, do not take the road, simply follow the path initially alongside the road and then through the picnic/BBQ area.

Continue along the path until you have to climb sixteen steps to the road. Turn right onto the road and follow the 'No-entry' road.

On your right is the St. Catherine's Sailing Club. The clubhouse was originally the carpenters' workshop for the breakwater builders.

Adjacent is the old lifeboat station now home to the Jersey Canoe Club.

Proceed to the St. Catherine's car park.

On the left is a German gun emplacement and bunker that has a substantial tunnel system at the rear. It is now a fish farm.

Return to the start.

Rozel Woods - Henry's Walk

Parish	St. Martin
Special Features	Picturesque woodland paths with streams and stepping stones.
	Usually plenty of water and mud nearby.
	Often a flock of sheep (wool gathering from the fence!) and in the Spring there should be lots of lambs.
	I have had such wonderful fun times here on 'adventures' with my grandchildren (Ella, George, Theo, Oscar, Henry, Oliver and have no doubt, number seven, Poppy will join us soon). All you need is imagination, old clothes and wellington boots!
	The water, mud, stepping stones and ropes appear very quickly into the walk and therefore, if you are accompanied by children, you will not need to travel too far to start the enjoyment or, indeed, have any need to do the whole walk!
	Why 'Henry's Walk'? My grandson Henry was two years old - he upped and offed – 'come on **D**randad'- scrambled up the steps and completed the full walk. This is now a ritual for all my new grandchildren – muddy clothes, wellingtons full of water and sheep's wool for mummy!
	Ideal for children of all ages (not suitable for pushchairs and prams.) But it is a lovely, indeed outstanding, walk for everyone.
	CAUTION
	Because of vegetation growth in summer on a small section of the paths, when walking at that time, although the paths are maintained, it is advisable to cover your legs.
Start	Public car park, Rozel Woods (St Catherine's Woods), St Catherine's.
	From the direction of Gorey -
	Follow the B29 coast road, signposted St. Catherine's, until you reach a junction - signposted B29 St. Catherine's Bay, to the right, and B62 St. Martin's Ch (sic) to the left. At that junction go straight across, turning left at the 'No-entry' sign some 20 metres ahead.

Rozel Woods - Henry's Walk

Start Continued...	Follow that byway/track, cautiously proceeding up to the car park. If possible, park in the second car park ahead.
	From the direction of St. Martin -
	Follow B30 signposted Gorey. Coming out of the village, turn left onto the B62 signposted St. Catherine and follow down. At the road junction at the bottom of the hill, signposted St. Catherine's straight on and B29 Anne Port and Gorey to the right, turn left.
	After some 20 metres, with a 'no entry' road ahead, turn left. Follow that byway/track, cautiously proceeding up to the car park. If possible, park in the second car park ahead.

Map Reference	**Jersey Telephone Directory**	Map 5 G4
	Official Tourist Map	70.6/52.4
	Jersey Street Guide	Map 26 C2

Terrain	Predominately woodland path, initially flat, with stepping-stones, but later with a steep climb - in part with steps - and some undulating, mainly downhill, byways.
Level of Difficulty	**SOME DIFFICULTY**
Time (approx)	1 hour
Distance (approx)	2½ kilometres (1½ miles)
Amenities	None

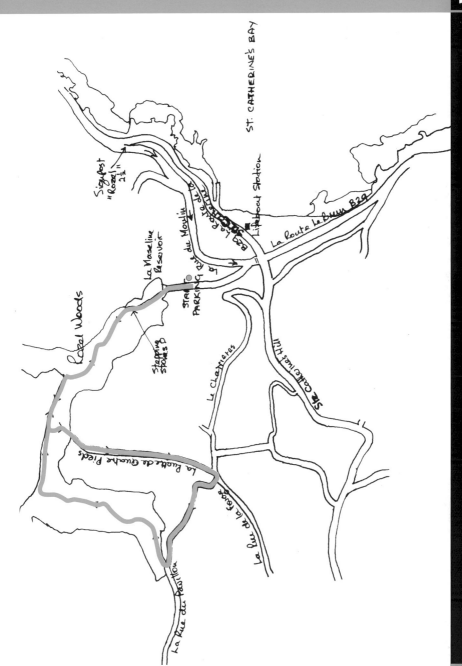

Rozel Woods - Henry's Walk
Walk Directions

Take the path towards the green locked gate and enter the woods.

As you approach the gate note the good works of the 14th St. Marks Scout Group shown on the plaque.

Go past the gate.

The area is known as Rozel Woods or St. Catherine's Woods or Valley. It runs roughly east to west and comprises some eighteen hectares of mixed woodland – the largest such area in Jersey. The reserve is a proposed site of special interest.

Absorb the information on the tree trunk Board to your left as you enter.

Follow the path along side the small reservoir.

Le Maseline Reservoir. It is a small reservoir built by the Germans during the World War II occupation. Now it is somewhat of a fisherman's retreat being stocked with some 40/50 carp. You may be lucky as I was (only once) to see a catch – a 13 lb. carp (and it was that big!). It was put back as they have to be.

On a sunny day you can see them basking below the surface.

Keep with the path, crossing a set of ten stepping-stones over a stream.

Again continue with the path, this time crossing a set of four stepping-stones to your left.

Follow for some 50 metres up the slight incline and then down to the stream again.

Proceed, keeping the stream to your right-hand side.

What opportunities for the children to play along this whole stretch of the stream - mud, water, fallen trees, rope swings and stream-crossing logs.

Continue on this main path ignoring all opportunities to turn right. When you reach a wet-meadow on your right-hand side keep going. After some 2/3rds of the length of the meadow you will see a 'Public Footpath' sign to your left.

Proceed up the steps of this steep footpath and continue as it meanders up the hill.

At the top a large meadow appears on your right-hand side, continue on the path.

Often there are sheep in this field and certainly there will be wool left behind on the wire fence.

Follow this path until you reach the road.

As you proceed, on your left-hand side, note the sea view with the French coast in the background.

Turn right onto the road and then immediately turn right again into Rue de Pavillon.

If you have not seen any sheep so far they are likely to be in the two or three fields immediately to your left.

As the road turns 90° to the left note that the right-hand granite gatepillar of the farm, unusually, also acts as a marriage stone with the date of 1849.

Granite carved marriage stones appeared in the 18th century, attaining maximum popularity between 1720 and 1880. They were usually rectangular lintels above the front door. They consisted of the initials of the husband and wife (the husband's on the left and the wife's on the right, using her maiden name), with one, two or entwined hearts, usually all within the date. The date recorded would be of significance to the couple, often the date of marriage or construction of the property.

What about the garden sculptures? To investigate fully, walk up to the granite pillars in the adjacent entrance.

Also, on the left-hand side, within the garden you will see a partially reconstructed apple crusher (used in cider making) around a horse chestnut tree. In 1795 over 20% of arable land was under orchard (15% of the whole of the Island, from 36% in St. Saviour to 4% in St. Ouen). In the 1830s cider was still the main source of the farmer's wealth. Every farm had cider-making equipment and in 1839, 270,000 gallons were exported to England. Although largely exported, much was also drunk locally – it was the main drink! The cider-making process usually took place inside. The apples were poured into the crusher and a horse would circle round pulling a large round granite stone to crush the apples. The resultant mulch then would be shovelled into the cider press and squeezed to make the final liquid for the barrels. Needless to say the quality was varied!

Follow this road down until you reach the St. Martin's Pumping Station on your right-hand side.

In front of the Pumping Station turn right and take the path, signposted 'Footpath to St.Catherine', back into the woods.

Just as you are to enter the woods and on the right-hand side, read again the St. Catherine's Woods information board on the log.

Rozel Woods - Henry's Walk
Walk Directions

Follow this path all the way down. Once over the bridge continue, now keeping the stream to your left-hand side.

This path is said to be part of the ancient 'perquage' from St. Martin's Church to the sea. Perquages were safe-conduct paths allowing criminals to escape arrest.

Perquages ran from a sanctuary – the parish church – to the sea and a waiting boat.

'The Sanctuary of the Church' dates from the earliest medieval times and was abolished at the Reformation. A criminal was allowed refuge in the church. He had then to either stand trial or sell everything and leave the Island taking an oath never to return. In the latter case the criminal was led by the priests to the sea along 'un perquage'. Each parish had a perquage and it always followed streams.

It says much for the fear of trial and imprisonment, and the rough and ready legal system, that a criminal would voluntarily emigrate promising never to return.

This path was last used in 1546 by a habitual criminal Thomas Le Seelleur but he did not escape the gallows. Caught again having been in trouble previously, despite being guarded, he escaped from the church using the path. Later he gave himself up and surrendered his right to sanctuary. A wayward character he was in trouble again in 1553 and falsely accused others. As an example to others seemingly, he was hanged, with his body left to rot.

At the path junction turn right (here you lose the stream) and follow down, this time keeping the wet-meadow to your left-hand side.

Retrace your steps, keeping with this main path all the way back - alongside the wet-meadow, then the stream, straight on through the trees, across the two sets of stepping stones and finally alongside the reservoir, to the car park and the start.

Queen's Valley Reservoir

Parish	Grouville
Special Features	Lovely water vistas. Straightforward walk around the reservoir. Ducks, geese and swans. **Ideal for prams and pushchairs.**
Start	Public car park at Queen's Valley Reservoir. (Care! - neither the car park nor the reservoir is signposted.) From the West (Five Oaks and Hougue Bie) follow the B 28 La Route de la Hougue Bie. Pass St. Saviour's Hospital to your right and the car park entrance is shortly afterwards on the right-hand side. From the East (Gorey and Faldouet) follow the B 28 La Rue D'Aval. The car park entrance is on the left-hand side as you approach St. Saviour's Hospital.
Map Reference	**Jersey Telephone Directory**　　Map 10　G1 **Official Tourist Map**　　69.9/50.4 **Jersey Street Guide**　　Map 34　G1
Terrain	Circular reservoir path with a good wide hoggin-based surface. Some undulation with one or two short inclines.
Level of Difficulty	⬤◯◯　**EASY**
Time (approx)	45 minutes
Distance (approx)	2¾ kilometres (1¾ miles)
Amenities	Portable toilet (soon after start)

Queen's Valley Reservoir
Map Guide

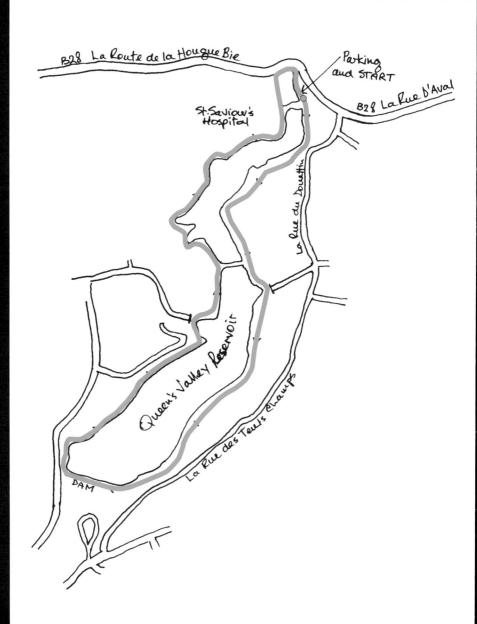

B28 La Route de la Hougue Bie

Parking and START

B28 La Rue D'Aval

St. Saviour's Hospital

La Rue du Douettin

Queen's Valley Reservoir

La Rue des Teuls Chauts

DAM

Queen's Valley Reservoir
Walk Directions

After a decade of real controversy, in the late 1980s, the Jersey New Waterworks Company - at the extremity of legal action - obtained a Royal Assent to construct the reservoir. Building work commenced, the dam was built, the valley flooded and the reservoir was brought into being in late 1991.

The reservoir holds in the region of 260 million gallons (1120ml) and will be able to yield 450 million gallons (2043ml) a year from its catchment and surplus water pumped from other areas. This capability has increased the Island's total reservoir storage capacity by 80%.

The reservoir water is pumped to either Augrès or Handois treatment works before entering the supply network.

The reservoir has more than proved its worth - the Island could not have managed without it.

Join the path by entering the first gateway on the left-hand side as you drive in. Then simply follow the path.

This first area of water to your right is a small shallow pond area – a silt pond – the prime purpose of which is to act as a silt trap for the reservoir. It catches any debris and sediment from the feeding stream.

An embankment separates it from the upper reservoir. The embankment has been deliberately designed to allow water to overflow when exceptionally large floods occur.

The pond is drained through a bypass culvert discharging directly into the reservoir.

Keep on the path all the way until you reach the intermediate dam to your right.

The upper reservoir to your right is comparatively shallow and was built primarily for environmental reasons – to save unsightly mud flats at high demand summer times.

The structure in the water on the far side is a stone-clad draw off tower that pumps water into the main reservoir in times of need.

Simply carry on along the path, passing the portable toilet on your left-hand side, until you reach the dam at the far end.

The main reservoir holds about 90% of the storage.

The round concrete structure in the reservoir near the dam is a combined draw-off and overflow tower controlled by valves. A scour pipe at the base allows water to be drawn from the very bottom of the reservoir. That water, often stagnant, deoxygenated and containing silt, is drawn off when there is surplus water, helping to improve the quality.

At the far end, as you pass through the open gate to reach the dam, note the commemoration plaque in the wall on the left-hand side.

Cross over the dam on your right.

As you cross turn round to your left and admire the view, with the white-topped tower of an old windmill on the skyline to the right of the Grouville Church spire, the spire of Grouville Church itself and, far left, the distant views of the Royal Bay of Grouville.

The windmill is Le Moulin de Beauvoir (Grouville Mill). Sites of 12 windmills (and 38 watermills) are known to have existed in island, some of them amongst the earliest occupied sites, dating from the 11th century. All of them would have been rebuilt many times.

Grouville Mill is one of only three windmills shown on an Island map of 1563 and windmills on the site can be traced back to 1331. Such windmills catered for areas remote from streams and for the summer when the flow of water might be inadequate to turn the water wheels. Their main function was grinding corn. Only four mills survive today – the others being St. Ouen, Rozel and St. Peter.

During the Occupation of World War II the tower was adapted as an Observation Post (M8) by the Germans. The heavy concrete top together with slit windows can still be seen. The mill is now part of domestic accommodation but still serves as a navigation marker.

The Royal Bay of Grouville was so named by Queen Victoria after her visit in 1859, having been much impressed with the scenery.

Now for the return half. Follow the path all the way, keeping straight-on at the intermediate dam (to your right) and ignoring left turns.

The reservoir has been stocked with trout and permit fishing is allowed. Interestingly, the presence of fish helps to monitor the quality of the water.

At the embankment near the car park, do not be tempted to cross over but simply veer left and continue with the path.

Plenty of ducks and geese and, indeed, swans here.

Follow round to the car park and the start.

The Ultimate Inner Grouville

Parish	Grouville
Special Features	Lovely distant views of Mont Orgueil Castle, Gorey, The Royal Bay of Grouville and France (Cherbourg Peninsular). Open countryside, at times with the feeling of real space. Short reservoir walk.
Start	The lower end car park of the Queen's Valley Reservoir.
	Opposite the Grouville Parish Hall, turn onto the B37 La Rue de Grouville, towards St. Saviour. After approximately one kilometre turn right (La Rue du Moulin de Bas) signposted Cycle Route 1. Keeping with this road (do not fork off left) and after some 400 metres, turn left into the car park at the base of the reservoir.

Map Reference	**Jersey Telephone Directory**	Map 10 F2
	Official Leisure Map	69.5/49.5
	Jersey Street Guide	Map 34 E5

Terrain	Predominantly undulating country roads and byways, but with one long steep climb early on, with a short reservoir section.
Level of Difficulty	● ● ○ **SOME DIFFICULTY**
Time (approx)	1 hour 40 minutes
Distance (approx)	6 kilometres (3 ¾ miles)
Amenities	Portable toilet at the start of the reservoir section

The Ultimate Inner Grouville
Map Guide

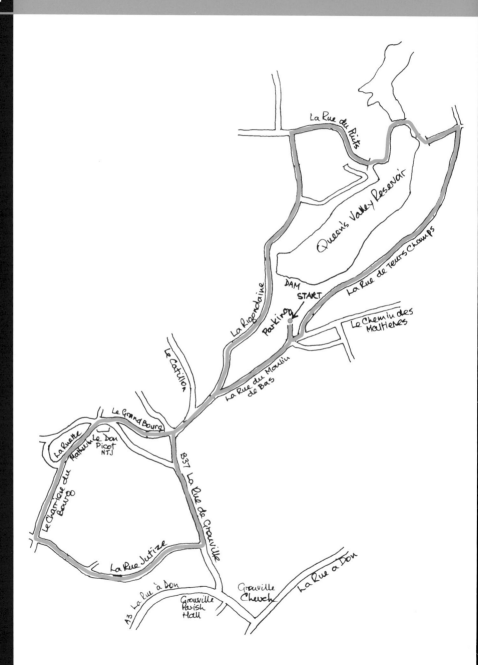

La Rue du Puits

Queen's Valley Reservoir

La Rue de Teurs Champs

La Rigondaine

DAM

START

Parking

Le Chemin des Maltieres

Le Catillon

La Rue du Moulin de Bas

Le Grand Bourg

La Ruette

Le Chemin du Bourg

Le Don Picot NTJ

La Maluin

B37 La Rue de Grouville

La Rue Jutize

La Rue à Don

A3

Grouville Parish Hall

Grouville Church

La Rue a Don

Leave the reservoir car park by turning left on to the road.

After some 50 metres turn left and proceed up the long steep incline to the top.

Ensure that you take time to absorb the wonderful views to your right, including later on Mont Orgueil (Gorey) Castle. The best views are firstly, as you climb, opposite the entrance to Les Teurs Champs, and secondly as you start to walk along the brow of the hill.

The tower far out in the bay is Seymour Tower. This tower, as it now stands, is the only example of a square Jersey tower and was built in the early 1780s as part of the Island's defences in the Napoleonic era. It is situated on an islet (L'Avarizon Islet) where previous defences had been built as far back as 1540. The tower is some two miles out to sea from the high tide mark, but is accessible with difficulty (dangerous tides) on foot at low tide. The tower provides a useful navigation aid. It was bought by the States from the Crown in 1923 for £120.

The golf course running along the coast is The Royal Jersey Golf Club. The club was opened in 1878 - a delightful and enjoyable sandy course of, now, 6116 yards - where Harry Vardon cut his golfing teeth. Deemed to be one of the most outstanding link courses in Great Britain.

The tower on the golf course is a Jersey round tower, Fort Henry, built in 1782 and again named after its builder Sir Henry Seymour Conway, Governor of Jersey 1772 -1785.

On the brow of the hill Mont Orgueil (Gorey) Castle comes into view - perhaps Jersey's most iconic structure, sitting at the head of the Royal Bay of Grouville.

Keep on this road for a total of some 1¼ kilometres.

As the road drops down you come to crossroads. Turn left at these crossroads and proceed down the 'No-through' road.

At the bottom join the reservoir path by turning right. This is best achieved by turning to your right in front of the locked entry gate and entering through the gap in the wooden fence adjacent to the portable toilet.

After a decade of real controversy, in the late 1980s the Jersey New Waterworks Company – at the extremity of legal action – obtained a Royal Assent to construct the reservoir. Building work commenced and the reservoir was brought into being in late 1991.

The reservoir has more than proved its worth - the Island could not have managed without it.

After approx 100 metres turn left over the (intermediate) dam.

A walk around the whole of the reservoir and more of its history are set out in a separate walk. See Walk 3 – Queen's Valley Reservoir.

At the end of the dam turn left onto the reservoir path.

Leave the path via the first gate on the right-hand side using the small side gate.

Proceed up the often moss-covered and slippery track to the top of the hill.

At the first junction join the road by turning left. Follow the road for some 800 metres.

Near the bottom, on the right-hand side, is a property, La Rigondaine. Note the old water pump.

At the 'T'-junction turn right.

When you reach the main road (Le Câtillon) 'T'-junction turn left.

Cross over to the other side of the road. After approx 50 metres turn right at the bend and continue with this road (ignoring the then immediate turning to the right). Keep to the left-hand side as you climb.

On the right-hand side is the property Springvale. After you have passed the entrance to the property note the 1790 marriage stone unusually positioned between two upper windows.

Granite carved marriage stones appeared in the 18th century, attaining maximum popularity between 1720 and 1880. They were usually rectangular lintels above the front door. They consisted of the initials of the husband and wife (the husband's on the left and the wife's on the right, using her maiden name), with one, two or entwined hearts, usually all within the date. The date recorded would be of significance to the couple, often the date of marriage or construction of the property.

On the chimney stacks note the protruding flat stones. These are excellent examples of dripstones that are often referred to as witches' stones or seats. In local superstition they were believed to be resting places for witches – well they had to rest somewhere! In fact, initially the roof would have been thatched so the stones were so placed to prevent rainwater seeping in at the vulnerable point where the thatch joined the chimney.

As you walk up the road, nearing the end of Springvale's granite front boundary wall, find another marriage stone with the same initials but with an earlier date, 1784. Could this be the date of their actual marriage, the stone taken from an earlier smaller property, with 1790 being the date when they built their grander replacement property?

Regardless, certainly a Jerseyman would not be averse to using up every bit of old stone in a new wall!

Next on the left-hand side of the road you will find the National Trust for Jersey sign Le Don Picot. Such gifts of land or property to the Trust are usually designated in this way. Le Don translates from the French as 'the gift' and, as a mark of gratitude, precedes the name of the donor often, as in this case, simply the family name. This small wooded côtil running alongside the road was gifted to the Trust in 1963 by Messrs L.C. and C.A. Picot, Mrs K.M. Picot and Mrs A.F. Le Sueur (née Picot).

Follow up the hill ignoring the 'No Entry' road to the right.

At the top, in front of Le Bourg House, turn left and follow the road round.

Continue the climb.

At the first crossroads turn left.

Follow the road passing Laurel House on your left-hand side.

> *Take time to look at the excellent view, initially to your left, featuring Gorey and Gorey Castle (Mont Orgueil), with France (Cherbourg Peninsular) as background.*

> *The bay in view is The Royal Bay of Grouville. This bay was so named by Queen Victoria after her visit to Jersey in 1859, having been very much impressed with the scenery.*

When you reach the main road at the bottom turn left.

> *As you turn notice on the right-hand side the old water pump in front of the property La Pompe.*

Proceed **very carefully** for approx 500 metres.

> *On the right-hand side you pass Home Farm.*

> *Note the marriage stones over the two entrances. The 1746 marriage stone is interesting as the date is different from the stone on the front of the house, which is 1741, and in any event Charles Malet married Elizabeth Touzel in 1719.*

> *Immediately on the left-hand side is a property Meadow Vale Cottage. There is not much of the old house here, but note the gable stone inscribed TGF 1689.*

Immediately left is a turning (La Ruette). Detour up this lane for a few metres.

> *On the right-hand side is a stream and in a recess a fine example of an abreuvoir - a drinking place for animals made by the creation of a break in the stream's flow using carved granite.*

> *Here the abreuvoir would be particularly appreciated by horses travelling to and from the higher ground where water was not so easily available.*

Return to the road and continue.

Take the first turning right (La Rue du Moulin de Bas) following Cycle Route 1 into a 'No Coaches' road.

Keep with the road as it bears right.

> *The tall oblong building on the left-hand side was built by the Germans during the Occupation as a power relay. It is now used as a seed potato store.*

> Proceed until you reach the turning left into the car park and the start.

Parish	St. Clement and Grouville
Special Features	Open countryside vistas. Coastal panoramas. Wet sand and pebble beach walking. Neolithic Dolmen. Good historical interest.
	CAUTION **This is a low-water walk. The beaches of this walk should be attempted only if the tide is out or going out. Otherwise the coastal road should be used instead, as indicated in the walk directions. (This alternative will be far less scenic and interesting.)**
Start	Public car park adjacent to the St. Clement's Parish Hall. The Parish Hall is situated on the A4 coast road, La Grande Route de la Côte (St. Clement's Coast Road) at Le Hocq.
Map Reference	**Jersey Telephone Directory**　　Map 9 D5 **Official Leisure Map**　　68.4/46.5 **Jersey Street Guide**　　Map 43 A7
Terrain	Country roads and byways, tracks, paths - including two reasonably steep inclines, one with steps – and wet sand and pebble beach walking.
Level of Difficulty	●●○　**SOME DIFFICULTY**
Time (approx)	1 hour 45 minutes
Distance (approx)	5¼ kilometres (3¼ miles)
Amenities	**Start and Finish** 　Public toilets 　Public telephone 　Pub/restaurant 　Slipway food shack **En Route (at Green Island)** 　Public toilets 　Public telephone 　Restaurant 　Takeaway kiosk

The Ultimate St. Clement's/ Grouville - *Map Guide*

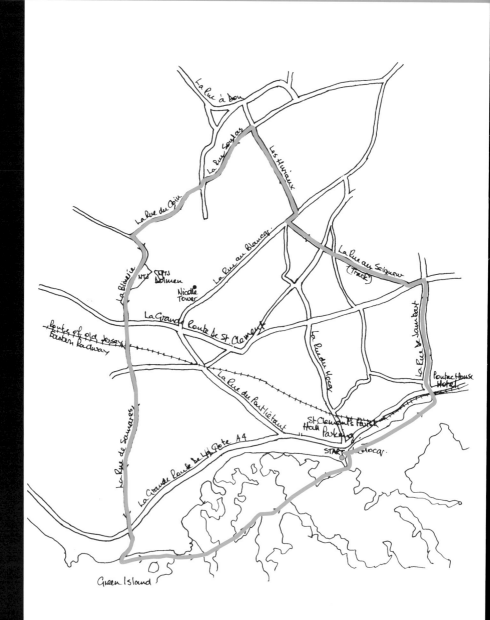

Leave the car park by crossing the coast road and proceed down the slipway.

To your right is Le Hocq Jersey Round Tower built around 1780.

Such towers are usually known by the inaccurate name 'martello'. Martello arises from Cape Mortella in Corsica where a round coastal tower caused the defeat of the British warships in 1794. The name has become very much generic for all round towers.

In fact Jersey Round Towers began to appear some fifteen years earlier based upon a plan to erect thirty-two. Twenty-two were built during the period 1780 – 1800, a number of which can still be seen around the coast. The plan called for beaches that were deemed vulnerable to attack from Napoleonic France to be protected by towers with corresponding batteries in all accessible parts of the coast. The round towers were of local design and quite different to the English Martello – taller, tapering, more elegant and of granite with machicolations – the protrusions at the top through which hot liquids and burning objects could be dropped on attackers.

Several types of English Martello were added in the early 19th century.

Slipways (or slips) are a common feature along the coastline. They act as a link between the coast road and the beach and were used mainly by farmers to collect seaweed (vraic – pronounced 'rack' or 'wrack') for use as fertiliser – the best natural replacement for the lack of chalk and lime in the local soil. (It is said that the vraic helped to give the Jersey Royal potato its unique flavour thereby helping to establish it as 'the king of potatoes'.)

Vraic was also dried to act as fuel.

The importance of vraic can scarcely be comprehended today. After spring tides, the beaches swarmed with carts. So popular was this free resource that collection had to be strongly controlled both as to timing and amount and was policed by vraic officers.

Note the craftsmanship in the slipway masonry, in particular that the paving stones are set at an angle – which helped horses' hooves to grip when pulling up the wet heavily laden carts.

(PROCEED ALONG THE BEACH ONLY IF THE TIDE IS OUT OR GOING OUT.) If you are in any doubt about the tide conditions follow the coast road to the Pontac slipway, walking on the seaward side, predominantly using the footpath.

Turn left onto the beach and follow along to the next slipway at Pontac. The slipway is just around the rocks on your left-hand side, initially hidden from view.

The Ultimate St. Clement's/ Grouville - *Walk Directions*

Jersey's south east coast represents the remains of the Island's former land bridge to the continent, an area that was submerged at the end of the last Ice Age. It now comprises of some of the most ruggedly beautiful and ecologically important inter-tidal habitats to be found in Europe.

It has been estimated that, within this rich and immensely valuable ecology, a single square metre of middle-shore mud contains the equivalent in energy of 25 Mars bars!

In 2000, The States of Jersey gave approval for 32.1 square kilometres (25% of Jersey's land mass at low tide) to be designated a United Nations Ramsar Wetland of International Importance. Surprised at the size? Remember that on a good tide one can walk over two miles before reaching the low water mark and the area stretches from Gorey pier to St. Helier harbour.

Head up the slipway.

Cross the main coast road into Rue de Jambart and follow. As the road bears right and becomes La Rue Hamel keep straight on up the 'No through' road to the end.

At the main road turn left and, where the pavement ends in front of the church, carefully cross over the road.

St. Clement's Church. Unlike most of the other Jersey churches, where the chancel is the oldest part, here the oldest part of the church is the nave. It formed the original Norman chapel with a low thatched roof and narrow windows, dating from the 11th century. The church went through turbulent times during and after the Reformation and was enlarged in the 15th century. The current bell was hung in 1828. An important and substantial restoration took place in the early 1880s when the frescoes or wall paintings were discovered.

At the end of the church wall turn right past the main gates.

Note the stone stile over the wall to the side of the church gates. Of no real use now, it was, at one time when the rector's sheep and cattle were put out to pasture in the churchyard.

Head up La Rue au Seigneur, marked 'No Entry – footpath only – except for access to the fields'.

It is said that this path was used by the ladies of Samares Manor to walk to church. They would remain cleaner and drier than if they had used the lower – then marshy – road.

Follow this path all the way to the top.

Near the top turn round to view the coastal panorama, noting the inland lighthouse to your right.

The lighthouse is Mont Ubé lighthouse - one of two (the other is on the shore at Grève D'Azette) leading lights of the western passage to St. Helier harbour.

At the road cross over, continuing on the path.

On your right-hand side is the Parish's Millennium Standing Stone.

The Société Jersiaise and Ronez Quarries jointly gave each parish a standing, undressed granite stone to commemorate the Millennium. The stone acknowledges earlier paganism. Note the plaque giving the names of the benefactors involved.

Additionally The States of Jersey presented each parish with a round section granite cross 2.475 metres high on a simple stepped plinth.

The cross symbolises and is in recognition and celebration of the second millennium of the Christian faith.

At the next road again cross over and follow the path.

The path/track that you have been walking along, is a 'chemin de corps' – a route along which funeral processions passed on their way to the St. Clement's Church – thereby making the path a public right of way in perpetuity.

As you proceed look to the left for continuing views of the coast. Also note the iniquitous four Le Marais tower blocks – surely one of the Island's worst planning decisions!

At the end of the path follow the road right.

After some 50 metres turn left into the road marked Cycle Route 1 (Les Huriaux) and follow.

When you reach the crossroads turn left and proceed down hill.

Once at the 'T'-junction turn left and follow the road round.

Keep following the road for a further 200 metres when you will reach the bungalow Fernvale on the left-hand side.

Immediately after the bungalow in the bank on the left-hand side of the road and sometimes hidden by undergrowth is the old parish boundary stone, carved 'G, le' (Grouville) on one side and 'St. C' (St. Clement) on the other.

Shortly thereafter note the St. Clement Green Lane sign on the right-hand side showing how one parish can denote the same road a Green Lane and the other not.

Proceed to the end of the road.

At the 'T'-junction turn left (in the opposite direction to the Cycle Route).

After approx 150 metres the road turns through 90° – follow round.

After a few more metres, in front of the semi-detached red-brick houses, turn left and proceed up the steps marked 'Dolmen de Mont Ubé, Société Jersiaise'.

The Dolmen du Mont Ubé is the property of The Société Jersiaise. The wooded côtil, through which this path runs, is owned by the National Trust for Jersey. It was bought in 1966 with funds from an anonymous donor.

The Dolmen is at the back of the côtil at the top. At the first path junction turn right and follow. After five metres turn left up the nine steps, again turning left at the top step.

Keep with this main path, ignoring two turnings to the right. Climb seven steps and then turn left to reach the top.

At the little grass plateau you will see the dolmen on your right-hand side.

Proceed to the dolmen.

The first farming folk to settle in the Island were the Iberians who arrived some 2,000-3,000 years BC. They left their traces in these great passage-graves.

(Dolmen is derived from two Breton words, dol – table, men –stone.)

In the early 19th century this dolmen was used as a pigsty and in the mid-century the capstones, or roof stones, were broken up for building material. But its twenty-eight uprights remain, forming a passage to the burial chamber. The whole dolmen was originally covered with a mound of earth.

On your right-hand side read the information board relating to the 'Neolithic Passage Grave 4250/3250 BC. Le Dolmen de Mont Ubé'.

Turn back down the path. This time, when you reach the fork in the path turn left and follow the main path to the far left.

Keep with this path all the way to the tarmac, turning right at the private driveway to reach the road.

At the road, with the property La Blinerie in front of you, turn left and follow down to the bottom.

At the main road **very carefully** cross over into Rue de Samares.

Keep with this road all the way to the coast road.

Near the end of this road on the right-hand side take a closer view of the four Le Marais tower blocks.

At the main road **carefully** cross over, signposted 'Green Island' and head for the beach and the slipway.

At the top of the slipway on the left-hand side read the memorial stone to three brave Jerseymen.

At the top of the slipway, on the left-hand side, take the steps down to the beach.

PROCEED ALONG THE BEACH ONLY IF THE TIDE IS OUT OR GOING OUT. If you are in any doubt about the tide conditions proceed along the coast road to Le Hocq, the car park and the start. Use the footpath on the seaward, right-hand side for as long as possible, then switch to the other side. (Interestingly, after 100 metres on the right-hand side, in the front garden of the property Rocque Berg, you will see the actual Witches Rock outcrop mentioned below.)

Green Island, to your right, was originally called La Motte (small island). The islet is now 300 metres from shore but in the early 17th century was likely to have been part of the Jersey mainland. The islet is vulnerable to coastal erosion and is now very carefully protected.

It is a prehistoric (roughly 2000 BC) cemetery site where 18 cist-graves, which are graves built of small stone slabs in the form of a box, were found. Some contained human remains of the New Stone Age (Neolithic) period. Several of these graves have been moved to La Hougue Bie, Grouville.

Head left, initially along the sandy beach, around the outcrop of rocks to your left.

The round tower seaward is Icho Tower, one of the English Martello towers mentioned previously. It was built in 1810, during the Napoleonic Wars, on the islet Ic-Ho (or Croix de fer). It is 8.4 metres high and cost £6263.

Originally garrisoned by 30 men, later reduced to 11 and finally abandoned, it was sold by the UK War Office to the States of Jersey in 1923 for £80.

Then pick a path, mainly through wet sands and pebbles, along the beach aiming for the first tower on your inland side.

The point to your left is called Le Nez.

The Ultimate St. Clement's/ Grouville - *Walk Directions*

In a private garden to your left is a rock outcrop some twelve metres high called Rocqueberg, also known as Witches Rock.

With simple and credulous inhabitants great ignorance and superstition prevailed in the Island over centuries. The belief in fairies, both good and evil, the notion of the devil and witchcraft was widespread. In the 16th and 17th centuries St. Clement became notorious as a centre of witchcraft. Witches Rock was so named because it is said that devil worshippers, men and women (not all witches were women!), used to meet at this, then very remote, spot for their ceremonies and to raise storms by their songs. 'Le Tchéziot' was the Devil's deputy and lord of the witches and charmers. He summoned them to come and dance when the moon was full – those with an evil eye had to leave whatever they were doing and go and dance.

You will find a slipway (Le Hocq) immediately to the far side of the tower.

If you are lucky you may find one or two people with their forks looking for cockles.

Proceed up this slipway to the road.

Cross over the road returning to the car park and the start.

Byways of St. Saviour and Trinity

Parish	St. Saviour and Trinity
Special Features	Straightforward, hilly tarmac byway walking. A short section of woodland path, particularly beautiful during daffodil time in early spring. Outstanding historical interest.
Start	Sports facilities car park adjacent to Grainville and FCJ Schools. Entrance in La Rue de Deloraine, off St. Saviour's Hill (A7). From Town, proceed up St. Saviour's Hill (A7) past Government House and St. Saviour's Church. Pass Grainville Playing Fields on the left-hand side then turn first left into La Rue de Deloraine. From the roundabout at Five Oaks, take the A7, St. Saviour's Hill exit. Pass Victoria Cottage Homes on your right-hand side and then take first turning right into La Rue de Deloraine. The entrance to the car park is 200 metres on the left-hand side at the end of the playing field. (Although a free car park, note you are asked to display arrival time.)
Map Reference	**Jersey Telephone Directory** Map 9 B2 **Official Leisure Map** 66.6/50.0 **Jersey Street Guide** Map 33 A2
Terrain	Predominately tarmac byways, but with inclines. One short section of woodland path walking, often muddy in places, some stepping stones and a short climb by steps.
Level of Difficulty	⬤ ⬤ ◯ **SOME DIFFICULTY**
Time (approx)	2 hours 45 minutes
Distance (approx)	10 kilometres (6¼ miles)
Amenities	None

41

Byways of St. Saviour and Trinity
Map Guide

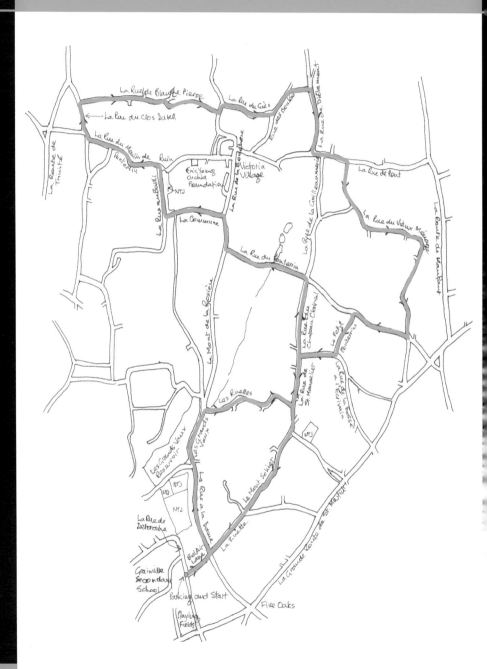

Exit the car park the way you entered.

Turn left onto the road and immediately take the first turning right into Bel Air Lane and follow to the crossroads.

At the crossroads turn left into Rue à la Dame and follow down to the end.

At the end turn right onto the main road, Grand Vaux, and follow the sign (slightly in front of you to your right) towards Victoria Village.

> *Immediately on you left-hand side, in the little crescent-shaped roadside grassy area, is the Parish of St. Saviour's Millennium stone. The Société Jersiaise and Ronez Quarries jointly gave each parish a standing, undressed granite stone to commemorate the Millennium. The stone acknowledges earlier paganism. The Jersey Field Squadron of the Territorial Army erected the stones. Note the plaque on the nearby stone giving the names of the benefactors involved.*

> *At the same time The States of Jersey presented each parish with a round section granite cross 2.475 metres high on a simple stepped plinth. The cross symbolises and is in recognition of the Christian faith. The St. Saviour cross is situated on a small triangular oak tree island adjacent to St. Saviour's School, alongside the main road La Route de Bagatelle at the junction with Chasse Brunet.*

Proceed along the road keeping the reservoir to your left.

After 300 metres turn right into Les Ruettes and follow up as it narrows and bends to reach the end.

At the 'T'-junction turn left and follow.

Keep with the road as it continues straight on and becomes Rue du Chateau Clairval (the road name is on the left-hand side, just past a turning to the right).

On the left-hand side look out for the '1850 Clos des Pauvres de St. Sauveur' granite plaque in the boundary wall of the St. Paul's Football Club.

> *Land would be given or bequeathed to the parish, or bought by parish from monies given or bequeathed, to bring in an income for the parish poor. The fields (Clos des Pauvres) were rented by the highest bidder at parish meetings.*

> *The poor ('pauvre' in French) were cared for in this manner in Jersey since medieval times.*

> *The name of the donor of the Clos des Pauvres was occasionally remembered in granite at the site. In this case 'Jeanne Gruchy' is most recognisable of the names so inscribed. In her lifetime, thought more thrifty than wealthy, she died in 1848 somewhat surprisingly leaving a substantial sum for the relief of the parish poor. Her will required each parish to purchase a plot of land at her bequest and apply the income generated to help the needy parishioners. Her remembrance was always in this form, sometimes more elaborate than this plaque, sometimes not.*

Byways of St. Saviour and Trinity
Walk Directions

Take the first left into La Rue du Ponterrin and follow to the end.

On the left-hand side you will see the property Oakvale. Note the protruding flat granite stones at the bases of the two chimneys. In folklore such stones were referred to as 'witches' seats' - they had to sit somewhere, most probably to rest when flying! Originally the property would have had a thatched roof. At the level of the original thatch, these stones were used to deflect rainwater at the vulnerable point where the thatch joined the chimney stack.

You will see a number of examples on this walk.

At the 'T'-junction turn right and follow.

Take the first turning left into La Commune and follow down. After leaving behind all the houses and buildings on the left-hand side and, as you start to see the end of the road, on the left-hand side of the road a short section of wooden pole fencing appears with a gateway entrance gap leading into woods. Enter the woods through the gap.

Take the lower, right-hand path and follow.

Keep with the path, bearing right as it joins another path. Then cross a probably muddy section aided by stepping stones and wooden platforms.

Follow all the way straight, stopping in front of a boundary gate.

In front of the gate turn left and climb 35 steps and keep with the now narrow path as it proceeds bearing to the left.

A lovely walk at anytime but particularly beautiful with the daffodils in the spring. (Mind where you are treading!)

Eventually, descending a final five steps, you will reach a path 'T'-junction. Turn right and follow the new path back to the entranceway and the road.

Rejoin the road turning left and follow down the short way to the end.

At the 'T'-junction turn right, but before you do note the National Trust for Jersey sign 'Le Don Sybil Perrée' on your right-hand side.

Such gifts of land or property to the Trust are usually designated in this way. Le Don translates from the French as 'the gift' and, as a mark of gratitude, precedes the name of the donor, often the family name only. In this case, as one of five sites gifted, Miss Sybil Perrée donated this wet-meadow area, Le Pré de Ponterrin, on the east side of La Rue au Bailli, to the National Trust for Jersey in 1974.

As you start to go along the road look to your left-hand side to see a classic example of a roadside well-head.

Again this road is flanked each side by daffodils and snowdrops in the early spring.

Keep with this road as it bears left at the end of the straight and proceeds uphill.

As you reach that point where the road bears left and climbs, look to your right, to notice the ruins of a watermill - Moulin du Ponterrin. Walk the 40 metres to investigate!

There are 38 known sites of watermills in the Island and they were in action from the 11th to the 19th century, with most activity during the late 16th and 17th centuries. Their main work was grinding corn. (Also a few were called back into service during the German Occupation and did work of vital importance.)

In mediaeval times every mill belonged to a seigneur, be he the king, an abbey to which the seigneur had granted his revenues, or a local fief holder. The tenants of any fief were obliged to grind their corn at the seigneur's mill and also to render services in the form of labour, cartage and materials for the upkeep of the mill. To the tenant the mill was essential, as the only means of grinding corn for bread. To the seigneur it was an important source of revenue in the fees he charged - usually paid in kind - in essence a tax.

Over time, seigneurs sometimes sold their mill and abbeys and priories were dispossessed, so the feudal system gradually faded away. Helped by favourable protection laws and inter-marriage, by the 18th century the power that came with mill owning was in the hands of the milling families. Feudal taxing had been replaced by millers' monopoly, with the general public no better off. Milling controlled the price of bread leading to discontent and sometimes to disturbance and riot.

In 1847 the town erupted over the price of bread. Grain boats had their rudders stolen. Hungry workers marched into The Royal Square in St. Helier. Rioters raided the town mill (its site where The Ceasarean Tennis Club is now) baying for the head of Pellier, the miller. Returning towards town with ill-gotten grain they were met head-on by troops near the Robin Hood Inn. Eventually order was restored and a deal struck. The States agreed (again) to sell bread at below cost, a town relief fund was set up, to which the rich also contributed, and the scale of parish relief was increased.

Despite all this, with wages pegged at two shillings (20p) a day, many of the poor were still forced to emigrate, particularly to Australia, New Zealand and the Americas.

Return to the road on which you were walking and continue to climb up the hill.

At the 'T'-junction turn right and then after 50 metres and around the bend, turn right again into Rue du Clos Durell.

After descending 240 metres, keep with the road a short way taking the first turning right into Rue de la Blanche Pierre and follow. At a right-hand bend in the road, on the left-hand side, look out for the property La Blanche Pierre.

Continue with the road around the bend. On the left-hand side in the garden of the property you will see an apple crusher (sometimes wrongly referred to as a cider press), often used today - as here - as a garden feature.

In the late 17th century it is said that virtually every house had at least one apple orchard. By 1795 over 20% of arable land was under orchard (15% of the whole of the Island), ranging from 36% in St. Saviour to 4% in St. Ouen. By 1801 the Island was producing two million gallons of cider annually, much exported but by far the majority drunk locally (pre coffee and tea!). 30 years later cider was still the main source of the farmer's wealth - every farm had an apple crusher and cider-press and all the required equipment. The cider making process usually took place inside an outbuilding known as a pressoir. The apples were poured into the crusher and a horse would circle round pulling the large round stone to crush them. The resultant mulch then would be shovelled into layers within a substantial press and squeezed to make the final liquid for the barrels. Needless to say quality varied enormously!

Stay with the road as it drops into a valley and climbs up the other side.

At the bottom of the valley listen to the sound of water as the fast flowing stream disappears under the road to carry on its journey down the valley to your right-hand side.

Over the centuries this stream, one of the Island's twelve main streams, supported up to six watermills, two upstream to your left and three downstream. The first one downstream from here was the Moulin de Ponterrin, the ruins you have seen earlier. Nowadays the stream flows into the Grand Vaux Reservoir.

At the 'T'-junction at the end of the road turn left, then take the immediate first turning right and proceed up the steep incline. Follow to the end of the lane.

At the 'T'-junction turn left and follow along the winding road to the end.

At this 'T'-junction turn right, immediately passing the property East Beaulieu to your left. Follow this byway to the end.

At the 'T'-junction turn left (into La Rue de la Guilleaumerie) and keep straight on as it virtually immediately becomes Rue du Pont.

Having proceeded 150 metres down Rue du Pont, take the first turning right into Rue du Vieux Ménage. Follow this winding road for some way.

As you proceed look out for the property Vieux Ménage, standing a little way back from the road on the right-hand side.

Again this is a very old historical house.

You are in the Vingtaine of Maufant in the Parish of St. Saviour. Eleven of the twelve parishes of the Island are sub-divided into 'vingtaines' i.e. originally areas, or little communities, that comprised twenty or so properties (vingt being the French for twenty). The exception is St. Ouen where they use the word 'Cueillette' (from the French verb 'cueiller' - to gather).

The name Maufant has been written in several different ways over the centuries - Malfanc, Malfang, and Maufang. It probably comes from two old French words, 'mau' for mauvais (bad) and 'fanc' or 'fang' or 'fange' , for mud; thus indicating heavy, muddy ground.

There is a likelihood that it is the site of La Chapelle de Maufant. In 1488 there is mention of La Chapelle de Malfanc, but all that remains to testify to the chapel are four window lintels, three appear to have been made by the same man.

Talking of men, one Damyan Poingdestre living here, in 1609 was fined 60 francs for having diluted the cider which he sold. It was mentioned earlier that cider quality varied enormously!

At the junction at the end of the road, take the immediate turning to the right. Follow the road until you reach the first turning left, named 'Petit Ponterrin' and rather hidden as you approach.

Stop at that road junction and opposite the turning, cross-over to the road-side buildings on the right-hand side of the road you have just come down.

Behind these converted farm outbuildings is a most wonderful property with an incredible history - an absolute classic example of an old Jersey property - not to be missed - Le Ponterrin - a most picturesque and interesting Manor House and farm that date from about 1500.

But first some background history. In the Middle Ages the Channel Islands were annexed into the Duchy by the Duke of Normandy. Feudalism and the seigneurial system flourished in Jersey. All land was claimed by the Duke which he then granted to his favourites in return for services and rentes (a type of Mortgage). Such grants were fiefs and their being may pre-date even the existence of parishes.

In 1204 Normandy was lost to the French and the landowners had to choose between remaining Norman or switching allegiance to the King of England. Those who returned to France lost their land to the Crown, whereupon the King re-granted their land to his favourites.
In essence the seigneur enjoyed the benefits and the duties (taxes) from the people who lived within the fief's boundaries. Tenants paid rent, gave 10% of their crop to the church and also had to work for the seigneur (remember previously in respect of the seigneur's mill)- not only beholden, they barely eked out an existence.

The fief, from which the manor house takes its name, was granted originally - together with Le Moulin de Ponterrin (the mill seen earlier) - to the Abbesse de Caen (France) by William The Conqueror in about 1066. The Abbesse of this famous abbey, otherwise known as L'Abbaye aux Dames, was his daughter, Cecile. The name Le Ponterrin probably derives from the Ponterre family who were living in Trinity in 1274. Confusingly the fief and mill are in Trinity and this house in St. Saviour. It was not until 1641 that the house and fief became joined and all became known as Le Ponterrin. The then Seigneur was Phillipe Falle.

On the roadside outbuildings, now next to you, Phillipe Falle's initials can be seen in the keystone dated 1643 at the apex to the window arch (originally a front door), to the left of the impressive double-doored courtyard entrance arch.

However the manor house behind is undoubtedly much older. Internally it is derelict with no stairs or floors and has not been lived in for over two hundred years - owners lived in the front roadside buildings.

To see the superb old manor house without intrusion, take several paces back down the road to the entrance to the fields. First notice the two pigsties adjoining the end of the roadside outbuildings. Then see the superb old manor house and finally, behind the house, the wonderful example of a well-head, complete with an ingenious capability to pour the well-water straight into the cattle trough.

The manor house is simply stunning - the integrity, the proportions, the irregularity of the windows, the simple grandeur and the impressive solidity: all remain intact. Features of the inside structure (fireplaces and arches) all ooze importance, strength, quality and social standing.

Note the front door arch with the three arch stones - probably the biggest in the Island - giving that feeling of immense strength. Note the holes or sockets around the windows. These were to hold the iron bars across the windows, further confirming the age of the property to a time before glass was fitted in windows.

Around 1930 the house was considered by the Société Jersiaise for conversion to a 'folk museum' but the cost was too great. Compromise was reached by arranging the Jersey Kitchen room, still on display at the Jersey Museum in St. Helier.

In summary, undoubtedly the manor house is a crown jewel of Jersey's heritage that, however it can be done, must remain with its integrity totally intact in perpetuity, preserved for future generations.

Return to the walk and the road.

Turn left into Petit Ponterrin and follow the road to the end.

At the 'T'- junction turn right.

Continue with the road, passing the property La Maison Clairval on your left, until you reach the end.

At the 'T'- junction turn left into Rue de St. Mannelier.

Follow the road to reach the property on the left-hand side 'St Mannelier - La Vielle Maison d'Ecole'.

The name St. Mannelier is derived from St. Maglorius or Magloire, which had become Magnely in 1477 and Mannelier in 1660. He was a refugee from Wales who came to the Island in the 5th century and died in 586, having founded a monastery.

In 1477, only nine years after the end of the French Occupation, a school was founded, connected to the St. Mannelier chapel by Jehan Hue, Rector of St. Saviour, to serve the eastern part of the Island. A similar school for the west of the Island was founded in 1494 by Vincent Téhy and Jean Néel at St. Anastase. The education - in those days for boys only - was free. These two were the only schools in the Island for well over three centuries.

Rectors were expected to do their best with a few promising pupils - seigneurs, particularly those with chapels, would have employed priests to teach their sons. Teaching was religion based concentrating upon divinity, latin and the classics.

Religion and education were very much linked. The Church, then much in missionary mode, seized the opportunity to spread its gospels and garner congregations through the eager, open-minded young. Rectors were expected to play their part.

Despite all their faults and shortcomings, the two schools fulfilled a real need. Over a period approaching 400 years they were very instrumental in preparing many local boys for university, where they would not otherwise have been educated sufficiently to take up university scholarships offered locally and by King Charles I.

However it took to the early 19th century before education really took off. Local schools sprang up in varying degrees across all the parishes, with Sunday School in every parish - paramount to the poor.

For example: as well as a national school for the infant poor (many of them clothed annually by charity), St. Helier's 7,000 population had 40 day schools taking 700 pupils, paid by the parents; St. Brelade included separate schools teaching girls sewing; St. Martin included 13 Dame's schools averaging 14 children and a Sunday School for 115 children.

In spite of many changes of fortune the St. Mannelier school (unlike St. Anastase) managed to continue until after the foundation of Victoria College in 1853 (when English became the educated language), but finally closed in 1863.

St. Mannelier school and chapel became a farm and now only the name survives. But the name will always survive locally to remind us of the time when religion and education were so closely allied.

Continue with the road, noting the surprising number of buildings on the left-hand side associated with the name St. Mannelier, and descend to the valley floor.

Still continue with the road as it becomes Mont Sohier and climbs.

Carry straight on some distance to the crossroads.

At the crossroads go straight across into Bel Air Lane and follow to the end.

At the 'T'-junction turn left and immediately right into the car park and the start.

Byways, Tracks and Paths - St. Saviour and Grouville

Parish	St. Saviour and Grouville
Special Features	Expansive and open countryside walking. Straight-forward tarmac byway walking. Sections of grassy tracks and paths.
Start	Small public car park on the east side of Les Varines, St. Saviour, at the end of a very short 'No-through' road adjacent to the 'No-entry' road La Rue de Beauvoir.
	From St. Helier, follow the A3 Georgetown and Bagot Roads. Opposite a petrol station and virtually as Bagot Road becomes Longueville Road, turn left into Les Varines. After 700 metres, on the right-hand side is a 'No-through' road, also signposted 'Public Footpath, La Fréminerie'. This no through road is immediately in front of the signpost for the 'No-entry' road, La Rue de Beauvoir, (also on the right-hand side). The small car park is at the end of the no through road.
	From Maufant and St. Martin, follow the A6 towards St. Helier. At the first major crossroads after St. Saviour's School turn left into Les Varines (opposite Wellington Road). Proceed down the hill. After 400 metres there is a 'No-entry' road on the left (La Rue de Beauvoir). Immediately after that junction and in front of a property entrance, turn left into the short 'No-through' road, also signposted 'Public Footpath, La Fréminerie'. The small car park is at the end of the no through road.
Map Reference	**Jersey Telephone Directory**　　Map 9 C3 **Official Tourist Map**　　66.8/48.6 **Jersey Street Guide**　　Map 33 B7
Terrain	Predominately easy tarmac byways, but with inclines, some long. Several sections of grassy paths and tracks, often in places muddy and occasionally slippery underfoot.
Level of Difficulty	⬤⬤◯ **SOME DIFFICULTY**
Time (approx)	1 hour 50 minutes
Distance (approx)	6 kilometres (3¾miles)
Amenities	None

Byways, Tracks and Paths - St. Saviour and Grouville
Map Guide

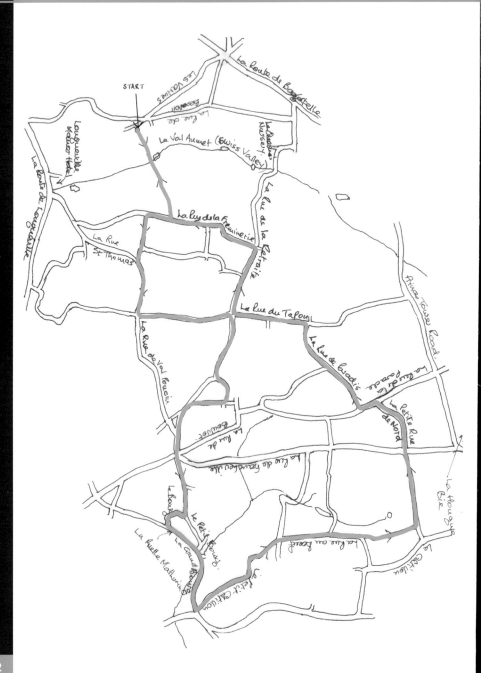

Leave the car park by the gateway you entered. Immediately turn right and pass the signpost to join the Le Val Aume footpath (often muddy in places) and follow.

Drop down into the valley, cross over the stream and continue straight ahead, climbing with the path all the way to the road.

At the road turn right and follow for 100 metres.

After the 100 metres turn left into a narrow grassy path and follow to the road.

At the road turn right and follow the short distance down to the 'T'-junction.

At the main road 'T'-junction turn left . Cross over to use the initial pavement and then continue to stay on the right-hand side, **taking care** (fast moving traffic) as you proceed up the incline.

At the first road junction (crossroads) turn left and proceed up the hill.

After 120 metres stop at Le Tapon Farm on your right-hand side.

> Looking through the pillared entrance notice the excellent, if unusually recent, example of a marriage stone over the door on the farm-house in front of you: PFFO.LMC.1912.
>
> Granite carved marriage stones appeared in the 18th century, attaining maximum popularity between 1720 and 1880. As here, they were usually rectangular lintels placed above the front door. They consisted of the initials of the husband and wife (the husband's on the left and the wife's on the right, using her maiden name), with one, two or entwined hearts all within the date. The date so recorded would be of significance to the couple, often the date of the marriage or construction of the property.
>
> Also notice the old water pump to the right-hand side of the yard.
>
> At the base of each entry pillar, at ground level is a smooth shaped granite stone. These are two excellent examples of 'Heurteurs'. Such stones were positioned in vulnerable spots to prevent carriage wheels, often of heavy carts, from damaging property - their shape ensuring that the wheels moved away from the pillar or wall.
>
> These days one often sees granite stones similarly placed to protect from cars and lorries.

Continue up the hill.

> In the next gateway to the farm notice the rather grand granite piggeries to the left-hand side of the entrance.

Again continue uphill passing Enderley Court on the left-hand side.

At the next road junction (crossroads) turn right into Le Boulivot de Bas and follow.

As you pass, on your left-hand side, make sure that you see the exquisite traditional pink granite house, Le Petit Boulivot.

Just before the front gate of the property, in the roadside boundary wall, notice the Parish Boundary Stone 'SS/G' - confirming that you are leaving St. Saviour and entering Grouville.

Turn left at the next road junction (after 250 metres) and follow up the hill.

At the next road junction, in front of The Barn/Boulivot Farm, turn right and follow downhill to the end.

At the ' T'-junction turn left and follow (beware of fast moving traffic).

The road narrows. Ignore the turning off to the right and proceed to the end.

At the 'T'-junction bear left and follow, passing a 'give way' sign as you approach a five-road junction.

At the five-road junction take the road **straight** across (leaving two roads to your left-hand side).

Immediately passing a football field to your right-hand side, continue with the road until you are alerted by a no entry sign to a track/path on the left-hand side. Ignore that turning. Continue by bearing right with the road you are on and pass through a delightful grouping of character properties.

At the end of these properties, at the road junction on the right-hand side adjacent to Le Bourg House, turn left with the road and proceed down the hill.

As you proceed down the road, the land on the right-hand side - a small wooded côtil on this south side of Le Grand Bourg - is called Le Don Picot. The côtil was donated to the National Trust for Jersey in 1963 by Messrs L.C. and C.A. Picot, Mrs K.M. Picot and Mrs A.F. Le Sueur (née Picot).

Le Don translates as 'the gift' and, as a mark of gratitude, precedes the name of the donor (usually, as in this case, simply using the family name) of the land or property to the Trust.

You will see the National Trust for Jersey's familiar sign to that effect on the right-hand side as you pass the end of the côtil.

Next, on the left-hand side is the property Springvale - much enlarged, renovated and enhanced from its original 18th century build. Note the 1790 marriage stone with the inscription JP and MVA , unusually between the eighth and ninth first floor windows. Here the initials stood for Jean Payn and Marie Vivian Amy.

Byways, Tracks and Paths - St. Saviour and Grouville

Walk Directions

When you are about to reach the main road and immediately in front of a 'Give Way' sign, take a left turn into a narrow road and follow up the long incline.

The road gets even narrower! Keep going to reach a turning off to the left. Ignore the turning, keeping straight on for another 400 metres.

In the early spring, there are lovely wayside daffodils all along the right-hand side of this stretch of road.

After the 400 metres, just as the road veers right and after being alerted by five bend-alert posts on the left-hand side (care - sometimes two, at least, are hidden by undergrowth), take the grassy track off to your left and follow to the end.

Once around several bends and when the left-hand hedging allows, look across left to the farm complex and in particular to the highly unusual if not unique, lovely walled pond.

At the road turn left and follow to the end.

Again take the opportunity to view the farm complex with the walled pond in the background.

At the road junction go straight across into the narrow road and follow that road to the end.

At the 'T'-junction turn left and after 50 metres turn right into Rue du Paradis, again to follow to the end (taking care to ensure that you ignore a turning off to the left as you proceed).

At the 'T'-junction at the end of the road turn left and follow to the crossroads.

At the crossroads turn right into Rue de la Retraite and follow.

Take the first turning left into La Fréminerie and follow down.

Proceed through the 'S'-bend and past some agricultural buildings and sheds on the right-hand side.

Keep straight on past Route des Champs on your left-hand side.

Continue down the road for a further 200 metres. Then you will reach the 'Le Val Aume Footpath' signpost on your right-hand side. **Care though**, it is carefully hidden behind you as you walk!)

Hairpin right onto the footpath and follow to the duck pond on your right-hand side. At the pond be sure to keep straight on (ignoring the path bearing off to the left) to reach the car park and the start.

Adapted from N.V.L.R. 1928

A Quirky Sunday Town Stroll

Parish	St. Helier
Special Features	It is impossible to do justice to everything on offer as you walk around St. Helier. This walk has taken on a different style from the others in the book, but I have, hopefully, been disciplined enough to ensure that the basic tenets remain - interesting and enjoyable walking - and not simply a route march from one must-include historical or interest point to another.
	Quirky in the title allows me a much needed freedom to be selective on a personal basis. **Sunday** in the title allows me to (virtually) ignore commercialism, consumerism and retail therapy - despite the now anticipated wider Sunday shop openings. Sunday in the title also allows the walker a greater capability to **stroll** with relative freedom away from weekday hustle and bustle, hordes and traffic - to really see a quieter, different St. Helier.
	Make sure that you pick the right Sunday and enjoy this varied and quirky selection!
Start	Green Street Car Park (free on a Sunday).
Terrain	Mainly flat town walking, but some inclines and steps.
Level of Difficulty	◉ ◑ ○ **SOME DIFFICULTY**
Time (approx)	2 hours 30 minutes (Allowing plenty of time for a real stroll and leisurely sightseeing.)
Distance (approx)	5 kilometres (3 miles)
Amenities	**Start and Finish** All the Sunday town amenities Public toilet and public telephone at entrance to car park

A Quirky Sunday Town Stroll
Walk Directions

St. Helier - named after a 6th century Belgian child Helerius, whose rich noble and pagan parents were unable to conceive. As a last resort, they begged Saint Cunibert to pray that they would have a child, agreeing that any first-born child would be given to God. A son was born, named Helerius, and was duly converted to Christianity and became a zealous and pious missionary under the wing of Saint Marculf, whose name is intimately connected with the conversion of Jersey to Christianity.

Many legends are attached to Helerius's early life: How he was cured of paralysis by Saint Cunibert on condition that he gave himself up to God; how later he performed miracles; how he became the centre of much unwanted attention; his need to get away and becoming reclusive. Around AD 525 it was Saint Marculf that recommended he go to Jersey - an island then of some 30 souls. Helerius felt that the more uncomfortable life was, the closer he would get to God. He chose the life of a hermit, cut off from land in a shallow cave on a rock or islet near Elizabeth Castle. He died prematurely - beheaded in AD 555, by Saxon pirates and became a martyred Saint - Saint Helerius.

The town still honour him with an annual July pilgrimage to Hermitage Rock (near to his cave) on which his mentor, Saint Marculf, had erected a monastery in his memory.

St. Helier - from a few thatched fishermen's huts on marshy land huddled around the Church to the bustling metropolis, home to a third of the Island's population.

St. Helier - from fishing, shipbuilding, maritime trading and the production of stockings to a major international finance centre.

In the 16th century
Beyond Charing Cross were only sand dunes, and beyond Snow Hill, only fields and orchards. The main streets were La Rue de Derrière and La Rue du Milieu, known today as King Street and Queen Street. (Both of the original names appear on the road signs as you walk.) To the north of those streets was only open countryside. Running parallel to those streets was La Grande Rue, now Broad Street. To its south was only the seashore.

To protect the inhabitants from the ravages of the high spring tides and the gale blown seas there was a seawall, stretching from Charing Cross to what is now called Bond Street. It was extended by the cemetery wall of the Town Church, against which the sea lapped.

Two main streams ran through the town. The northerly, La Faux Bie, reached the sea where the Esplanade car park is now. The other stream, Le Grand Douet, was near today's Conway and Bond Streets.

With streams running down the middle of unmade streets and the streets used as rubbish tips and dumping grounds for everything, the town environment was filth, stench and disease. In those days, long before hygiene was associated with health, the plague and, later cholera, were frequent and deadly visitors and if you survived birth and childhood (which many did not) life expectancy was not a half of that of today.

You are to walk within the town as it is today with snippets relating to the following five centuries. Mission impossible is always a challenge!

So welcome to my personal 'Quirky Sunday Town Stroll.'

Exit the car park the same way as you entered.

At the road, cross over and turn left passing Channel House.

At the end of Channel House turn right into Regent Road and proceed up the incline.

At the 'T'-junction turn left onto the 'No-through' road and follow.

Continue up the road keeping the massive Fort Regent granite walls to your right-hand side.

Before Fort Regent was built the hill (Le Mont de la Ville - Town Hill) was an open common on which the townsfolk grazed their cattle. In 1785 part of it was levelled as a parade ground for the Town Regiment.

During the parade ground's creation a dolmen was discovered. It was known that Sir Seymour Conway, The Lieutenant-Governor of the Island at the time, was a keen archaeologist, so the town officials gifted the dolmen to him. He had it re-erected at his home in England, near Henley, Oxfordshire.

In 1804 this open common land was sold to the British Government for £11,280, with plans for nothing more elaborate than a gigantic earthworks. However, in 1805 it was decided to build a strong modern fortress. The foundation stone was laid in November 1806 by General Don and construction was completed in 1814. It was named Fort Regent after the Prince of Wales (later George IV). The Fort was occupied by units of the British army until 1927.

It was sold to The States of Jersey in 1958 and then developed as a leisure and conference centre and the rest is history - a somewhat chequered history!

Where traffic is banned and the road becomes more of a path, keep straight on to the top.

At the main road **carefully** cross straight over.

In front of you is the new JEC 90 kiloVolt switching station. At the time of going to press the station was expected to be completed later in 2011, at an estimated cost of £10m.

This station will become a critical network hub, connecting the Jersey grid to the submarine cables from France and the La Collette standby electric-generation facility.

The network will feed into a new 200 megawatt grid system, which is anticipated to be completed by 2018/2019 .

In the ten years from 2000 Jersey had joined with Guernsey to import electricity from France. In that time Electricité de France (EDF) has exported 500 million euros of electricity to the Channel Islands through a sub-station on the Normandy coast. Another undersea cable is planned to be completed in 2013 and a new 10 year deal to guarantee a billion euros worth of electricity to the Islands has been signed.

As you face the switching station, go to the plaque on your left-hand side and read the detail relating to a prisoner of war camp.

Here is the site of a 1944/5 Prisoner of War Camp for 41 Americans and 9 British prisoners brought from France or picked up in coastal waters.

With your back to the plaque go straight across and proceed along a short tarmac path past the cement bollard, through a tarmac circle and on to reach a small oblong car park.

At the car park turn left and aim for the gateway in the far corner. Stop at the gateway.

Read the plaque on the right-hand side of the gateway relating to Le Petit Mont de la Ville - a fortified outwork of Fort Regent, known as South Hill Battery.

Carry on up the path for 40 metres.

After 40 metres take the path left, hairpin back on yourself and follow the narrow path up to the top.

At the top of the path turn right and cross over the grassy area to exit via the pathway at the far end.

Keep straight on with this sometimes rather indistinct grassy path, eventually climbing the twelve steps in the far corner to reach the top.

What contrasting views above and around St. Helier -

From old to new - with Elizabeth Castle and the Energy from Waste Plant.

> *Elizabeth Castle. It took over 7 years, but the Castle was finished in 1600. Sir Walter Raleigh was the first Governor to live there. Extensions and additions continued throughout the period 1626 -1647.*

> *The Energy from Waste Plant. It cost £100 million and is capable of processing 105,000 tonnes of waste a year and is complete with a generating capability to produce 7% of the Island's electricity from its waste.*

From ugly to attractive - with the reclamation and industrial site to the harbour and town vista.

Head across to the right passing two World War II German gun emplacement sites on your right-hand side.

To really understand the size and shape of the emplacements, take the opportunity to walk across and explore their other sides.

At the extreme left proceed down thirteen steps to the lower level and proceed to the far extremity.

Again, an opportunity to take in the views and vistas of the harbour, St. Helier, St. Aubin's Bay and St. Aubin itself.

Looking out from here it is astounding to think that until 1844, other than by boat, the sands had been the only means of direct communication between St. Helier and St. Aubin.

Turn back and keeping on this lower level, head for the exit in the corner on the far left-hand side.

Exit the gateway leaving the tall granite wall to your right-hand side. Carry straight on past the buildings and flats to your right.

Continue down the path, through the gateway and into the car park.

Follow through the car park for 20 metres. Then turn left onto the concrete path, descending 12 steps, to go across the children's play area.

With the help of a further 13 concrete steps down, proceed through the whole of the children's play area exiting through the wooden pole path-barrier.

After 10 metres turn right onto the smaller path leading to the road.

Go straight across the road to the top of some steps leading down to the lower road.

Proceed down the 22 steps. At the bottom continue with the pavement for 20 metres to reach a memorial stone.

Note the World War II Prisoner of War Camp information relating to the French North African soldiers who were brought here from France and Alderney from August 1943 to June 1945.

At the adjacent bench, cross over the road to the top of more steps down to a lower road.

These steps overlook the English Harbour. The road in which you are standing is Pier Road. It is so named because, prior to the 1830s, it was the only road to the harbour from the town - a tortuous and long way round to a very inconvenient harbour.

Below you to the left is La Folie Inn, until very recent times, the tavern that served the harbour. (More below.)

Proceed down the 38 steps.

At the bottom of the steps read the plaque relating to the building of the wall extension in 1819/20.

Turn left and start to walk 60 metres on the pavement on this side of the road (and be ready to count!).

*Before you start to walk look carefully at the wall. It housed 27 openings ('les runs à calfaîtage'), used as small storage areas for the tools and oakum (loose fibre obtained by untwisting old rope) used by the caulkers (workers who made boats and ships watertight by stopping up any gaps in the hull) from adjacent shipyards that operated in this area during the 19th century. **Count the openings as you proceed**. The first 15 openings are blocked up but the outlines remain, then there are four that are open and finally another 8 that are blocked up.*

A Quirky Sunday Town Stroll
Walk Directions

After 60 metres (at the end of the openings and in front of the public toilets opposite), cross over the road and carry straight on, past the side of the toilets, out on to the old stone quay straight ahead.

This quay area, known as La Folie, was built in the early 1700's. The stone fronted quay was open to the south-west gales and provided little protection. The tavern bore the brunt of the gales which were a definite deterrent to its trade - to many the tavern literally was a folly.

As early as 1768, the berths on the town (right-hand) side, became known as the English Harbour, whilst in 1769, those on the south (left-hand) side were known as the New Harbour and later the French Harbour.

At each end of the quay note the granite bollards. A sailing vessel would be moved along or away from the quay by the crew hauling on a rope wrapped around the bollard (known as warping).

On the quay turn right and start to follow along towards the far end. However, stop at the second vertical ladder down to the sea.

In the 18th century cannon barrels were set into the quayside for ships to tie onto. By this ladder look to your immediate right, you will see the rusty remnants of one.

Carry on to the far end to reach the second granite bollard.

Take the opportunity to view the harbour area around you.

Go back twelve metres and turn left to follow alongside the granite wall of the buildings, heading towards to the road. Stop as you enter the car parking area.

Note the second cannon barrel.

Continue to the road.

At the road take time to look across to the other side of the road where you now have a better perspective of 'les runs à calfaîtage'.

The objective now is to reach Commercial Buildings; this requires walking around the harbour using the two 90° bends ahead.

Turn left, crossing the road to use the pavement on the other side - it is the safest way.

Proceed towards the first bend.

After 50 metres, note the plaque in the wall relating to the '1,000 ft wall built circa 1820'. Where is the 1,000 feet (300 metres) of wall? Well it was the precursor to the shoreline reclamation for the construction of the whole length of Commercial Buildings and the much needed harbour access road in front. Yes, mainly it runs behind the Buildings, supporting and buttressing Pier Road.

While at the plaque look closely at the row of buildings in front of you starting at the corner. Surprisingly to a lot of people, these buildings actually are the first of Commercial Buildings. A closer look at the facades will show some of the original entrances and stonework, somewhat identical in style to the main row around the next corner.

Follow round the two 90° bends.

Commercial Buildings, or to give them their very descriptive original French name - Le Quai des Marchands (the quay of the merchants).

The dignified row of 31 granite merchants' buildings emphasising strength, solidity and importance, stretching now almost to the tunnel, was built piecemeal between 1818 and 1831, on land reclaimed from the foreshore.

They were built by individual merchants for their businesses, which often included ship building. The ground floors were used as offices, while the area between the buildings and the Pier Road wall housed their equipment, installations and working areas. Living accommodation was above. Rest assured, 'living over the shop' for these merchants was certainly in comfort, even luxurious.

As mentioned earlier, until the merchants' initiative, the only way to the then small and very distanced harbour was by the tortuous and inconvenient Pier Road.

Walk along Commercial Buildings towards the tunnel. If traffic allows cross over the road - a better perspective can be seen from the other side.

As you walk along, where there has not been major alteration or modification, look at the similarity of the buildings. Note in particular the original numbering over the various entrances. Your first, No. 14, was the last built in 1831; No. 15, 1823 was placed back within wholesale renovations; ensure you see Nos. 19 and 20. No. 19 was the first to be built and supports an interesting plaque to be read. Sadly the remainder, both numbers and facades, start to fade as the Norman's yellow takes over!

If you had crossed over the road, cross back over in front of No.26 (in Norman's yellow).

Proceed to the road and the traffic light crossing at the end of the pavement (the one nearest the tunnel). Cross over the road and turn right towards the tunnel. 20 metres before the tunnel entrance and behind the building, turn left and climb up six steps into a courtyard area. Carry straight on to go under the first floor of the building on the far side.

Opening out before you could be a film set of a Dickensian novel- a scene of little courtyards with their original granite cobbles and setts. Use your imagination as to who might be just around the corner...

Carry straight on with the cobbled road.

A Quirky Sunday Town Stroll
Walk Directions

Immediately past the turning right (leading to steps up to Pier Road) on the right-hand side notice the excellent example of original shore-side warehousing. Note particularly the fourth storey hoist.

As stated before, in the early days St. Helier's harbour was primitive and inconvenient. Accordingly vessels would beach between Elizabeth Castle and the Town Church, unload at low tide and bring their cargo up the beach on carts to such merchants' warehousing. (Also, because of a lack of adequate shelter, Jersey's large and highly prosperous fishing fleets would winter elsewhere, usually St. Malo.)

Note on your right-hand side you will see the street name Le Passage Gosset.

The name originates from the Gosset family who had interests in the adjacent properties between at least the late 18th and the late 19th centuries. Amid some controversy, it was Abraham Gosset who successfully proposed the erection of the statue to King George II in the Market Square. The statue was unveiled in 1751 (see later).

With building extensions, the Passage has now become probably the shortest public right of way you will ever see.

As the road bends, again on the right-hand side, note the road sign Ordnance Yard (referencing its earliest usage of handling military supplies). Bear left and proceed to the end of the road.

As you proceed you pass the Jersey Museum on your right-hand side. It is an exceptional museum and a separate must-visit.

The story at the museum begins 250,000 years ago marking the time of the first arrivals to Jersey. It continues through the centuries to explore the factors that shaped this unique Island and its people.

At its core is what was No. 9 Pier Road, a fine example of a prosperous Victorian merchant's town house. The house had been superbly well built around 1817 and is now perfectly restored to enable the museum to have an amazing and unique display for the benefit of past, present and, indeed, future generations. The rooms have been meticulously re-created to their original state, down to the traditional gas lamps and period furniture.

As plaques in the walls on the roadside indicate, the museum has been extended from time to time to incorporate originally adjoining properties, thereby enabling art and other exceedingly worthwhile, sometimes short-term, displays.

The buildings also house the Headquarters of the Société Jersiaise. Note the commemorative stone over the Museum's garden entrance. La Société Jersiaise was founded in 1873, for the study of Jersey archaeology, history, natural history, the ancient language Jèrriais and the conservation of the environment.

With no satisfactory headquarters, in 1893 Jurat Josué George Falle, a founder member, passed a life interest in the Pier Road properties to the Société for as long as the Société should exist and function.

A Quirky Sunday Town Stroll
Walk Directions

WALK 8

As you leave Ordnance Yard you enter the open public space of Weighbridge Place. Bear right and diagonally cross the open area to reach the zebra-crossing adjacent to the two yellow telephone boxes near the taxi rank.

Over to your left perhaps there is a competitive game of boules for you to watch and, at certain times, also the attraction of a market or special event.

Go over the zebra-crossing and, with the help of another zebra-crossing bearing left, you enter Liberation Square.

As you enter the square, just to the left not prominently placed nor grand in style - in fact surprisingly rather inconspicuous for so important an event in Jersey's history, note the stone to commemorate the Liberation of the Island on 9th May 1945 .

Then, ahead of you is the Liberation sculpture 'Monument to Freedom', commissioned by the Jersey Public Sculpture Trust, with public funds. It was unveiled by HRH The Prince of Wales on the 50th Anniversary of The Liberation, 9th May 1995. Sculpted in bronze in 1995 by Philip Jackson, the sculpture is a wonderful masterpiece of art which more than adds to the significant degree of symbolism included in the design of the square itself. The sculpture depicts the feelings of elation on liberation - the two figures, on the left as you look, represent the business community, the soldier represents the liberating forces, the fisherman represents industry, and the family on the right represent the farming community. The 12 fountains represent the 12 parishes and the moat the sea around Island Jersey.

Take a few moments to digest the information on the plaque and reflect on the meanings, thoughts and hopes.

Again, it is surprising that such an ordinary plaque illuminates the extraordinary that has been left here, in word, mind and deed, for the benefit of future generations.

Proceed towards the entrance of Liberation Wharf itself.

But before you do, on the facade over to the left of the entrance, read the names of the two naval officers who, on Liberation Day, first draped the Union Jack flag from a window on the facade above the plaque.

Again, before entering, note the plaque on the facade to the right which confirms that the building was the terminus of The Jersey Railway Company 1895 - 1936.

A railway between St. Helier and St. Aubin had opened in 1870. In 1884 a line was built from St. Aubin's Hospital to the Corbière quarries to carry granite for export.

In 1885 this line was linked to St. Aubin and in 1899 was extended by branch line to Corbière. An eastern line from St. Helier, Snow Hill (see later in the walk) to Gorey was started in 1872, but the final stage was not in place until 1891.

A Quirky Sunday Town Stroll
Walk Directions

The railway zenith was 1924/5 when, for each of these two years, over one million passenger journeys were made. By way of comparison, in 2010 some 3.2 million journeys were made by (Connex) bus, island-wide. Numbers then declined. Rail-cars replaced trains, buses were used to link stations, winter services were dropped, but all in vain - a fire at St. Aubin station was the final straw and the lines were finally closed in 1936 - a victim to car and road transport.

Note too that, unusually, the building was constructed using not only the pink granite of Jersey, but also with the contrasting dark stone imported from Guernsey.

Enter the Wharf. At the time of going to press, the actual shopping mall is closed on Sundays. An opportunity therefore simply to view the new development emphasising the café, restaurant and bar areas, including undercover 'outside' seating.

Exit as you entered and turn left. Continue to the zebra-crossing and cross the main road (The Esplanade) into Conway Street.

In 1786 the Parish Assembly of St. Helier decided to construct Conway Street to make access from the beach to the town more convenient.

The road follows the route of the original (main) town stream, Le Grand Douet, now underground and which now exits into the Town Harbour.

The Street was named after Marshall Conway (Sir Seymour Conway), who was Lieutenant- Governor of Jersey at the end of 18th century and was responsible for the building of the numerous Jersey Round Towers around the Island's coastline.

Proceed towards the end of Conway Street but stop opposite the third turning right, Bond Street.

Look down Bond Street.- that was the line of the 16th Century sea-wall with the Church wall further down on the left - you have just come out of the tide and up from the beach!

At end of Conway Street turn left into Broad Street (La Grande Rue).

As you turn, on your right-hand side of the corner is a large obelisk and surrounding fountain honouring Pierre Le Sueur (1811 - 1853). An outstanding Constable of St. Helier - he was elected five consecutive times. He instigated the construction of underground sewers and provision of clean water for the cholera affected and disease prone town; streets were widened, enabling better transportation to the harbour; street names were posted; the town's houses numbered and a fire brigade formed (see later). In 1847, he quelled the bread riot (see Walk 6, Page 45), calming the hundreds of starving rioters and immediately set up a fund to ease the plight of the poor of St. Helier. He died aged 41, possibly of overwork.

Over 400 people followed his cortege - a real tribute and a final accolade to the town's greatest constable.

A Quirky Sunday Town Stroll
Walk Directions

Proceed along Broad Street.

On the left-hand side you pass the Post Office. Read the small commemoration plaque on the external (path-side) wall. Erected by The States of Jersey in 1976 - the bi-centennial year of The United States of America - the plaque was placed in commemoration to Sir George Carteret (1609 - 1680) a founder of New Jersey, 'a man of the sea and of great affairs'.

Sir George Carteret was the nephew of Sir Phillipe de Carteret, an autocrat, who had been appointed Bailiff in 1627 and later also Lieutenant-Governor.

Sir George had dropped the 'de' from the family name at the start of a successful career in the Royal Navy - it sounded too French. In the 1630s, during an era when Jersey's involvement in piracy and privateering was at its height, he showed himself to be of exceptional resource in his naval exploits to raise funds in support of King Charles I and the Royalist cause.

On the commencement of the English Civil War he retired from the navy, returned to Jersey and in 1640 married Elizabeth, the daughter of his uncle Sir Phillipe. On the death of his uncle in 1643, Sir George inherited the office of Bailiff and was appointed Lieutenant-Governor by King Charles I. He held office for 8 years, 1643 - 1651. His rule was severe, but profitable for the Island and he did much local good. In addition in 1644 he became Vice-Admiral of The Channel Islands - a much needed title to legitimise his privateering on behalf of the king. Needless to say, this appointment came from the King and not as would have been usual, from the Admiralty - then under the control of Cromwell. In 1645 he also received a knighthood and baronetcy.

In the turmoil of the English Civil War he remained strongly and personally devoted to the cause of the king. Sir George also ensured that Jersey remained loyal to the King as the Island disintegrated into its own lawlessness and internecine warfare - in essence, between the parliamentary majority and royalist minority of influential Islanders. Further, under his personal leadership the Island became a refuge for Royalists, amongst whom, in 1646 and again in 1649 - 1650, was Prince Charles. During the second visit, on the execution of Charles I in England in 1649, Jersey proclaimed Prince Charles as King - the first place to do so - Prince Charles said he would never forget all this personal support. Certainly no one could have defended the king's cause more passionately than Sir George or helped so much in preserving the continuity of the English monarchy.

Although Prince Charles was not to be crowned King Charles II in England until the Restoration in 1660, Sir George was not forgotten. He was sworn of the Privy Council, appointed Vice-Chamberlain of the Household, and constituted Treasurer of the Navy. He became a very close advisor to the king and a contemporary of Samuel Pepys.

Knowing of his long interest in the colonies, and the Americas in particular, Charles II also gave Sir George a large grant of land in the American Colonies, which Sir George immediately named New Jersey.

Sir George ensured that many of the Island's poor, who wanted to emigrate, went to the Americas and New Jersey in particular, where many of their descendents still exist.

(In the interests of brevity and space, much has been omitted from Sir George's extremely colourful later life, with its various ups and downs. Suffice to say he remained loyal and amongst the King's favourites.)

Follow down to reach Charing Cross and stop at the tall toad-topped column. This is Le Bouan Crapaud stone, sculpted by Gordon Young in 2004.

Commissioned during celebrations marking Jersey's 800-year link with the Crown and donated anonymously by an islander, this piece of public art sits at the western end of the old historic town, on the site of the 1693 prison demolished in 1811. The column text comes from the 1771 Code of Jersey Laws.

Jersey was the last Channel Island to be cut off after the Ice Age, so the common toad is found only on this particular Channel Island - thus the reason why Jersey people are known colloquially as 'crapauds', taken from the Jèrriais language.

Keeping 'the toad' topped column to your immediate <u>left</u>, carry straight on, initially still in Charing Cross but leading straight into York Street, for fifteen metres.

As you walk down, after fifteen metres, in the pavement read the first of what will be a total of sixteen carved granite paving stones on both sides of the road - the Occupation Paving Stones. Laid in 2005, on the 60th anniversary of Jersey's Liberation, these sixteen stones are inscribed with the words of islanders who lived through the Occupation and slave workers brought to Jersey to work on the German fortifications.

Keep to this left-hand side pavement and proceed.

As you continue down the road read another six paving stones.

Stop at the next turning left (Seale Street).

Do not turn at this road junction, but take time to admire the architecture of the impressive Town Hall building on the opposite side of the road.

Go straight across the zebra-crossing to reach the Town Hall (Salle Paroissiale de St. Helier). Start walking down the pavement in front of the Town Hall.

As you walk continue reading three more stones - all in front of the building.

Stop at the third and last inscribed paving stone.

Turn to face the façade of the Town Hall and, opposite this last paving stone, look at the end ground floor window and its supporting stonework. Then compare with the rest of the ground floor windows. Yes, it is different! The window is bigger and the stonework underneath is different. Folklore, at least, suggests that at the time of building the Town Hall in 1872 this window did not exist, but there were doors here instead behind which the town fire engine was kept.

In the early 18th century the authorities started to become very concerned about buildings as a possible source of fire. Bye-laws of 1715 stated property owners had to have two good leather buckets as a fire precaution. Also any new and replacement thatched roofs were banned and owners were given up to ten years to replace existing thatch with slate or tiles.

The late 17th century saw the birth of property insurance through English companies e.g. Sun Fire Office, Royal Exchange, The Phoenix - those and many more born out of The Great Fire of London of 1666. Eventually, for identification purposes, the insurance companies introduced fire marks: properties were marked with the company's plaque which included the fire policy number (you will see an example later). Each company made its own individual arrangements to deal with fire. If a fire occurred, company fire-fighters would turn out but, if the building was insured by another company, blaze or no blaze, it was not their problem, so they would just walk away or sometimes even positively thwart attempts to put out the fire. Such hindrance was seen by some as good marketing, as were the fire-fighters smart, even outlandish, uniforms.

To get over the problem, in 1845 the town parish, with the drive and initiative of Constable Pierre Le Sueur and with the help of donated fire buckets and a fire engine, took the decision to form a fire brigade. Initially the fire engine was based in Don Road prior to it being moved to the Town Hall, which was built in 1872. As the service expanded - yes, you have guessed it - the fire engine left the Town Hall, the Town Hall was re-modelled, a new window and its stonework replaced the 'garage' doors - hence the differences you see.

Using the zebra-crossing in front of the Town Hall, cross over the road and turn right to return back up York Street staying on the pavement on this side of the road passing four more inscribed paving stones.

Again, read these next four paving stones (this time much easier as the words face you).

Do **not** take the next turning left (Dumaresq Street) but cross over the road and carry straight on with the pavement to find the last two inscribed paving stones.

Again, read the final two.

Keeping with the pavement, proceed into the pedestrian precinct - King Street (La Rue de Derrière). As you enter look for the Cross on the right-hand side.

The Cross (La Croix de la Reine) was erected by The Town Vingtaine (Vingtaine de la Ville) in 1977 to commemorate The Queen's Silver Jubilee. Good at French? Read all the detail, including that on the plinth!

Proceed up King Street and, at the next road junction, turn left into New Street (La Rue Durell).

As you turn see, and hopefully hear, the clock - the Rivoli Revolving Clock -on your right-hand side above the jewellers. A marketing gimmick, the clock celebrates Jersey's three principal industries - finance, agriculture and tourism - and chiming on the hour between 10am and 6pm each day. Try joining in with the well-known tunes!

Proceed down New Street for 80 metres to reach, on the left-hand side, the National Trust for Jersey property, No 16 New Street.

The house is undoubtedly the finest remaining early Georgian house in St. Helier. Bought in 2003 for £1 by the Trust in a very dilapidated condition, the house has been lovingly and meticulously restored, at a cost in excess of £1 million, internally to reflect the property's most dominant period - the early 19th century.

Originally in isolation on the edge of town, with rather wet marshy land and stabling, the house was built around 1740 when the road was called La Rue Durell, and built right on the town stream (Le Grand Douet) which now flows underground.

The property is so worth an internal visit, when it's history will be revealed and full information available. If it is not open (at the time of going to press it was planned to open to the public by the end of 2011) you must return another time.

Retrace the 80 metres back to King Street. At the road junction turn left into the shopping precinct (King Street).

After 20 metres, turn right into Brook Street (Petit Douet).

Both names indicate water (with its, then, accompanying mud, filth and squalor), and confirm the link to the nearby main town stream - Le Grand Douet.

Ignore the turning left (Vine Street) and carry on the short way to the 'T'-junction.

At the 'T'-junction turn left into Library Place.

Almost immediately, over the road on your right hand side, as indicated by the plaque on the wall, is the building which housed the Island's first public library.

The Very Reverend Philippe Falle (1656 - 1742) first made his offer of a library and books in 1729, but the project was fraught with difficulties and building did not commence until 1737. It was finished five years later, but sadly not until shortly after his death. The library stayed in this building (The Old Library) until 1886. It then moved to rooms in the States building in The Royal Square and moved again to its existing site in 1989, with that fine building being opened by Her Majesty The Queen.

Architecturally, this library was one of the first buildings in Jersey to be built using brick. The ground floor was to house the librarian. The library was on the first floor. Around 1830 it was extended for the ever growing library, when the attics became another storey and, invisible to the road, new attics were added above.

Note the Philippe Falle 'PF' initials on the hoppers at the top of the two down pipes.

The road now veers right and becomes Church Street. Do not take that road but carry straight on with the paved walkway leading into The Royal Square.

*However, **before** you carry straight on, take the opportunity to look up Church Street. In the plague ridden days of the 16th and 17th centuries, the street was notorious for the filth, squalor and stench - it was virtually impassable. Its original name was La Rue Trousse Cotillion (Tuck Up Your Petticoat Street).*

Proceed towards the Square.

As you proceed, notice the last building on the left-hand side, with the old blue 'Police' sign outside.

Built on the site of the old meat market, the building, Piquet (Picket) House, was used by the military police until 1924. In 1995 it was acquired by The States to establish a police station in the town centre. The station closed after only a few years. However, with a change of strategy, after an absence of more than a decade, the police station re-opened in 2011, to house a new Town Policing Unit with high-visibility 'bobbies on the beat'.

In the wall to the left of the door is an original blue emergency phone, or police alarm, 'No. 2'. (It had been installed in 1901 in another part of town. There were a total of eight such alarms around the town at that time.) The detail given of its workings makes interesting reading.

Also note the sundial - if the sun is out, check the opinion that says the sundial runs about four minutes ahead of GMT.

Enter The Royal Square.

The Royal Square was originally the town market, known as Le Marchi or Le Vier Marchi. (As far back as the 12th century King Henry II had given the Right to establish a market near the church.) In those early days shopping as we know it did not exist. The wealthy went to France or sent their representatives to some continental fair. The poorer people made or produced all that they needed for their very frugal existence but occasionally came to town, to the market place, where they brought their produce, animals and knitted goods for sale.

Adjacent to Le Marchi were the corn and meat markets. Until it was paved over in 1668 the market was an area of mud, filth and squalor and nearby roads were almost impassable. However, the paving did not solve the total problem and noise and congestion added increasingly to the general mêlée. Eventually the adjacent Court House found it impossible to operate effectively so the decision was taken to move the market to a marshy site on the then edge of town. The new market was opened in 1803 but was knocked down in 1881 and replaced in 1882 on the same site by a larger and much grander market - the one we still have today.

A Quirky Sunday Town Stroll
Walk Directions

Having entered the Square, to your right, within the paving is a large rectangle with the word 'Vega' inside, of which the 'V' is outstanding. Proceed to the spot and let us start there.

The word was originally laid during the Occupation by Joseph Marie Le Guyader, a local stonemason, at a time when he was doing remedial work on the Square paving.

With the Occupation by German Forces in June 1940 came real hardship. By 1944 food, medicines and fuel were almost non-existent and the Island, both the occupier and the occupied, was starving. However, there was good news: a Red Cross ship was on its way bringing food and medicines. On 31 December 1944 the 'Vega' unloaded 250 tons of provisions - by way of individual parcels, courtesy of the Canadian Red Cross.

Until Joseph Le Guyader had finished his work, the extra large letter remained hidden under a cover. The outstanding 'V' was a 'V' for victory and to have been caught in such an act of defiance would have ensured at least a prison sentence.

However, according to gathering folklore, for some reason, reflecting on such a large symbol 'V', directly under the noses of the Occupiers, seemed to kindle thoughts that brought much needed light relief to many long suffering local people!

Read the more recently added inscriptions forming the rectangle now surrounding the original 'Vega', reflect and you in turn, also smile!

Move across the Square to the Statue of George II.

Erected apparently in gratitude for monies the king gave (or was about to give - how could he then refuse) for harbour improvements, the statue was unveiled in 1751. At the same time the Market Place was re-named The Royal Square. However, until the market finally moved to its new site in 1803, the Square was still referred to by most as the market place - Le Marchi or Le Vier Marchi.

On the plinth of the statue note the marking 'B↑M'. It stands for 'benchmark' and the arrow points to the exact mark in the plinth from which, historically, all distances in the Island were measured.

As you face the statue from the way you joined the Square, over to your left on the corner is a jeweller's shop. Proceed towards the jewellers.

High on the right-hand side of the jeweller's shop-front facing you notice a small plaque. This is the fire insurance company fire mark mentioned earlier - the number being policy No. 22985, the company London Insurance and the year 1747.
However, so valuable, vulnerable and unique is this fire mark that it is a fibre-glass replica. The lead original is safely in a locked cabinet on public display within the shop.

Start to exit the Square through Peirson Place, by the side of the jeweller's shop, but almost immediately stop at the plaque in the wall of the public house on your right-hand side.

Synonymous with the Square is the Battle of Jersey on 6 January 1781, one of the major turning points in the history of Jersey, fought between two adversaries Jersey and France, led by Major Peirson and the Baron de Rullecourt respectively and won by Jersey. Both men lost their lives in the short but bloody battle centred finally in the market place, with Major Peirson and his men having entered by your exit route, which was then named Avenue du Marché.

The Peirson Plaque on the wall of the public house to your right must be read and the filled-in holes of the musket balls, within the wall, seen.

Snatched from political capitulation, by an only just 24 year old and only recently promoted Major Peirson, his courageous victory was also a victory for personal strength of character, conviction, initiative and leadership.

Proceed the short way through Peirson Place to the main shopping precinct- King Street.

Turn right into King Street and proceed the few metres to Halkett Place crossroads.

Go straight across the crossroads into Queen Street (thus continuing down the shopping precinct) and follow.

As you proceed, ignore window shopping and look to the upper floors to see the varying architecture and often ornate and quality detailing.

For example, on the first shop on the right-hand side making the corner, note the delft-style blue tiling and the marble-esque columns.

At the end of the precinct the immediate area encompassing all the roads is known as Snow Hill (Pompe de Haut). Stop at the sculpture on the pavement.

Known as Les Jongleurs (a group of musicians) sculptured by Carole Vincent, the sculpture was donated to the town by The Jersey Public Sculpture Trust in 1996. With its seating, it was designed to create a focal point at the junction of Queen Street, Bath Street and Snow Hill.

Leaving the art to your left, proceed right, remaining on the pavement, to reach the road (Hill Street to the right and La Colomberie to the left). Cross over the zebra-crossing and turn left.

Take an immediate turning right into Regent Road (Ruette de la Comédie) and proceed up the steps of the road.

As you climb up the steps, the area to the right was the terminus area of the Island's second railway, the Jersey Eastern Railway Company, which ran from here to Gorey from 1873 to 1929. But like the other company, the Jersey Railway & Tramway Company mentioned earlier, it finally found that it could not compete with the car and road transport and went into voluntary liquidation in 1929.

As you start to walk up the road, notice the huge amount of excavation it took to create the line of the railway track, now a car park.

Continue up the road passing four sets of wrought iron-rail protected front door steps, and stop at the fifth (No.16 Regent Buildings).

Note the plaque in the wall relating to Lilian Mary Grandin.

She was born in 1876, was one of the earliest pupils at the Jersey College for Girls (founded in 1880 as the Jersey Ladies College) and was the first lady in Jersey to become a doctor. She was twenty when she offered herself for medical work in the West China Mission of the United Methodist Church in the remote Chinese Province of Yunnan (some 2,000 miles up the Yangtze river from Shanghai) where, as well as being a much travelled hospital doctor, she set up clinics and a leper colony and trained Chinese women to become midwives and nurses. She died 28 years later of typhus still in China, aged 48. Her hillside grave in Zhaotong is marked with the words 'a beloved physician'. A House at JCG Prep is named after this inspirational and legendary former pupil, in whom the school has great pride.

Continue down the road for a further 30 metres to reach a locked gateway with a large rather simple mural behind.

This was the gateway to a property known as Beau Regard. The Latin over the 1831 gateway translates to 'this corner of the world beyond all others smiles upon me'. As the mural shows, at that time the house had extensive and magnificent country and coastal views.

A poignant reminder of the negative side to progress?

Ignoring the next turning left, La Chasse, proceed down the road for a further 120 metres to the road junction.

At the road junction bear left and proceed to the main road, with the car park in front of you.

At the main road turn left and then cross over the road to the car park entrance and return to the start.

Fern Valley

Parish	St. Helier
Special Features	Undoubtedly one of Jersey's prettiest inland spots. A short tranquil and reflective walk. Liberation Wood. Often ducks in the reservoir and sheep (from 2011) in the central wet-meadow. **Fern Valley also features in a longer walk - Walk 11 - Two Valleys.**
Start	Very limited parking at the entrance to the National Trust for Jersey, Fern Valley, located adjacent to the pumping station some 400 metres to the left as you proceed down the one-way very narrow Fern Valley from Mont Cochon/La Route de Mont Cochon.
	From St. Helier/First Tower proceed along the inner road - A1, La Route de St. Aubin. At First Tower turn right onto the B27, (Le) Mont Cochon and follow up the hill for 1600 metres (approx 1 mile), then turn right under a canopy of trees into Fern Valley.
	From St. John follow the B27, initially La Rue Du Bel au Vent, leading into La Route du Mont Cochon, virtually 3 kilometres (nearly 2 miles), then to turn left into Fern Valley.
	Please park prettily and considerately at your own risk. As you leave, remember it is one-way.
Map Reference	**Jersey Telephone Directory** (for the turning off the B27 - Map 8 I1 Map 8 H1) **Official Leisure Map** 63.9/51.0 **Jersey Street Guide** Map 22 D7
Terrain	Track and path, with areas of decking over streams and water; steps and some inclines (including one climb of 31 steps).
Level of Difficulty	◓ ◑ ◯ **SOME DIFFICULTY**
Time (approx)	45 minutes
Distance (approx)	1½ kilometres (1 mile)
Amenities	None

Fern Valley
Map Guide

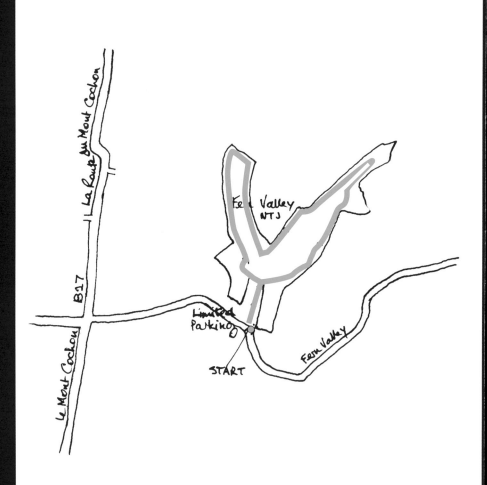

Fern Valley (Le Côtil au Cacher) was acquired by the National Trust for Jersey in 1989. The land covers some 24 vergees (11 acres) and was bought from The Jersey New Waterworks Company at the time they compulsorily acquired Trust properties in Queen's Valley needed for the construction of the Queen's Valley Reservoir.

Fern Valley represents in microcosm everything that is good about country walking. Undoubtedly one of the prettiest inland spots in Jersey and to me one of the best jewels in a wondrous crown. It consists of a central wild flower rich wet-meadow with a stream surrounded by mixed broad leaf woodland. The Valley takes its name from the numerous ferns in the woods, seen throughout the walk.

The reservoir is fed from the stream you will see in the valley and the pumping station pumps the water to the Millbrook Reservoir - these days by electric pump having converted from diesel in the 1960s.

Keeping the pumping station and adjoining small reservoir to your left walk around the locked gateway, using the steps to the side, and follow down the track until you reach the meadow where it divides into two paths.

Take the path to the left and follow the decking across the water and stream.

Stop and listen to the lovely soulful sound of the water.

At the end of the decking keep with the path bearing left and climb up the steps.

Follow the path along. Where it turns 90º to the right keep with the path and descend the steps.

Cross more water by using the decking. Afterwards bear left and follow.

Continue with the path eventually to climb up four steps to the path junction. At the path junction turn left and continue.

The path will bring you to a cleared côtil on the right-hand side - an area now known as Liberation Wood.

This new wood was created in 2005 to commemorate the 60th anniversary of the Liberation.

The project, a joint venture between the National Trust for Jersey and the Jersey Sculpture Trust, involved the planting of 60 saplings - 30 oak and 30 ash - in this unspoilt natural beauty spot - a symbolic reminder replacing some of the thousands of trees lost during the Occupation. In folklore the oak is a symbol of strength and wisdom and the ash renowned for its potent healing properties. They were chosen as a reminder that such times should not be repeated.

The final tree was planted by Michael Ginns representing The Channel Islands Occupation Society on the 16th December 2005.

The wood was designed to compliment the Freedom Tree sculpture on the waterfront commissioned by the Jersey Sculpture Trust and unveiled by H.M. The Queen on Liberation Day 9th May 2005 - linking the natural and built environments in the same project with both needing to be preserved for future generations.

Fern Valley
Walk Directions

The wood - seasonally a bracken covered côtil - is being maintained and preserved for future generations by the National Trust for Jersey rangers working alongside people serving Community Service Orders under supervision of the Probation Service who also helped in the path construction.

Keep with the path all the way along below the wood.

At the path sign bear right keeping with the path, initially up a total of 31 steps and then 12 more, to the top of the wood. Follow across the top to the viewing platform and Information Board.

Absorb the information on the board.

This will make an ideal spot to reflect again all aspects of the Occupation and the folklore symbols of the oak and ash.

Records show that 100,000 trees were cut down during the first four years of the Occupation. The rate of felling accelerated after that as fuel became more and more scarce.

Wood was used also for essential repairs to footwear and wooden clogs were made at a local factory. Wood was such a precious resource that it was illegal under the Forestry (Jersey) Order 1941 to fell trees without the permission of the German forces or the Labour Department.

Continue with the path.

In early summer a wonderful short section of foxgloves and bracken.

Later climb three steps and then descend with the help of twelve steps to the path 'T'-junction.

At the path 'T'-junction turn left to start to circle the wet-meadow and follow.

Stop along this straight section to admire the view and, once again, take in the peaceful tranquillity.

At the end of this straight section bear right.

Proceed down five steps and cross the marshy area and small stream using the decking.

Again stop and listen to the lovely sound of the babbling water!

Proceed up the steps and continue along the path around to the right as it follows the side of the meadow.

Keep looking right at the view and feel the serenity - 'Oh no, not an aeroplane to spoil it!'

You will be alerted to the end of the meadow circuit by several groups of steps.

As you descend to and then reach the original track turn left.

Follow the track back to the road and the start.

NOTE: If you have parked at Fern Valley you are reminded to drive away turning left.

Sights and Sounds of Water

Parish	St. Lawrence
Special Features	The seemingly constant soulful sight and sound of water. Lovely woodland, stream-side and road-side paths. The interesting and absorbing information given along the route where it follows the superb St. Lawrence Millennium Walk. **CAUTION** **Because of vegetation growth in summer on certain sections of the paths, when walking at that time, although the paths are maintained, it is advisable to cover your legs.**
Start	In Waterworks Valley (C118 - Le Chemin des Moulins) just 1400 metres up the valley from the main road (A1 - La Route de St. Aubin) and having just past Millbrook Reservoir on the right-hand side of the road, there is a turning right - Ruelle de St. Clair. Do **not** turn into the Ruelle; but <u>immediately</u> past that road, there is a very narrow brick- pillared entrance to a small car park. Turn directly and carefully into that car park. (The car park is in front of the cottages and on the far left-hand as you enter, you will see the Parish of St. Lawrence Board relating to the Millennium Walk.)
Map Reference	**Jersey Telephone Directory** Map 8 H1 **Official Leisure Map** 63.1/51.1 **Jersey Street Guide** Map 22 A8
Terrain	Mainly woodland, stream and roadside paths, at times undulating and with several steep climbs (including one of 74 steps); one section at least always muddy; some roads and byways on the return.
Level of Difficulty	⬤ ⬤ ◯ **SOME DIFFICULTY**
Time (approx)	2 hours 20 minutes
Distance (approx)	6¾ kilometres (4¼ miles)
Amenities	None

Sights and Sounds of Water
Map Guide

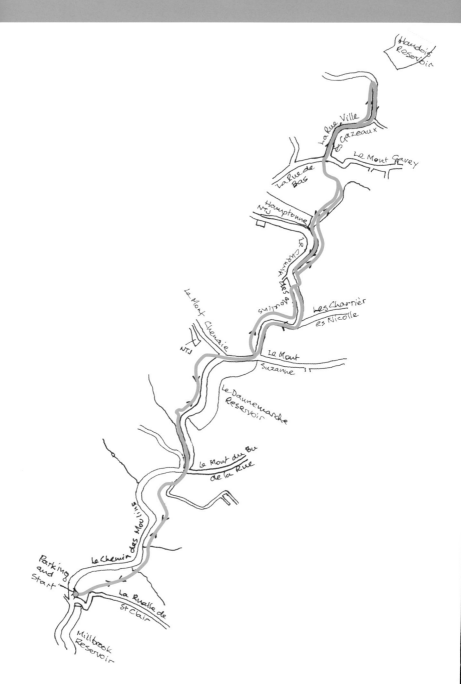

This walk largely follows the parish's superb Millennium path – Le Sentier des Moulins. The path was created, under expert advice, by some forty St. Lawrence parish volunteers. It was commenced in late 1998, virtually finished in 2000 and totally completed in 2002 – an amazingly quick time. It required much by way of permissions, agreements and approvals, hence had to be constructed piecemeal. Broadly it follows the sites of the valley's earlier six watermills.

The path is seen in importance not only for the achievement and its enduring nature, but for the community spirit within the parish the making engendered.

The creators were supported throughout with refreshments by the St. Lawrence Ladies Action Group who were affectionately known by the acronym SLAGS.

Waterworks Valley (Le Chemin des Moulins)

Between the 13th and 19th centuries there were as many as six mills in the vicinity, all dependent on the flow of water from the main streams flowing through St. Lawrence, now Waterworks Valley. The main stream, one of the swiftest in the Island and dropping well over 100 metres in nearly 5 kilometres, was powerful enough for the tusk – it was therefore known as Mill Brook.

As the town of St. Helier grew from the beginning of the 19th century, concern with regard to health intensified. The catalysts for piped drinking water were a terrible outbreak of cholera in 1833, bringing 348 fatalities and subsequent periodic outbreaks, including 1849 when nearly 300 died.

Subsequently the first waterworks company was established. Piped drinking water began to flow from the St. Lawrence streams to St. Helier from 1870.

Today, rather than just the streams and mills of Le Chemin des Moulins of bygone days, we speak of Waterworks Valley, because of the large reservoirs of Millbrook (1895), Dannemarche (1908) and Handois (1929) and the associated pumping stations, machinery and equipment that contribute to the capture and holding of water from those same streams and its piping to various parts of the Island.

Start the walk by following the arrow in the Parish of St. Lawrence Le Sentier/La Sente des Moulins board.

Cross over the brook and follow the path, turning left along side, and then crossing the water gully. Immediately after crossing climb the eleven steps.

When you come to a path 'T' junction turn left and follow that path, crossing over a wooden platform and then continuing until you come to a small trickle of water crossing the path. Cross that water, using the granite stepping stone. After ten metres turn left onto the main path and follow down.

Keep with this wide path passing a stone bench on your right-hand side.

Sights and Sounds of Water
Walk Directions

Can you read the total inscription?
'Jesus said come unto me and you shall find rest in your soul' (?)

Continue to follow the path all the way, still keeping with it as it narrows, climbs up and passes several lengths of boundary fencing on the right-hand side.

Follow to the end. At the road turn left and follow the short distance to the main (Waterworks Valley) road.

Cross over the main road aiming slightly left towards the Pine Tree Kennels but finding the no-entry sign (to Le Mont Misère).

To the right of the no-entry sign take the wooden raised path down three steps in the wet meadow.

Follow this raised path around.

Absorb the Le Sentier des Moulins information plaque.

Cross three platform bridges.

At the third bridge note the names nailed into the wooden floor.

You will see such First names along various parts of the walk - they are those who helped with the particular sections of the Millennium path.

Also read the 'Streams' information plaque.

Still with the path take the four steps up. Turn left at the top following the 'Footpath' arrow.

After a few metres climb nine steps. Shortly after climb another sixteen.

Then cross over the track and climb another 74 steps.

Continue to follow the path. Finally, after a climb of a further 45 steps, descend, still with the path.

Above the reservoir absorb the information on the two plaques on the tree trunks on your right-hand side - 'Valley Structure' and 'Valley Mills - Le Moulin de Dannemarché'.

When you are virtually at the bottom of the path follow the last steps around to the right and follow in that direction until you reach the main road.

Turn left onto the main road and follow its white lines for some 100 metres.

Re-join the footpath as directed by the sign by turning left through the cleft in the rock. Initially crossing the bridge over the water channel, follow the path to the end - crossing several more bridges particularly as you approach the end.

En route absorb the information on the plaque, on the tree trunk to your left, relating to the 'Red Squirrel'.

A final bridge indicates the end of this section of the path.

On the last bridge again look out for the names nailed into the floor.

Also read, on the right-hand side, the adjacent plaque relating to 'Moulin de la Haye'.

As you come off the bridge continue left.

Immediately on your left-hand side on tree trunks are twin plaques relating to trees and flora. Absorb the information.

Continue with the sometimes indistinct path near or alongside the stream to your left which runs roughly parallel to the road.

Do not forget to listen to the babbling water. Also note the tree planted to commemorate the 60th Anniversary of the St. Lawrence W.I.

At the end, climb the seven steps and cross the main road (Le Chemin des Moulins) and aim for the twin plaques on the left-hand side of the open space that you enter.

Absorb the information on the twin plaques concerning the 'Jersey Cow' and 'Roadways - The Occupation'.

Take the path immediately to your left, descending seven steps. Cross over the stream and head-on up the path alongside, but 'below' the road and on the edge of the meadow.

When you reach the plaque, at ground level on your left-hand side - showing you where you are – turn right through the small gate. Enter the marshy field to the left using the much needed stepping stones. Then go up seven steps and join the lower more indistinct path by turning right.

Keep with this path. Amongst others, in due course this will take you over Mark and Ted's steps. Continue over the bridge (again with helpers' First names), across more stepping stones and at the end, five more steps.

At the top of the steps turn right onto the path and follow. When it opens out, cross the field to reach the gate, sign-post and the plaque.

Absorb the information on the plaque 'Valley Mills –Le Moulin de Quétivel'.

Cross over the road and, noting the modernised mill on your left-hand side, head up the road Ville ès Gazeaux.

Nominated by the Parish in 2005 Rue de Ville ès Gazeaux won the Société Jersiaise Annual Scenic Lanes award for the second time. The judges representing a cross section of associations felt that it "captured the essence of the Island's lanes".

Ignore the first opening on the left-hand side at the end of the metal railings. However after a full 100 metres, at the path marker post, turn left onto the path, initially using the stepping-stones. Keep with the path following the stream around, at times minding your head and not slipping in the mud.

Cross over the bridge and turn right still with the path.

Absorb the information on the plaque on your right-hand side 'Beech and Sweet Chestnut' (trees).

Cross back over the stream and follow the path alongside the road until you reach the Parish of St. Lawrence Board at Handois Reservoir.

Absorb the interesting and varied information on the St. Lawrence Le Sentier/ La Sente board.

Turn right onto the road - back the way you came.

The road walking gives you a better chance to appreciate the award winning scenic lane.

Keep on the road, walking on the right-hand side, until you reach the renovated and converted mill house (now on your right-hand side). The waterwheel is now clearly visible. Proceed to the 'T'-junction.

Cross over the road and re-join the path across the field to the left and follow. Keep with the track/footpath. Almost immediately, in front of the gateway/barrier, bear right with the, now, path and head towards the bridge over the stream. Ignore the turning left, this time carrying straight on over the bridge and keeping with this path all the way to the main road.

As you near the main road note the plaque on your right-hand side relating to the gift by Sally Chambers' family in her memory.

At the main road turn left and follow down for 400 metres, walking on the left-hand side.

After 400 metres, as you approach the first turning left (Les Charrières Nicolle) cross over to the right-hand side of the road into the small car park area.

Go through the car park area and head towards the footpath platform bridge. However ignore the bridge and take the path to its left.

Follow that often marshy path keeping the stream to your right until you reach the main road again.

At the main road turn right and follow (best using the left-hand side), subsequently alongside the reservoir to your left.

What a surprising number of platforms for the fishermen on the sides of the Dannemarché Reservoir.

Keep with the left-hand side of the road, passing the reservoir, to reach the junction with Le Mont du Bu de la Rue. Then continue to follow the main road round for another 30 metres.

Opposite Pine Tree Kennels turn left onto the footpath, passing the Electricity sub-station and the Jersey Water Pumphouse to reach the excellent 'Produced with Pride' St. Lawrence Millennium - Le Sentier des Moulins Information Board - on the far side.

Absorb the board's full range of information - no doubt whetting your appetite for even more.

On your right-hand side is the parish's Millennium Standing Stone. The Société Jersiaise and Ronez Quarries jointly gave each parish a standing, undressed granite stone to commemorate the Millennium. The stone acknowledges earlier paganism. The Jersey Field Squadron of the Territorial Army erected the stones on 5th September 1999. Note the plaque on a nearby stone giving the names of the benefactors involved.

(Additionally The States of Jersey presented each parish with a round section granite cross 2.475 metres high on a simple stepped plinth. The cross symbolises and is in recognition and celebration of the second millennium of the Christian faith. The St. Lawrence cross is situated at the junction of Le Mont Cambrai and La Grande Route de St Jean.)

With the board to your left and the stones to your right look for the 'Footpath' sign ahead and follow the arrow, taking the path in the left-hand corner to enter the woods.

Follow the path straight ahead (keeping the stream to your left)

Stop when the stream passes underneath to the right-hand side.

Ensure you read the information plaque on your right-hand side relating to 'Valley Mills and Le Moulin de Vicart'.

With the aid of a marker post in due course on your right-hand side, continue with this path until you reach the main path.

As you approach the main path, here to the left are the remains of the cellars of the old mill.

At the main path turn right and follow.

Sights and Sounds of Water
Walk Directions

Keep with this path past the stone bench on the left-hand side and still with the stream to your right.

After some 150 metres, at the marker post on your right-hand side turn right.

After ten metres step over the small trickle of water crossing the path and continue with the path.

At the next path marker post take the right fork and follow the path, descending eleven steps, crossing over the stream and following down, to return to the start and the car park.

Two Valleys

Parish	St. Lawrence
Special Features	Lovely woodland paths. Picturesque country lanes. Fern Valley – one of the best jewels in a wondrous crown.
	CAUTION **Because of vegetation growth in summer on certain sections of the paths, when walking at that time, although the paths are maintained, it is advisable to cover your legs.**
Start	The one-way road between St. Lawrence Parish Hall and St. Lawrence Church. Situated on the A10, La Grande Route de St. Laurent.
	Good parking all round the Church and the Parish Hall. Preferably park in the start road between the two.
	You will need to undertake a short one-way circuit, first turning into La Route de L' Église (the other side of the church). Follow that road behind the church and then turn right.
Map Reference	**Jersey Telephone Directory**　　Map 3 B5
	Official Leisure Map　　62.5/51.7
	Jersey Street Guide　　Map 21 F4
Terrain	Predominately undulating paths and tracks, sometimes muddy in places, but with some lanes, byways and roads including a very long and very steep lane to finish.
Level of Difficulty	◉ ◉ ◖ **VERY HARD**
Time (approx)	2 hours 20 minutes
Distance (approx)	7 kilometres (4¼ miles)
Amenities	**Start and Finish** 　Public telephone 　Pub (with food) 　Village shop

87

Two Valleys
Map Guide

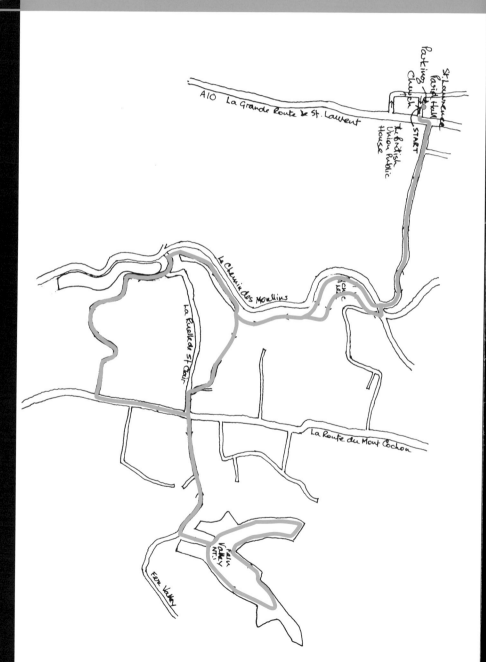

The church is believed to be the oldest building in the parish and amongst the oldest churches in the Channel Islands with records dating back to 1198. However no part of the original structure remains. It has been progressively enlarged, particularly in the 14th and 16th centuries, with the building today largely re-created by a restoration scheme in the late 19th century.

In 1550 the King's Commissioners, apart from leaving one in each church, ordered the Island's church bells to be sold. Half the value raised was used to improve fortifications at St. Aubin. The remaining single bell in the belfry is inscribed 1592 and is the oldest in the Island.

Much speculation surrounds a broken, 1.5 metres high, Roman pillar on display in the church. It bears an inscription that may be as early as the 6th century. It was found beneath the church during the 19th century renovations. The find suggests that the site has been a centre of worship since the 6th century and as such makes the pillar perhaps one of the most interesting and important single historical objects in the Island.

The St. Lawrence Parish Hall was opened in 1882. The siting completed the uniqueness of the parish in having all of its public buildings and other basic amenities within one small area.

Cross over the main road in front of the parish hall and turn to your left; immediately turn right into the signposted 'NO ROAD' (Le Mont Misère).

Once you leave the tarmac still follow the lane past the central yellow barrier post and descend.

Le Mont Misère (Misery Hill) may have been so named because it was so steep.

Proceed with caution - as the byway drops down to the bottom it gets much steeper and can be slippery.

You are now in the main parish valley Le Chemin des Moulins known these days as Waterworks Valley. Between the 13th and 19th centuries there were as many as six mills in the vicinity, all dependent on the flow of water from the streams flowing through the valley. The main stream, one of the swiftest in the Island and dropping well over 100 metres in nearly five kilometres, was powerful enough for the task – it was therefore known as Mill Brook.

As the town of St. Helier grew from the beginning of the 19th century, concern with regard to health intensified. The catalysts for piped drinking water were a terrible outbreak of cholera in 1833, bringing 348 fatalities and subsequent periodic outbreaks, including 1849 when nearly 300 died.

Subsequently the first waterworks company was established. Piped water began to flow from the St. Lawrence streams to St. Helier from 1870.

Two Valleys
Walk Directions

Today, rather than just the streams of Le Chemin des Moulins of bygone days, we speak of Waterworks Valley because of the large reservoirs of Millbrook (1895), Dannemarche (1908) and Handois (1929) and the associated pumping stations, machinery and equipment that all contribute to the capture and holding of water from those same streams and its piping to various parts of the Island.

At the main road cross over turning left, then immediately (before Le Mont du Bu de la Rue, but to that side of the road) turn right into the road marked 'VICART' on the stone to your right-hand side as you turn.

Climb the hill and, at the end of the barbed wire after 80 metres on the right-hand side, turn right into the footpath.

Keep with this path for some distance passing several lengths of boundary fencing on your left-hand side and later a stone memorial bench.

Can you read the total inscription?
'Jesus said come unto me and you shall find rest in your soul' (?)

Continue on this path, later bearing left and ignoring all the opportunities to turn off right.

The path starts to rise, eventually steeply, and turns into more of a track with water gullies, initially on the right-hand side. Proceed to the top.

At the top turn left onto the road (Ruelle de St. Clair) and proceed up to the main road (B27 La Route du Mont Cochon).

At the last property on the left-hand side, along the base of the boundary wall, are rounded protruding stones. These are known as 'heurteurs'. Their purpose was to protect properties from damage by heavy carts. These days you often see ordinary granite stones similarly placed to stop damage from cars and lorries.

At the main road cross over and under a beautiful canopy of trees proceed into Fern Valley.

Follow the Fern Valley lane, some 400 metres, until you reach the pumping station and adjacent small reservoir on your left-hand side.

The reservoir is fed from the stream you will see in the valley. The pumping station pumps the water to Millbrook reservoir – these days by electric pump having converted from diesel in the 1960s.

At that point turn off the road into the National Trust for Jersey Fern Valley.

Fern Valley (Le Côtil au Cacher) was acquired by the National Trust for Jersey in 1989. The land covers some 24 vergees (11 acres) and was bought from The Jersey New Waterworks Company at the time they compulsorily acquired Trust properties in Queen's Valley needed for the construction of the Queen's Valley Reservoir.

Two Valleys
Walk Directions

Fern Valley represents in microcosm everything that is good about country walking. Undoubtedly one of the prettiest inland spots in Jersey and to me one of the best jewels in a wondrous crown. It consists of a central wild flower rich wet-meadow with a stream surrounded by mixed broad leaf woodland. The Valley takes its name from the numerous ferns in the woods, seen throughout the walk.

Keeping the pumping station and adjoining small reservoir to your left walk around the locked gateway, using the steps to the side, and follow down the track until you reach the meadow where it divides into two paths.

To your right are areas of gorse and bracken. In the bygone days the local inhabitants collected gorse and bracken to use for fuel and bedding.

Take the path to the left and follow the decking across the water and stream.

Stop and listen to the lovely soulful sound of the water.

At the end of the decking keep with the path bearing left and climb up the steps.

Follow the path along. Where it turns 90º to the right, keep with the path and descend the steps.

Cross more water by using the decking. Afterwards bear left and follow.

Continue with the path eventually to climb up four steps to the path junction. At the path junction turn left and continue.

The path will bring you to a cleared côtil on the right-hand side - an area now known as Liberation Wood.

This new wood was created in 2005 to commemorate the 60th anniversary of the Liberation.

The project, a joint venture between the National Trust for Jersey and the Jersey Sculpture Trust, involved the planting of 60 saplings - 30 oak and 30 ash - in this unspoilt natural beauty spot - a symbolic reminder replacing some of the thousands of trees lost during the Occupation. In folklore the oak is a symbol of strength and wisdom and the ash renowned for its potent healing properties. They were chosen as a reminder that such times should not be repeated. The final tree was planted by Michael Ginns representing The Channel Islands Occupation Society on the 16th December 2005.

The wood was designed to compliment the Freedom Tree sculpture on the waterfront commissioned by the Jersey Sculpture Trust and unveiled by H.M. The Queen on Liberation Day 9th May 2005 - linking the natural and built environments in the same project with both needing to be preserved for future generations.

The wood - seasonally a bracken covered côtil - is being maintained and preserved for future generations by the National Trust for Jersey rangers working alongside people serving Community Service Orders under supervision of the Probation Service who also helped in the path construction.

Keep with the path all the way along, below the wood.

Two Valleys
Walk Directions

At the path sign bear right keeping with the path, initially up a total of 31 steps, then 12 more plus 4 more later, to the top of the wood. Follow across the top to the viewing platform and Information Board.

Absorb the information on the board.

This will make an ideal spot to reflect again all aspects of the Occupation and the folklore symbols of the oak and ash.

Records show that 100,000 trees were cut down during the first four years of the Occupation. The rate of felling accelerated after that as fuel became more and more scarce.

Wood was used also for essential repairs to footwear and wooden clogs were made at a local factory. Wood was such a precious resource that it was illegal under the Forestry (Jersey) Order 1941 to fell trees without the permission of the German forces or the Labour Department.

Continue with the path.

In early summer a wonderful short section of foxgloves and bracken.

Later climb up three steps and then descend with the help of twelve steps to the path 'T'-junction.

At the path 'T'-junction turn left to start to circle the wet-meadow and follow.

Stop along this straight section to admire the view and once again take in the peaceful tranquillity. Also note the amount of tree planting on the left-hand side undertaken by Jersey Trees for Life.

At the end of this straight section bear right.

Proceed down five steps and cross the marshy area and small stream using the decking.

Again stop and listen to the lovely sound of the babbling water.

Proceed up the steps and continue along the path around to the right as it follows the side of the meadow, descending steps as you proceed.

Keep looking right at the view and feel the serenity - Oh no, not an aeroplane to spoil it!

You will be alerted to the end of the meadow circuit by several groups of steps.

As you descend to and then reach the original track turn left.

Follow the track back to the road leaving the meadow gate behind you.

Once at the road turn right and follow (Fern Valley) back up to the main road.

At the main road turn left and proceed past the houses and bungalows for approx 400 metres, walking on the right-hand side.

Immediately after Orlagh House turn right and walk down the road (the red postbox in the wall just as you have turned will confirm that you are on the right road).

Keep with the tarmac road as it meanders, initially right, eventually passing 'Newfield' on your right-hand side.

Carry on across the short hoggin area and join the narrow grassy path straight ahead.

While proceeding downhill soak up the glimpse of the sea (St. Aubin's Bay) to your left.

Shortly after the path enters the woods take the path down to the left through the gap in the wooden post fence. Proceed down 70 steps towards the reservoir.

Welcome back to Waterworks Valley. The reservoir is Millbrook Reservoir.

The only sound is water (and the rustle of leaves in the autumn).

Follow this path to the end and then turn left and follow the next path.

Drop down passing in front of Lakeside Cottage. Join the road left and follow down to the main road.

Facing you on the opposite side of the main road is an abreuvoir – a drinking place for animals.

In this instance it was built to enable horses to be watered as they went through the valley laden with stone from the Mont Mado Quarry to St. Aubin for the building of the seawall. Previously steam traction engines had been used but their weight so badly damaged the roads that a change back to horse-drawn was enforced.

Turn right at the main road and then immediately turn right again through the brick pillars into the small front car park.

Cross over the car park, re-joining the path as arrowed by the Parish of St. Lawrence Le Sentier/La Sente des Moulins Board.

Cross over the water channel and follow the path, turning left along side another channel.

Did you notice the water pipe largely concealed in the bottom of the channel?

Cross this channel and climb up the eleven steps to a main path.

Turn left onto the path and follow along crossing over a wooden platform and continue quite a way until you reach a small trickle of water which crosses the path. Cross that water. After ten metres turn left onto the main path.

Continue with this path until you reach the stone bench on your right-hand side.

Are you still sure about the inscription?

After the bench follow the path for some 100 metres. At that point a path turns off left in front of a track marker-post. Take that path and, initially guided by another marker post on your left-hand side, meander with the path down through the trees.

Two Valleys
Walk Directions

Absorb the interesting plaque on the left-hand side relating to 'Valley Mills – Le Moulin de Vicart'.

Continue straight along the path (with the stream to your right-hand side) into the open grassy area to reach the excellent 'Produced with Pride' St. Lawrence Millennium Information Board.

Absorb the board's information –no doubt whetting your appetite for more!

Also on your left-hand side is the parish's Millennium Standing Stone.

The Société Jersiaise and Ronez Quarries jointly gave each parish a standing, undressed granite stone to commemorate the Millennium. The stone acknowledges earlier paganism. The Jersey Field Squadron of the Territorial Army erected the stone on 5th September 1999. Note the plaque giving the names of the benefactors involved.

(Additionally The States of Jersey presented each parish with a round section granite cross 2.475 metres high on a simple stepped plinth. The cross symbolises and is in recognition and celebration of the second millennium of the Christian faith. The St. Lawrence cross is situated at the junction of Le Mont Cambrai and La Grand Route de St. Jean.)

Carry on along the grass on this side of the road.

Keep to the path, passing the Jersey Water pump house and the JEC sub-station to your right, until you reach the 'You are here' information plaque on a tree trunk on your right-hand side.

Cross over the main road and proceed back up Le Mont Misère – beside the dog kennels on your left-hand side and identified by the 'No-entry' sign and the central granite stone barrier.

Prepare yourself for the strenuous and possibly slippery climb up the hill, carry on to the main road and cross over to the parish hall and return to the start.

West St. Lawrence

Parish	St. Lawrence
Special Features	Lovely small valley vista. Long straight stretches of flat country roads and byways with open countryside. Good for striding out. Several places of historical interest. **CAUTION** **Because of vegetation growth in summer on certain sections of the path near the start, when walking at that time, although the path is maintained, it is advisable to cover your legs.**
Start	The one-way road between St. Lawrence Parish Hall and St. Lawrence Church. Situated on the A10, La Grande Route de St Laurent. Good parking all round the church and the parish hall. Preferably park in the road between the two. You will need to undertake a short one-way circuit, first turning into Route de L'Église. Follow the road behind the church and then turn right.
Map Reference	**Jersey Telephone Directory** Map 3 B5 **Official Leisure Map** 62.5/51.7 **Jersey Street Guide** Map 21 F4
Terrain	Predominately straightforward country roads and byways, with one very long, not too steep, incline; one path near the start (often muddy in places) with a reasonably steep incline.
Level of Difficulty	◓ ○ ○ **EASY**
Time (approx)	1 hour 30 minutes
Distance (approx)	5 kilometres (3 miles)
Amenities	**Start and Finish** Public telephone Pub (with food) Village shop

West St. Lawrence
Map Guide

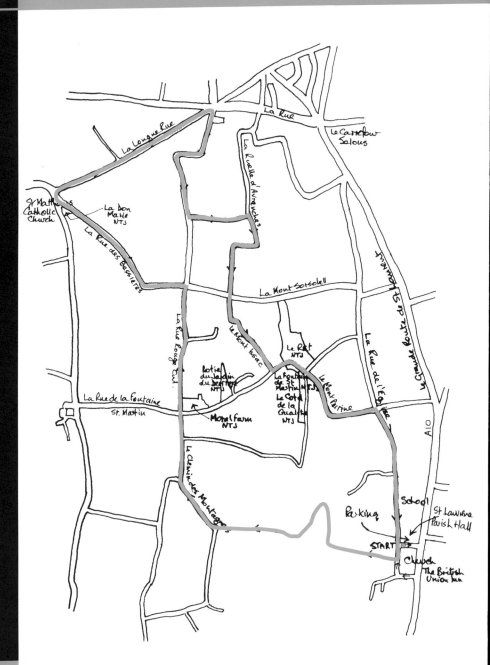

La Rue

Le Carrefour
Selous

La Longue Rue

La Ruelle d'Avranches

St Matthews
Catholic
Church

La Bon
Marie
NTJ

La Rue des Bessières

La Mont Sorsolell

La Mont Isaac

La Rue Rouge Cul

Le Rat
NTJ

La Grande Route du St Laurens

La Rue de l'Eglise

La tie
du Jardin
du bed tree
NTJ

La Fontaine
de St
Martin NTJ

Le Mont Farine

La Rue de la Fontaine
St. Martin

Le Cotel
de la
Qualite
NTJ

Morel Farm
NTJ

A10

La Clemin des Montaignes

School

St Lawrence
Parish Hall

Parking

START

Church

The British
Union Inn

Start in the road between the church and the parish hall.

The Church is believed to be the oldest building in the parish and amongst the oldest churches in the Channel Islands, with records dating back to 1198. However, no part of the original structure remains. It has been progressively enlarged, particularly in the 14th and 16th centuries, with the building today largely re-created by a restoration scheme in the late 19th century.

In 1550 the King's Commissioners, apart from leaving one in each church, ordered the Island's church bells to be sold. Half the value raised was used to improve fortifications at St. Aubin. The remaining single bell in the belfry is inscribed 1592 and is the oldest in the Island.

Much speculation surrounds a broken 1.5 metres high Roman pillar on display in the church. It bears an inscription that may be as early as the 6th century. It was found beneath the Church during the 19th century restoration. The find suggests that the site has been a centre of worship since that 6th century and as such makes the pillar perhaps one of the most interesting and important single objects in the Island.

The Parish Hall. *St. Lawrence decided to build its own parish hall which was finished in 1882. The siting completed the uniqueness of the parish in having all of its public buildings in one small area.*

Turn away from the main road and proceed down the road to the end.

At the end of the road turn left into the 'No- entry' road.

Immediately before the first house on the right (Abbey Gate) turn right, taking the track down the side of the house. After the end of the house carry straight on entering a narrow, often muddy, path and proceed down into the valley.

This is one of the earliest paths in St. Lawrence. It is a 'chemin de corps' (a coffin path). Such paths were the most direct routes for funeral processions to take to reach the church. The paths thereby became public rights of way in perpetuity.

At the valley bottom you reach a stream.

Stop here! Take time to listen to the stream and admire the lovely valley view, particularly to your left-hand side.

Cross over the stream and continue climbing up as the path turns into a track.

This part of the path is reputed to be also 'un perquage'.

In part, perquages were safe-conduct paths allowing criminals to escape arrest. Perquages ran from a sanctuary – the parish church – to the sea and a waiting boat. 'The Sanctuary of the Church' dates from the earliest medieval times and was abolished at the Reformation. A criminal was allowed refuge in the church. He had then to either stand trial or sell everything and leave the Island taking an oath never to return. In the latter case the criminal was led by the priests to the sea along 'un perquage'. Each parish had a perquage and it always followed streams. It says much for the fear of trial and imprisonment and the rough and ready legal system that a criminal would voluntarily emigrate promising never to return.

Keep straight on by the side of the building complex (Badier Farm) to reach the road.

Badier Farm is a beautiful farm with an enclosed courtyard and a double arched entrance. The keystone of the main arch bears a shield with initials and the date 1684. Initials also appear above the arched front door. The initials are those of Jean Ramon who married Sara Gruchy in 1676. Around that time heraldry was often used to indicate the owner of the house and to record the date of some important event in his life. In this case, as we know the marriage date to be 1676, it could be the date of construction of the house or arch.

Join the road and follow round to the right.

The narrow path virtually straight across as you reach the road is a continuation of the 'chemin de corps'.

Keep with the road for a total of 400 metres (in due course ignoring a road off to the left - Les Charrières Malorey).

After some 400 metres you come to crossroads. Turn right into La Rue de la Fontaine St. Martin. However proceed for **only a few metres** stopping at the entrance to the farm on your left-hand side.

This farm is Morel Farm, (hopefully the gateway is open) one of the more important properties now owned by the National Trust for Jersey. Note the wonderful colour of the granite. The property was gifted by Mr Arthur J. Morel in 1939. From Morel family documents there seems little doubt that a property on this site had belonged to them since 1560. The first Morel came from Lisieux, being a Huguenot refugee, one of three brothers, one of whom had been burnt at the stake for his religion.

The site consists of a farmhouse and a range of outbuildings, including a pressoir (containing a fine example of an apple crusher), piggeries and a boulangerie (bakery), clustered around a cobbled courtyard.

The double roadside arch is one of the most perfectly proportioned in the Island. The main arch bears the date 1666 - coincidentally the same year as The Great Fire of London. Note the smaller arch has a Fleur-de-Lys emblem.

To the right of the arch are mounting-steps ('abordas') to assist in mounting one's horse.

The date on the central chimney stack of the house shows 1716. The building with the belfry is much later – 1858. The building is commonly known as The Chapel, but was never used for religious purposes and is currently used for storing potatoes. On the gable, note the belfry in which hangs a ship's bell inscribed 'John Morel 1837'.

Return to the crossroads – this time turning right into Rue Rouge Cul (carrying on in the same direction as before).

Doesn't this vicinity make a lovely traditional setting.

Keep on this road for approx 400 metres. At the first crossroads turn left into La Rue des Bessières.

Follow this road to the end.

On the left-hand side of the corner at the end of the road is the National Trust for Jersey sign Le Don Marie. This small triangular plot of land was gifted to the Trust in 1980 by Miss Leonie Marie.

At its apex on the ground is a stone, roughly the shape of a cube, known as La Pierre des Baissières. On it are five cup marks indicating a Stone Age origin. It may have served as the base of a wayside cross or even as a tribal boundary stone, or possibly may be an early form of heraldry, but nothing can be said about it with certainty. Adding further intrigue is the fact that it is exactly where the boundaries of the three parishes of St. Lawrence, St. Mary and St. Peter meet.

At the end of the road turn right. Immediately to your left is the churchyard of St. Matthew's Church. Enter.

On the left-hand side is a lovely example of a Grotto to Our Lady of Lourdes. The little girl below is St. Bernadette. The grotto is well used particularly by the Portuguese community.

While in the church grounds proceed along the side of the church towards the 'Coffee Room' sign. At the end of the church turn right and go through the iron gate.

Immediately look down to the bottom of the church wall on your right-hand side to see the first building stone, (Premiere Pierre) dated 23 May 1871.

The buildings behind the church housed a Catholic school.

Return to the road and cross over into the 'No-entry' road, La Longue Rue.

West St. Lawrence
Walk Directions

As you turn round the corner notice the very large building (currently looking in a somewhat drab and sad state) on your left-hand side.

The Victorian period witnessed a resurgence of Roman Catholicism. Anti-clerical laws on the continent towards the end of the 19th century led to the arrival of a number of teaching and nursing orders e.g. 1886, De La Salle Brothers and Little Sisters of the Poor, 1909, Faithful Companions of Jesus (FCJ).

This building was built as a convent around the 1880s by a Belgian Order and believed to be in conjunction with St. Matthieu's Church. The Sisters left in 1915. The forerunner of Beaulieu School started there in 1924, remaining until moving to a town site at the end of 1950, when they purchased the beautiful Beaulieu Convent from the nuns - the Helpers of the Holy Souls - who left Jersey after 70 years of devoted work among the poor and needy.

During World War II some 100 German soldiers were billeted here.

It became a furniture depository and has escaped the developers. It is presently used predominately for charity storage.

It is reputed to be very beautiful inside, retaining Saints' names on the doors and still housing the original small chapel.

Keep on this road (La Longue Rue) for some 500 metres.

At the junction with the main road turn sharply right into La Rue Rouge Cul.

Follow this road for approx 400 metres, passing through two 90° bends and then turn left into La Ruette d'Avranches.

Avranches Farm is on the left-hand side as you walk down and is believed to have been built about 1750. It is the first wall that runs down the side of the road that is interesting. Can you find the small stone in the middle with some initials - or is it a date? Can it be AGB?

On the short side-wall protrusion at the end of that wall note the 1767 marriage stone. The marriage stone is somewhat unusual as it does not follow the normal pattern.

Granite carved marriage stones appeared in the 18th century, attaining maximum popularity between 1720 and 1880. They were usually rectangular lintels above the front door. They consisted of the initials of the husband and wife (the husband's on the left and the wife's on the right, using her maiden name), with one, two or entwined hearts, usually all within the date. The date recorded would be of significance to the couple, often the date of marriage or construction of the property.

At the first road junction (a virtual 'T'-junction) turn right into the road 'barred to cars and motorcycles except for access'.

Follow its narrowing and twisting route to the crossroads.

At the crossroads go straight over into Mont Isaac.

Follow the interesting road to the end.

At the 'T'-junction turn left.

After 50 metres, on the left-hand side, note the excellent example of an Abreuvoir.

Abreuvoirs were watering places for farm animals. They were formed by trapping water with stones, usually rectangular of construction and sometimes in trough style.

After 30 metres, on the other side of the road, there is a fountain. This fountain is one of the old sacred springs, La Fontaine de St. Martin, said to have healing properties. Along with the adjoining very small côtil, the fountain was purchased by the National Trust for Jersey in 1958.

Adjoining that land is a much larger côtil, which was given to the Trust by Mrs Saranne Lort-Phillips, Le Côtil de la Qualité, again in 1958.

West St. Lawrence
Walk Directions

Proceed for another few metres and on the left-hand corner of the junction with Le Mont L'Évesque, stop and view the National Trust for Jersey property Le Rât Cottage.

Le Rât Cottage was purchased by the National Trust for Jersey in 1937 for £200 (some of which had to be borrowed) – it was their first property purchase.

Turn left into Le Mont L'Évesque and proceed some 20 metres to the front gate of Le Rât.

It is a classic and fine example of a small and fairly humble early 17th century Jersey dwelling. However, there are 'voliers à pigeons' (pigeon holes) built into the exterior walls. Only seigneurs, in their manor houses, were allowed the luxury of keeping such birds in any number. They kept hundreds of pairs of birds in a separate round building, called a 'colombier' (dovecote), ensuring that there was always a meat pie during the winter months when meat was scarce. If permission had been granted by the seigneur, a small number of birds could be kept by persons of some standing.

Thus, despite the humble nature of this property, it must have been occupied by someone of importance. It is particularly interesting that Le Rât's name is possibly connected with rate collecting.

The cottage is built without any foundations (sur l'herbe) and is compensated with very thick walls.

Return to the road you were on and carry on up the hill (Le Mont Perrine).

At the crossroads at the top turn right and follow the road down towards the School.

On the right is a large farm complex, Oaklands. It is a site that has been occupied and frequented for many purposes from the earliest times with stone items illustrating this from as early as the 17th century. It was owned by a Langlois family for over 200 years, but passed into the Pipon family in the 20th century. The family were perhaps the last on the Island to use horses rather than tractors and continue to exhibit that tradition at Island country shows today.

Carry on past the school, then take the first turning left between the parish hall and the church to bring you back to the start.

St. Aubin to Noirmont and return

Parish	St. Brelade
Special Features	Wet sand and pebble walking. Lovely headland paths and views. Array of World War II German fortifications. Good historical interest. **CAUTION** **This is a low water walk and should be attempted only at, or within an hour or two of, low tide.**
Start	Public car park opposite The Old Court House and adjacent to The Royal Channel Islands Yacht Club, St. Aubin. Follow the A1 from St. Helier to St. Aubin. At St. Aubin's harbour turn left into Le Boulevard, St. Aubin and follow to the end. (If this car park is full there are other car parks and street parking nearby.)
Map Reference	**Jersey Telephone Directory** Map 7 D3 **Official Leisure Map** 60.6/48.5 **Jersey Street Guide** Map 29 E9
Terrain	Pebble and sand beach, woodland and headland paths and roads, including a steep incline.
Level of Difficulty	● ● ○ **SOME DIFFICULTY**
Time (approx)	2 hours 10 minutes
Distance (approx)	7 kilometres (4¼ miles)
Amenities	**Start and Finish (in St. Aubin)** Public toilets Public telephone Restaurants Pubs Cafes and takeaways Shops

St. Aubin to Noirmont
and return - *Map Guide*

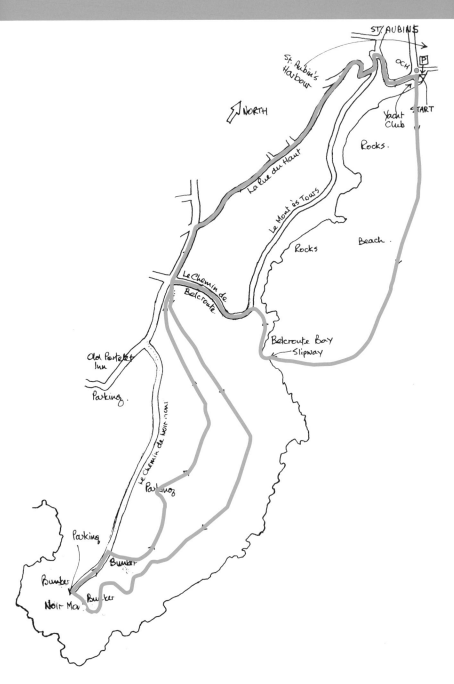

ST. AUBINS

St. Aubin's Harbour

OCH

NORTH

START

Yacht Club

Rocks.

La rue du Haut

Le Mont ès Tours

Rocks

Beach.

Le Chemin de Belcroute

Belcroute Bay
Slipway

Old Portelet Inn

Parking.

Le Chemin de Noirmont

Parking

Parking

Bunker

Bunker

Bunker

Noir Mon.

ST. AUBIN

Named after the 6th century Bishop of Angers.

St. Aubin became a thriving and affluent community during the 17th and 18th centuries when, with no real port facilities at St. Helier, the fishing and merchant fleets made use of its sheltered harbour – the safest anchorage in the Island, sheltered from the prevailing south-westerly gales.

St. Aubin's Fort has a long history. In the 16th century a tower was built on the rock, remaining for 100 years. In the Civil Wars it became a fort with a bulwark. Then came granite ramparts and the building of an extra storey on the tower. That lasted for another 100 years. It was then remodelled, but its present appearance dates from its reconstruction in 1840. Finally, the Germans updated it to a fortress in 1940.

St. Aubin's harbour started with a pier from the Fort in 1675. It still remains. 1754 saw the first works for the actual harbour. In 1790 the owners of the land facing the harbour constructed the existing quay (the long gardens in front of the properties show how much land was reclaimed from the sea). The north pier was added in 1819 giving the harbour the look it has today.

In the 17th and 18th centuries St. Aubin became the shipping and commercial port of the Island. During the wars with the French, Jerseymen were skilled privateers capturing French shipping for the King. In 1798 a visitor counted 30 ships tied up to the pier. In 1779 there were 150 French prizes at anchor in the bay.

From those times merchants began to build their spacious and grand houses, using basements for goods storage – The Old Court House (now a hotel and public house) is a good example. The date 1611(the earliest known in the vicinity) is carved over the fireplace. It was in this building that captured cargoes were distributed, with a judge deciding on the validity of each share and ensuring that the King received his percentage.

Another is a property – La Vieille Maison built in 1687 on the road that brought you to the car park – The Bulwarks or Le Boulevard. In a tiny back yard there is a pump, a stone trough and a well. There is a story that the owner's horse used to be led through the house into this back yard but this is questionable!

Until 1810 the only highway to St. Helier was across the beach and there was no direct road until 1844. In 1910 a second-hand motorbus began to chug its way along the road much to the amusement of contemptuous cabbies whose horses were often seen with their heads buried in nosebags of hay – so much better than the heads in the sand of those fearing change!

St. Aubin to Noirmont
and return - *Walk Directions*

A railway built to link with St. Helier opened in 1870 – the inaugural train from St. Helier taking less than ten minutes for the 3½ miles. In 1884 a line was built from St. Aubin's Hospital to the Corbière Quarries to carry granite for export. In 1885 this was linked to St. Aubin and in 1899 was extended by a branch line to La Corbière. An eastern line from St. Helier to Gorey was started in 1872, but the final stage to Gorey was not finished until 1891. It closed in 1929. The railways zenith was 1924/5 when it is said that for each of the two years over one million passenger journeys were made. (By way of comparison, in 2010, some 3.2 million passenger journeys were made by (Connex) bus, island wide). Numbers then declined, rail-cars were substituted for trains, buses started to link its stations, winter services were dropped, but all in vain. A fire in St. Aubin station was the final straw - and the lines finally closed in 1936 - a victim to car and road transport.

THIS SHOULD BE ATTEMPTED ONLY WHEN THE TIDE IS OUT OR GOING OUT.

Drop down onto the beach by using the steps in front of the Royal Channel Islands Yacht Club.

This beach is sometimes called pebble beach from the stones dumped here by the Germans from tunnel excavations.

Head down, diagonally to your right towards the sea (southerly), onto the sand and set a line that takes you seaward of any protruding rocks. (You are heading for the next bay.)

Within fifteen minutes you will come automatically to the bay - Belcroute Bay - where you turn and head up right, over the pebbles, to the slipway.

Around the 18th century when St. Aubin was the Island's main port, Belcroute Bay was used as the anchorage of ships back from faraway ports, suspected of carrying cases of the plague. Being held in quarantine they were not allowed to let anyone or anything land in Jersey until they were cleared - weeks could pass.

The plague was intermittent but a menace and certainly one of the greatest fears of the time. The first outbreak occurred in St. Helier in 1518. Accordingly the Royal Court moved to Grouville and stayed there until 1536. In 1563, in similar circumstances, they convened to St. Saviour's Church. In 1565 the disease struck St. Lawrence, one of its victims being the Rector. In 1626 it struck St. Brelade on such a scale that many victims had to be buried in their own gardens.

The most famous of the Belcroute plague victims was Captain Phillipe Janvrin who died on board his ship 'Esther', in 1721 having returned two days earlier from Nantes, where the plague was rampant. His body was not allowed to be brought ashore so he was buried by his own crew on the islet (île au Guerdain) in the middle of Portelet Bay within sight of his home – the court ruling that this was acceptable 'because the sea surrounded it'. (See later.)

Climb up the slipway and head up the hill.

As you leave the slipway, on your right-hand side is a World War II German 'Resistance Nest' comprising an open emplacement for a 7.5cm field gun.

As you climb, on the left-hand side you will come to the gilt-eagled entrance of Noirmont Manor – a fief with which came the title and benefits of seigneur. Jersey fiefs and their siegneurs were the fabric of Island life for over 600 years.

In the Middle Ages the Channel Islands were annexed into the Duchy by the Duke of Normandy. Feudalism and the seigneural system flourished in Jersey. All land was claimed by the Duke, which he granted to his favourites in return for services and rentes (a type of mortgage). The lands granted were known as fiefs, and their being may pre-date even the existence of the parishes.

In 1204 Normandy was lost to the French and land owners had to choose between remaining Norman or switching allegiance to the King of England. Those who returned to France lost their land to the Crown, whereupon the King re-granted their land to his favourites.

In essence the seigneurs enjoyed the benefits and dues (taxes) from the people who lived within the fief's boundaries (a percentage was then sent to the Crown). However, with the last of their feudal dues abolished in 1966, the title is now very much nominal.

Unusually this fief did not have other properties. Unique also was that it was once the personal fief of the Dukes of Normandy. Again, at one time the fief was owned by the Monastery of Mont St. Michel. The manor also had the dubious distinction of manorial gallows - one of only three manors on the Island allowed this status - again proving the importance of this particular fief.

The first manor house was built in 1695. This was demolished in 1810 and replaced by the present property during a period of great affluence in Jersey. Very fine houses appeared, based more on prosperous English than the previous Normandy style. The design concentrated more on the grandeur of the reception rooms than anything else. Noirmont was perhaps no exception. Seaward its situation is beautiful and the view breathtaking; it is also far more imposing inside than outside which has quite a modern look.

The current Manor is where Lillie Langtry, the famous and notorious beauty, spent her honeymoon in 1874. Unique is the dining room windowpane on which she scratched her initials with her diamond ring.

When you reach the top of the hill and the junction with the main road, turn left and then almost immediately turn left again onto the path into the woodland, indicated by a yellow horseshoe-topped marker post.

Ignore the bridle path straight in front of you by immediately taking the path off to the right. After a few metres go through a path entrance-way and follow.

Keep with this main path for some 110 metres until you reach a wooden bench on the right-hand side.

Keep with this main path straight on, leaving the wooden bench on your right-hand side and ignoring all opportunities to turn off right or left.

Carry on for some 65 metres, passing through the pine trees, to reach a path 'Y'-junction. With the Rotary Club of Jersey 1990 stone on the ground in front of you, bear left leaving the stone to your right-hand side.

Keep with this main path until the next 'Y'-junction. Then bear left and follow to the end, keeping the wire fencing to your right-hand side.

At the end of the path turn right and proceed into the left-hand footpath, ignoring the two paths to the right.

Follow the path keeping the fence immediately to your left and taking time to absorb the views through the trees to your left.

The backdrop to the extensive grounds of Noirmont Manor includes St. Helier, St. Aubin's Bay and St. Aubin itself.

Prominent on the landscape is the tall chimney of La Collette Power Station (now being used also by the new energy-from-waste plant). Also very noticeable is the stark outline of the leisure and conference facilities known as Fort Regent.

Fort Regent – named after the future George IV, then Regent to the indisposed George III - was built by General Don as part of Jersey's defences during the Napoleonic wars. It took ten years, 1804-14, and was built on common land on the top of Town Hill that had been compulsorily purchased. Over recent times it has been a leisure and conference centre but currently is said by some to be in need of revitalisation or find a new destiny. There has even been thoughts of privatisation.

Keep following the path alongside the fence all the way round.

Eventually emerge from the trees and continue until you reach a relatively small concrete base with two short rusted rail runners on the ground on your left-hand side.

Continue straight-on with the path.

After the path has veered inland, and where you have the first guns well in sight, at the fork bear left with the 'worn' path.

After 15 metres, at the 'T'-junction in front of the wire fencing, turn left.

Stay on this path ignoring a turning to the left and to the right. Keep left at each of the next two junctions.

To confirm that you are on the correct (coastal) path you will then pass two benches on the small headland to your left-hand side.

The Germans occupied Jersey from 1st July 1940 to 9th May 1945.

Hitler was obsessed with the idea that the British would try to recapture the Channel Islands. On 20th October 1941 he issued an edict that the Islands be converted into an impregnable fortress - 'the mailed fist of the Atlantic Wall'.

By 1945 there were 146 artillery guns in 37 battery sites in the Channel Islands. All were destined to see little action.

In Jersey a massive programme of defence works was ordered, the magnitude of which is not generally recognised and defies belief.

Railways were constructed to transport materials - sand from Grouville Bay (estimated at over one million tons) and crushed stone from Ronez and other sites.

About 500,000 tons of concrete were laid in less than two years (one-fifth of all the concrete in mainland Europe's Atlantic Wall that stretched 2,700 kilometres from Norway to the Spanish border).

There were up to 11,000 German troops and 6,000 foreign workers, mainly French and Spanish but including 1,000-2,000 Russian and Polish slave workers. In the region of 300 concrete structures, 7,400 running metres of anti-tank wall and 23,500 square metres of floor space within tunnels on numerous sites were built in the Island.

Despite all post-war attempts to dismantle and destroy, particularly by the British army in 1946 and the scrap-metal merchants in 1953, the local fortifications include some of the best surviving examples of their kind in Western Europe.

The fortifications must be viewed as part of the Island's heritage in the same light as the remaining fortifications, mainly castles and towers, from earlier centuries and treated as such for the benefit of future generations.

Recognised since the 19th century as a headland of strategic importance, Noirmont Point was the first headland to be fortified and became the most heavily concentrated in the Island. In 1947 the headland that is ahead was purchased by the States of Jersey as a memorial to World War II and the Occupation.

Collectively known as 'Batterie Lothringen' (Lorraine) – named after a German battleship - there were four main gun positions with supporting ammunition and personnel bunkers plus the operations' nerve centre, the formidable underground command bunker ('Leitstand') – the only one in Jersey. All four guns were to be fired electronically from the command bunker.

St. Aubin to Noirmont
and return - *Walk Directions*

In addition, the headland positively bristled with a formidable array of defensive installations and works - guns, searchlights, barbed wire and minefields - twenty-two guns ranging from field guns to machine guns, two mortars, sixteen defensive flamethrowers and three searchlights.

The artillerymen who manned the guns above ground numbered 180 and were quartered above Portelet Bay in what was subsequently the Jersey Holiday Village, before being redeveloped as apartments and houses. Some have returned to Jersey from time to time as holidaymakers.

Follow the path round, initially to the right and continue as it meanders. Stop at the concrete gun base on your right-hand side.

Read the memorial in honour of the men of PT Squadron 34, United States Navy, who died in action off this point on 9th August 1944.

Continue with the path where immediately afterwards on your right-hand side is a two roomed personnel bunker.

Read the Channel Islands Occupation Society plaque on the bunker.

Again continue. Ignore the steps turning down to your left. Keep on until you reach the large gun emplacement (Battery Lothringen No 2 gun) on your left-hand side.

This is the most visited emplacement in the Island with a 15cm gun that was recovered in 1979 from the sea (the 'gun graveyard') at Les Landes. The gun weighed 5,730 kg, and the turret 17,000 kg - no wonder they required a 2.5 metre thick reinforced concrete base! The emplacement was linked directly to two ammunition bunkers and the personnel bunker you passed 50 metres back.

The path you came along was then the latter's communication trench.

Read the Channel Islands Occupation Society plaque on the gun-site.

Climb up onto the gun emplacement and admire the view.

The black and white tower to your left is Noirmont Tower (La Tour de Vinde) built between 1810-14 as one of a chain of coastal towers as a defensive measure against French attack - now very much more simply, a navigation aid for shipping.

Proceed up and into the car parking area.

Respect the plaque on the right-hand side commemorating the men and women of Jersey who perished in World War II.

Immediately cross over the car park to seaward.

Somewhat inconspicuously there hides the incredible Noirmont command bunker ('Batterie Leitstand').

This bunker of two floors and a depth of twelve metres, was blasted out of the granite cliff in a massive 'L' shape. In its main functions of firing control and position-finding, the bunker was equipped with a six metre base range-finder and two periscopes that magnified to a factor of ten.

The bunker was assisted by secondary observation stations and spotting devices. It controlled not only the four main guns but also six anti-aircraft guns protecting the battery. The bunker was operated by 25 men working up to three weeks out of four, 24 hours a day, with one week off.

The two external cupolas retain the original 18cm-thick armoured plate that protected the two periscopes, but the other revolving armoured turret that protected the range-finder is a 1997 replacement incorporating the original arms.

The bunker has been meticulously restored by the Channel Islands Occupation Society and is open to the public on a regular basis.

Adjacent to 'Batterie Leitstand' is the massive and impressive structure of the naval artillery direction and range-finding tower ('Marine Peilstand und Meßstellung') MP1. The observation slits are set in two metre thick concrete.

Each floor was intended to control a separate artillery battery. In the event it was used for simple observation purposes and had an anti-aircraft gun on the roof.

Of nine planned, only three were built – the others being at Corbière and Les Landes. This brooding cliff-top tower was unique in that it had its entrance on the top floor. It was totally camouflaged, being grass-topped with granite walls and vegetation.

You should turn right onto the exit road and follow out of the car park, but before you do, walk over to the far side (left-hand side) of the car park and in front of you take in the wonderful view of the lovely little bay known as Portelet Bay with the islet in the middle.

Portelet is a picturesque bay. In the centre of the bay is L'Île au Guerdain (named after the family that owned it) which has become popularly known as 'Janvrin's Tomb'.

As mentioned earlier, Captain Phillipe Janvrin was buried on the Île. His burial was somewhat bizarre. The body was rowed across by three crewmen. On the cliff side was the minister and the family mourners. On their signal began the burial service. His widow later obtained permission to exhume his body and to have it re-interred in the cemetery at St. Brelade's church.

Some 90 years later, during the Napoleonic Wars, the Martello Tower was built on top of the original grave.

In Victorian times the upper levels of the Bay were quarried and the granite shipped from a jetty in the bay to London, where it was used to line the Thames Embankment. In 1918 the quarry and surrounding land was sold for £2,000. An intended house did not materialise, but a holiday camp developed.

In 1940 the German occupying forces took over the campsite and used it as a base for their troops. They left it virtually destroyed. Post war it reverted to a holiday camp and later became in the hands of developers, finally to build what you now see on the top - love it or hate it!.

Head towards the exit road.

Take the opportunity to read the unusual inscription on Alessandro Ferrero's memorial bench (probably to your left-hand side).

Join the exit road and proceed up the incline.

On the immediate left is No. 3 Gun. It is up to 80 metres away from its ammunition and personnel bunkers, which follow behind further up the road again on your left-hand side. The reason for the distance is that the support bunkers were already in place when the gun was re-sited from its planned closer initial position.

The gun was extensively camouflaged to resemble a small grassy knoll.

Follow up towards the brow to the gun and concrete structure on the right-hand side. The concrete structure was the Battery Lothringen Water Reservoir.

All batteries had to be self sufficient for water. This 5.5 metre square structure supplied the entire battery. Eventually it carried a sandbagged machine-gun position on its top.

Read the Channel Islands Occupation Society plaque on the reservoir.

Adjacent is No.1 Gun, note the impressive retaining granite walls to one of the two ammunition bunkers.

Immediately after the Reservoir turn right onto the path, proceed past the wooden locked path-entry barrier and follow.

Immediately to your right see again granite walls on the shallow path from the No.1 Gun to its personnel bunker. Again the Channel Islands Occupation Society's plaque on the personnel bunker is of interest.

Stay on this path following it around the meadow (keeping the fencing to your left-hand side), and ignore all opportunities to turn off right, until you come to a small car park.

Turn right on entering the car park and take the exit to your right through the gate, and join the path.

Continue with the path to the left keeping the pine trees immediately to your left until you reach the meadow.

Follow this path keeping the meadow to your left-hand side (at certain times of the year the meadow may be somewhat obscured), ignoring **all** opportunities to turn off right.

On the far side of the meadow stay with the path to cross the bridle path through the wooden barrier rails as indicated by the green-topped marker post.

Once across, carry **straight on** (ignore any opportunities to turn off right) to reach the bridle path again. As before, cross-over, passing through the wooden barrier rails as indicated by the green-topped marker post.

Having crossed again, follow the path ahead where shortly farm buildings will appear on your left-hand side. The path will also bring you back to the side of the meadow.

As the path leaves the side of the meadow and enters the trees keep left with this main path.

After approx 50 metres there is a granite plaque on the ground on your left-hand side, which acknowledges the Rotary Club. After 10 metres, again on the left-hand side, is a further stone plaque (more difficult to see and read) relating to The Men of The Trees. **At that point** (and no earlier) take the path to the right.

Keep following this path as it meanders through the trees until you reach a memorial bench.

Turn left at the memorial bench and keep with this main path until you reach the exit and the road.

Turn right onto the main road (Route de Noirmont) and **walking carefully** follow down to the second junction right, where you turn right into Rue de Haut.

Follow the road as it descends, becomes Mont ès Tours and finally Le Mont du Boulevard.

As you proceed down make sure that you again absorb the views of St. Aubin's Fort.

At the second hairpin bend, on the left-hand side, is a property called Rochebois. The original house was called La Maison du Val Essart and was built about 1630.

Then further down on the right-hand side, above the door of the first house beyond the high granite wall, there is a marriage stone dated 1694.

Coupled with The Old Courthouse, dating from 1611, the above examples reinforce how old this area of St. Aubin is. Just take a few moments to imagine how it must have been in the 17th and 18th centuries.

Continue down to the car park and the start.

Portelet Nature Reserve and Common

Parish	St. Brelade
Special Features	Stunning coastal views. A short, easy, very interesting circuit of differing aspects, including 250,000 years of history and World War II German fortifications.
Start	Car park, Portelet Common. From B57 La Route de Noirmont, turn right, signposted to Ouaisné and Portelet, then immediately bear left, signposted Portelet. Continue, joining the unmade 'no through' road and carry straight on to the car park - careful with the aggressive humps, particularly with low-slung cars.
Map Reference	**Jersey Telephone Directory** Map 7 C4 **Official Leisure Map** 59.6/47.3 **Jersey Street Guide** Map 39 A4
Terrain	Easy headland, woodland and copse paths.
Level of Difficulty	⬤ ◯ ◯ **EASY**
Time (approx)	45 minutes
Distance (approx)	2 ½ kilometres (1 ½ miles)
Amenities	None

Portelet Nature Reserve and Common - *Map Guide*

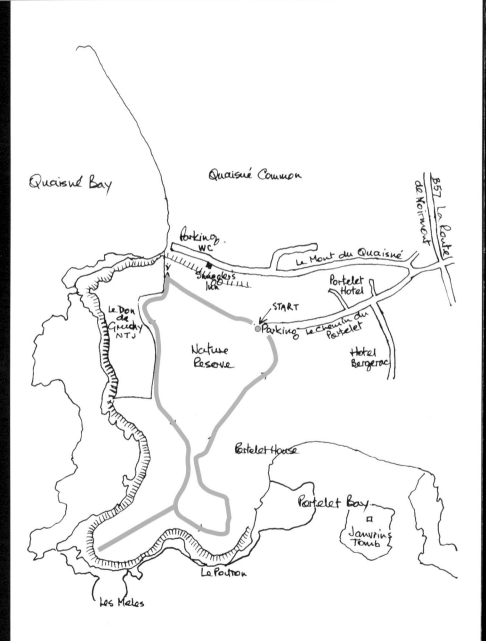

Quaisné Bay

Quaisné Common

B57 La Route de Noirmont

Parking WC

Le Mont du Quaisné

Smuggler's Inn

Portelet Hotel

START

Le Don de Grucchy NTJ

Parking

Le chemin du Portelet

Hotel Bergerac

Nature Reserve

Portelet House

Portelet Bay

Jamvrin's Tomb

Le Poutron

Les Meles

Portelet Nature Reserve and Common - *Walk Directions*

Start at the Information Board on the far side of the car park to the entrance.

Absorb the details contained on the Information Board.

In fact Portelet Common was designated an ecological Site of Special Interest in 2007, thus obtaining all the protections that the designation brings.

With your back to the board go across the car park to the far left, turning into the path controlled by a locked rusty gate with a small 'No Motorcycles' notice.

Follow the path. After some 250 metres turn off right and proceed to reach 3 granite stones with yellow painted triangular warning markers.

Admire the majestic view of Ouaisné and St. Brelade's Bay.

Turn to your left and walk some 20 metres to the National Trust for Jersey memorial stone.

This area of the headland is called La Cotte. It was gifted to the National Trust for Jersey in 1978 by Mrs Hope Dixon in memory of her father Jurat Guy Fortescue Burrell de Gruchy, Seigneur de Noirmont.

The gift included the small recently renovated building on top of the cliff over to your right - La Cotte Battery (or Guard House). It was constructed as a defensive battery and magazine in 1759 and complimented the battery across the bay at Le Coleron. It was dismantled in 1816, a year after Napoleon was defeated at Waterloo, and thereafter was used for accommodation initially by quarrymen and most recently by private tenants (who survived with no modern amenities). It is now empty and receiving some renovation.

Keep straight on until you are out of the circle of stones.

Part way down the cliffs of the promontory to your right is La Cotte de St. Brelade Cave, one of the major middle-Palaeolithic sites in Europe. It is more like a split in the rock with an arch over the top and was hollowed out when the sea would have been higher than today and at a time when Jersey would have been joined to France.

The cave was a camping site for prehistoric hunters as far back as 250,000 years. From 100,000 years ago, the age of the Neanderthal Man – the forerunner of homo sapiens – thirteen human teeth were found and also the remains of at least five arctic mammoths and the skulls of three woolly rhinoceroses.

Man then was short in stature with jaws of brutal strength and ferocity and walked with a bend at the knee. He was, pure and simply, a cave dweller with a mentality of little more than a basic brute. These hunters would have killed the animals by driving them over the cliffs. They finally abandoned the cave some 50,000 years ago.

Such is the importance of the site that public access is not permitted.

Then bear left to pick up the headland path.

Portelet Nature Reserve and Common - *Walk Directions*

Follow this path, much within lovely heather and low yellow gorse, to reach a long stone wall. Turn right at the wall and follow to the end - **take great care at the end!**

However, ensure you stop and admire the stupendous and majestic views.

Turn back and, keeping the wall to your right-hand side, follow all the way.

Again, where the wall has been reduced in height, keep stopping to see the wonderful changing vistas.

In the far right-hand corner go through the gateway marked 'Portelet Common Nature Reserve'. Once through, immediately take the right fork of the path.

Follow this path until you have the opportunity to veer right to proceed to the headland. Take that opportunity and walk over the brow to the end. Make sure you see the railed track on the seaward side of the bunker. (Not the easiest section and can be omitted.)

The headland is known as Le Fret Point (La Pointe de Fret - French for 'turbulent headland')

On the end of the headland is a concrete World War II German searchlight bunker – part of the defensive system built around the Island at that time by the German Occupying Forces.

This unusual shelter housed the large 150cm coastal artillery searchlight mounted on a railed trolley. It was code named 'Max' (or 'Anton') and worked in conjunction with 'Batterie Lothringen' at Noirmont (which you will see in the distance, shortly).

In the vicinity you may have seen on your right-hand side other concrete structures that relate to the 'Resistance Nest Le Fret', including a coastal gun emplacement and an associated infantry personnel shelter.

Return to the original path. Keep following the path around to your right. Resist all further temptations to turn off right.

On the right-hand side admire the views across the bay to Noirmont. Also note the distinctive features of the huge multi-floor World War II German Observation Tower (Marine Peilstand und Meßstellung - MP1), set alongside Batterie Lothringen, with its observation slits set in two metres thick concrete. Note also the black and white Napoleonic Tower 'Le Tour de Vinde'– now very much a navigation point. (Walk 13 takes you all around that area.)

Eventually the path veers left and heads for the trees.

Keep with this path, virtually skirting the trees, which remain much on your right-hand side and follow back to the gateway.

Immediately after going through the gateway carry straight on, keeping the trees to your right-hand side, to reach a narrower path protected, as you enter, by a granite stone at its centre.

Follow the path all the way through the wooded area to return to the car park and the start.

L'Ouaisné and St. Brelade

Parish	St. Brelade
Special Features	Wide expanses of firm sandy beach. Wonderful views. Good historical and folklore interest. St. Brelade's promenade. CAUTION **This a low-water walk. The beach on this walk should be attempted only if the tide is out or going out and there is clear sand between L'Ouaisné and St. Brelade at the (Le Grouin) headland.**
Start	Public car park, L'Ouaisné. From the A13 St. Aubin/Red Houses road, turn off onto the B57 La Route de Noirmont. Take the sixth road right, signposted Ouaisné and Portelet. Then keep right, signposted Ouaisné (Le Mont du Ouaisné) and follow the road to the bottom. The car park is then on the right-hand side.
Map Reference	**Jersey Telephone Directory** Map 7 C4 **Official Leisure Map** 59.5/47.5 **Jersey Street Guide** Map 39 A3
Terrain	Flat, firm but wet, sand, coastal path (with some climbing including, at one point, 43 steps), promenade and a short stretch of road.
Level of Difficulty	⬤ ◯ ◯ **EASY**
Time (approx)	1 hour 25 minutes
Distance (approx)	4 kilometres (2½ miles)

Amenities	**Start and Finish**
	    Public toilets
	    Public telephone
	    Bar/restaurant
	    Pub/restaurant
	    Bay kiosk
	
	En Route (in St. Brelade's Bay)
	    All the usual amenities and more

L'Ouaisné and St. Brelade
Map Guide

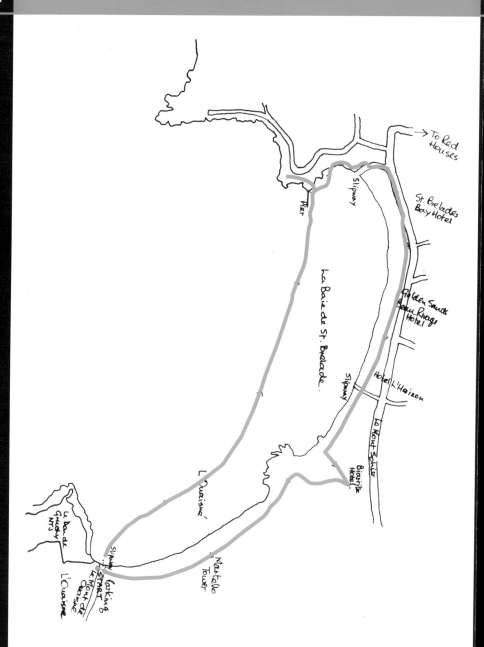

L'Ouaisné and St. Brelade
Walk Directions

Start at the 'Welcome to Ouaisné' information board towards the front of the car park.

Read the information contained on the board.

'Ouaisné' means anchorage in Norman French – a reminder of a lucrative business, of the late 17th to 19th centuries. Smuggling wine, spirits and tobacco into England was nearly as profitable as into France. The English Customs awoke to the fact that the Island was importing far more tobacco than it could possibly smoke. Enterprising merchants were buying it in Southampton, getting a rebate on duty, bringing it in to the Island and then landing it on moonless nights in remote Devon coves. When a customs officer arrived in 1681 he complained that the whole Island was in conspiracy against him as, whenever he tried to do his duty, he was affronted and beaten and could get no help from the jurats and constables! The Jersey smugglers defied all efforts to outwit them.

Anchorage again helped in the 19th century when ships took stone, quarried from the headland over to your left, around the Island.

Check the tide situation before proceeding further. You must see sand below the rock outcrop (Pointe le Grouin - the pig's snout) at the far end of this L'Ouaisné part of the bay before you continue along the beach.

Proceed down the slipway to the beach. Turn right onto the sand and head across, aiming for the seaward side of the rock outcrop (Pointe le Grouin).

Note the sea wall to your right.

The anti-tank wall (Panzermauer 6), built in 1942, formed part of the defences built by the German Occupying Forces during World War II, as part of Hitler's 'Fortress Europe' strategy. A total of seven walls (7400 running metres) of anti-tank wall were built. Note particularly that it is built in several different ways suggesting that the Germans were experimenting with wall design at that time.

The tower is a Jersey Round Tower - St. Brelade No 1. It was built around 1780 and was called La Tour du Hoinet. On the top would have been an 18-pounder carronade. Such towers are usually known by the inaccurate name 'martello'. Martello arises from cape Mortella in Corsica where a round coastal tower caused the defeat of the British warships in 1794. The name has become very much generic for all round towers.

In fact Jersey round towers began to appear some fifteen years earlier based upon a plan to erect 32 of which 22 were built during the period 1780 – 1800, a number of which can still be seen around the coast. The round towers were of local design and quite different from the English martello – taller, tapering, more elegant and of granite with machicolations – the protrusions at the top through which hot liquids and burning objects could be dropped on attackers.

L'Ouaisné and St. Brelade
Walk Directions

Several types of English martello were added in the early 19th century.

Over more recent times the tower has been painted red and white and been used as a navigation mark. Nowadays the tower is in private ownership.

St. Brelade's Bay had two such towers. The No. 2 Tower built at the same time is in the bay on the other side of the rock outcrop. The tower was the first one sold into private ownership and was converted into a private house in the 1970s. Although the old black and white painted navigation checks have long since gone, the house is still a landmark.

Walk seaward of the rock outcrop (Pointe le Grouin). If you wish you can cut through the lower part of the rocks – it is much easier than it looks!

(In an emergency there are steps to exit the beach adjacent to the German bunker.)

Legend has it that the parish church was to be built at Pointe le Grouin, near a pagan shrine. Many loads of stone were heaped up at the selected spot and workmen were said to have started laying the foundations. The next morning not a stone remained. The workmen walked to where the church now stands and found the stones neatly piled up with their tools beside them. Having once again laid the stones the same thing happened. It was then decided to build the church at this new spot.

In the pagan shrine where the little people (fairies) had lived undisturbed for centuries there was rejoicing and much fatigue - for it was they that had carried the stones to the new site upon their backs.

Pointe Le Grouin has harboured defences from the 18th century to World War II. Those from World War II are still very much in evidence.

In the corner on this side of the outcrop is a German bunker that formed part of the 'Strongpoint Le Grouin'. It is a casement that housed a standard 4.7 cm anti-tank gun and is sited in a usual position built into a rocky headland. Note also the two shooting openings (embrasures) adjacent in the anti-tank wall.

Continue, in as straight a line and as near to the sea as possible, across St. Brelade's Bay to the far side, heading for the church and the harbour on the far side of the bay.

Immediately you cross into St. Brelade, on the other side of the outcrop, notice another anti-tank gun casement, again part of the 'Strongpoint Le Grouin'. This is of a different type with a 7.5 cm gun. This too has the supporting two embrasures in the adjacent wall.

Because of the bay's vulnerability to attack, at that time it bristled with guns. As well as those at Le Grouin another gun was sited near St. Brelade's Bay Hotel. Additionally there were larger guns where Hotel L'Horizon now stands and in the churchyard.

As you near the church stay with the beach and walk towards the harbour on your left.

Go through the harbour to the far right-hand side, being careful to avoid the mooring chains and ropes.

Climb onto the raised walkway keeping the white painted protective railings to your left. Follow round onto the jetty and walk to the end.

Admire the different view of the bay.

Return to the end of the jetty and then climb the twelve steps directly in front of you.

At the top of the steps immediately turn left and climb the narrow (and initially tricky) path.

At the path junction turn left and proceed out onto the headland.

Le Coleron Battery. Tucked away isn't it!

Situated on this promontory adjacent to the St. Brelade's harbour and surrounded on three sides by the tide, an ideal site for the battery, built in the reign of George III. Dismantled in 1817 - after the Napoleonic wars - the stone 'paved' area is all that remains of the original battery. It was the cannon platform, changed from wooden plank by a law passed in 1778, when a levy of £4500 was ordered to urgently upgrade Island's defences, at a time of great concern internationally.

The site was gifted to the National Trust for Jersey by Mr G. R. Morley in 1956. However the footpath was in separate private ownership, where only more recent negotiations have enabled proper public access.

Turn back down the path you came - this time, where the path divides, turn right and follow down.

Within the private land to your left are the 18th century guardhouse and powder magazine of the battery. At the time of going to press there were plans to convert them into a living room, kitchen and toilet, to become a separate part of a weekend retreat on the site.

Descend the twelve steps to the jetty. Then turn left and follow the path back into the harbour.

Keeping as close as possible to the seawall to your left, head towards the beach.

L'Ouaisné and St. Brelade
Walk Directions

Within the seawall, just before the church and near a white painted navigation marker on the wall, there is a path leading up to the church. Take that path up to the churchyard gate.

This path purports to be a 'perquage' – the shortest one in the Island.

Perquages were safe-conduct paths, allowing criminals to escape arrest. They ran from a sanctuary -the parish church - to the sea and a waiting boat.

'The Sanctuary of the Church' dates from the earliest medieval times and was abolished at the Reformation. A criminal was allowed refuge in the church. He had then to either stand trial or sell everything and leave the Island taking an oath never to return. In the latter case the criminal was led by the priests to the sea along 'un perquage'. Each parish had a perquage and it always followed streams.

It says much for the fear of trial and imprisonment, and the rough and ready legal system, that a criminal would voluntarily emigrate promising never to return.

There is no doubt that there was a perquage the short way from the church to the sea. But there is also no doubt that during substantial renovations in the late 1800s, by the Reverend Balleine, he knocked a hole in the wall for the gateway from the steps you have just climbed into the churchyard. His actions therefore have created doubts as to the exact route of the original perquage.

Go through the gate and through the churchyard towards the side door of the church. In front of that door turn right and immediately right again into the Fishermen's Chapel - Chapelle de Ste. Marie.

The Fishermen's Chapel is a must. The chapel became associated with the fishing guilds of the late medieval period– giving rise to its present colloquial name.

The building dates back to the 11th – 12th centuries and is believed to be on the site of the original timber and clay-floored church. The wall paintings were completed in the 14th and 15th centuries, shortly after the stone chapel was built.

During the Reformation in the 16th century, like those in England, Jersey churches were ravaged - extravagance and grandeur giving way to a new austerity. The chapel and its wall paintings survived the Reformation only by its conversion in about 1550, into an armoury. It housed the parish cannon for some 300 years.

After the mid 19th century it had several different uses and disintegration continued.

Several major renovations in the 20th century restored the chapel to this present day austere and mystic place of prayer.

A visit to the church is also a must!

St. Brelade, a son of a Cornish King who lived in the 400s AD, is credited as founding the original Celtic religious community probably on the spot that he landed.

The present beautiful stone church was begun in the late 1000s and by the 1100s most of the present nave and saddleback tower had been built. Substantial additions were made in the 12th and 14th centuries and a last one – being the north aisle and an extension to the nave – in 1537. At that time there was a ring of five bells in the bell-tower, but an order of Council in 1550 ordered four of them to be removed and melted down (as similarly with other churches in the Island). The money raised was used to build up the Island's fortifications.

After more that 400 years, in the 16th century this church, along with the others in the Channel Islands, changed governance from France to England and the Diocese of Winchester.

During the 18th century, as the population increased, several galleries were built within the church including one for the honorary police and even a 'galerie des fumeurs' for men wishing to smoke during the sermon.

Substantial and much needed renovations were carried out by the Reverend Balleine in the late 1800s. In 1895 the plaster on the ceiling and walls was removed exposing the granite (from La Moye Quarry) and the beach pebbles. Through his careful work we have the buildings we see today.

On exit turn back past The Fishermen's Chapel (on your right-hand side) and reach the churchyard's seaward retaining wall. Follow along to the first (north-east) gateway.

On the wall to the left-hand side of the gateway is a plaque reminding us of a German military cemetery here. Prisoners of war during World War I, and the bodies of 213 German soldiers of World War II, were buried here, mostly in the northern part of the churchyard and a few in part of the Rectory Garden across the road. The bodies were exhumed and taken to France in 1961.

The churchyard and part of the rectory garden were commandeered by the Germans during the Occupation and parishioners had to be buried in the new cemetery across the road.

Exit the churchyard through the arched north-east gateway guarded by the two huge and very old evergreen oak trees known as holm oaks.

As you leave the gateway turn round to admire the arch and notice the old poor box, now on your right-hand side. The inscription translates 'Jesus beheld how people cast money into the treasury'.

Follow up the short road to the main road.

Note the property on the right-hand side as you go.

Certain of the appurtenances are not original to the property. The 1852 dated down-pipe and the eagles came from a Hall in Cheshire and the 1834 marriage stone (all 14 tons of it) was found in a field in La Moye.

At the main road turn right and carefully follow to beyond the wrought iron garden fence of St. Brelade's Bay Hotel.

During World War II the hotel was a Soldatenheim – a German Soldiers' Home.

Buried under the hotel gardens on the seaward side is a World War II air-raid shelter bunker.

Turn right down sixteen steps to the promenade and then turn left and follow this promenade until almost the very far end.

As you walk along admire the beautiful public gardens with the fountain to your left.

Virtually at the end of the promenade there are some public toilets (Côtil du Grouin) on your left-hand side, with steps leading down to the beach just before on the right-hand side. Stop between the two. Go through the gap in the low wall on your left-hand side, just before the toilets, and climb up the sandy path.

Keep with this main path all the way up, through the fir trees, until you come to some steps. Climb the 43 steps to the back of the Biarritz Hotel.

You now begin to realise that this area called Le Côtil du Grouin is sizable – over fifteen vergees (a good 6 ½ acres).

The land was acquired by the States in 1856 related to army and Militia gunnery use.

On the last step turn sharply right and follow that path back through the pine trees – which includes some very tall ones.

The tallest trees are among the few of that size on this side of the Island that survived the Great Storm of 1987.

Keep with the path ignoring all temptations to turn off right or indeed left.

The path eventually bears left and starts to descend towards L'Ouaisné. Keep with the path.

As you walk down ensure you take in the wonderful seaward vistas unfolding before you, but do not forget to look also at the view left and straight ahead.

To your left is the view of L'Ouaisné Common Nature Reserve. The reserve is one of Jersey's richest and most diverse wild habitats. However, since the building of the defensive sea wall by the Germans in 1942 the sand dunes have now stabilised, aiding a gradual progression to heath-land. Gorse is very prevalent and is controlled to prevent it dominating.

In bygone days gorse, together with bracken, was gathered by the local community and used for fuel and bedding. Here too the reeds would have been a valuable crop for thatching.

Ahead the promontory houses the remarkable cave La Cotte de St. Brelade. The cave, more like a split in the rock with an arch over it, has traces of civilisation back some 250,000 years - the age of the Acheulean man. Changes in sea level due to the melting Arctic ice caused the cave and probably the Island to be abandoned for a long period before being re-occupied some 100,000 years ago. At that later, Palaeolithic (Old Stone Age) time – the age of the Neanderthal man (the forerunner of Homo sapiens) – thirteen human teeth were found and also the remains of at least five artic mammoths and the crania of three woolly rhinoceroses (now in the Jersey Museum) – proof again that Jersey was once part of the European mainland.

Man then was short in stature with jaws of brutal strength and ferocity and walked with a bend at the knee. He was, purely and simply, a cave dweller with a mentality of little more than a basic brute. These hunters would have killed the animals, the remains of which were found, by driving them over the cliff. They finally left the cave some 50,000 years ago.

Carry on descending the now steeper path with the aid of the carved rock steps.

On your right as you descend you can now have a closer inspection of the anti-tank gun casement described earlier.

Continue with the path running across the bay alongside the seawall to the car park and the start.

Beauport and Les Creux

Parish	St. Brelade
Special Features	Stunning views of St. Brelade's Bay - perhaps one of the best vistas in the Island.
	Spectacular views of the rock formations - probably the most remarkable rock formations in the Island.
Start	St. Brelade's Church car park up the hill behind the church hall and office buildings.
	Descend to St. Brelade's Bay, from either the traffic lights at Red Houses via La Marquanderie (B45), or from St. Aubin on the A13 and turn left onto the B66 down to the bay.
	From the road along the bay, turn off between St. Brelade's Church and the vicarage.
	Follow the road to the end and then turn right, signposted 'Beauport Bay'. After some 90 metres, and after the church buildings, turn right into the car park.
	You may wish to leave a donation for the parking in the box on the right-hand side as you leave.
Map Reference	**Jersey Telephone Directory** Map 7 A3
	Official Leisure Map 58.2/48.2
	Jersey Street Guide Map 28 B9
Terrain	Coastal and country paths, with an initial fairly steep climb and sometimes difficult underfoot.
Level of Difficulty	◉◑○ **SOME DIFFICULTY**
Time (approx)	1 hour 10 minutes
Distance (approx)	2¾ kilometres (1¾ miles)
Amenities	None

Beauport and Les Creux
Map Guide

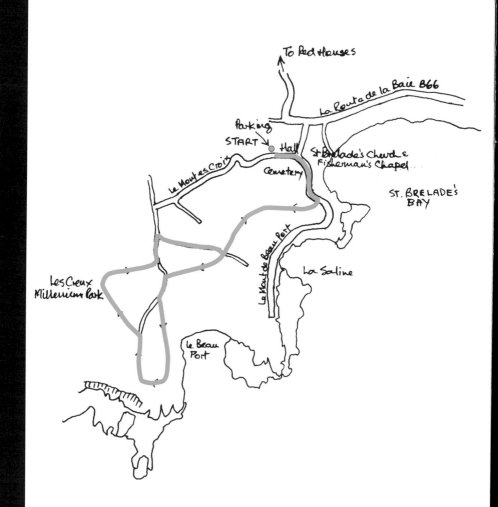

Turn left out of the car park and follow the road towards the church.

A visit to St. Brelade's Church and the Fishermen's Chapel is a must – perhaps at the end of the walk if you have time. (Some historical information at the end of this walk - pages 133 and 134.)

In front of the church gate turn right into the 'No-entry' road.

The lychgate at the main entrance to the churchyard was given in 1933 by Lady Florence Trent, who was born in Jersey, as a memorial to her husband, Jesse Boot, first Baron Trent of Nottingham. He was founder of Boots the Chemists and is buried in a private, sombre and rather sinister plot on the hillside a short distance away.

There is a signpost 'Footpath to Beauport' in the wall on the right-hand side as you turn the corner. Keep going up the road for some 125 metres, then turn right up the steps of the path marked 'Beauport Bay 20 minutes. Please keep to the Path' and follow.

Near the top, look back at the magnificent view over St. Brelade's Bay.

Keep with the path. Later, as it starts to drop down into some trees, still follow the path (ignoring the path to the right).

Drop down into the trees and up the other side until you reach the road.

At the road turn left and after a few metres enter the car park.

At the car park entrance bear left and follow the narrow path to the right of the stone marker 'Le Beau Port/Les Creux'. Carry straight on with the coastal path– do NOT take the left turn arrowed 'Beach (Steps)'. Cross over through the green railings and leave the small pumping (Beauport Pumping Station) and electrical works on your right-hand side.

Over time, in the Island agricultural industry it had been the practice to dump surplus potatoes in the open to rot. In 1992 huge quantities were dumped at Beauport with disastrous effect. Potato leachate began to flow down to the beach. Remedial action has been tankering – hence no longer the stream under your path and the evidence around you of pumping and civil works. One million gallons of leachate a year are collected and this is likely to have to continue until 2020.

Continue to follow the path.

At 'Bill Bates' bench on your right-hand side admire the view particularly of the magnificent rock formations to the right as you look out across Beauport Bay.

At the fork in the path take the seaward, left-hand path and follow.

Periodically look left at the lovely views.

Continue with this path until you reach the granite and wooden bench on the headland, in memory of Olive Clare Rogers.

Again make sure that you admire the incredible panorama to your left, sweeping from the Portelet headland, across L'Ouaisné and St Brelade's Bay to Beauport Bay below you.

The rounded low granite walled structure towards the end of the small headland on the other side of Beauport Bay is the remnants of the Beauport New Battery and magazine built in about 1870. It boasted 24-pounder guns mounted on carriages.

Go past the length-way sides of the bench and then bear right with the path. After five metres turn off to the right through a very narrow path opening in the gorse. Follow through the gorse (only two or three metres) and come out onto a grassy open space. (As a check, there should be a bench in the top corner on your right-hand side.)

Traverse the open space in the general direction of the houses and enter a very short meandering path straight ahead through some scrub into another small open grassy headland area. (As a check, this time with a white granite shell sculpture to your right.)

*With the shell sculpture behind you, you **must** go as far forward as possible, looking out to sea to take in the most incredible view of the rock formations, both ahead and below - probably the most remarkable rock scenery in the Island.*

Walk up to the shell sculpture keeping it to your right-hand side.

The sculpture is an initial part of the 'Art in the Environment' plan for Les Creux Millennium Country Park.

With the sculpture to your right, follow the path straight ahead until you reach virtually a five path junction.

At that junction take the second left path and proceed through the granite pillared gateway.

Go through the granite pillared gateway and then turn right with the grassy path. However, immediately turn left up the path that veers 45° towards the houses.

Carry straight on through the next granite gateposts keeping with the path.

Continue with the path until you reach a ground-level granite stone signpost on your right-hand side. Then turn right to (sic) 'St Brelade's By', ignoring the misleading arrow, and follow the grassy path.

Keep straight on, ignoring a path to the left.

Where, instead of being grassy, the path has a hoggin base for a few metres turn right and follow through the narrow granite pillared gateway. Continue to the road.

Beauport and Les Creux
Walk Directions

At the road turn left following the granite marker on your left-hand side with the green lizard and 'La Moye'.

The green lizard is the logo of the park.

After some 70 metres take the path to the right signposted by granite marker with an arrow and a drawing of a green lizard.

Green lizards can be seen in the thick vegetation around the park. Jersey is the only area in Britain where they can be found naturally.

Follow this path and continue left as it joins another path.

The initial view ahead is of Ouaisné bay with its red and white Jersey round tower.

Continue with this path all the way down to the road.

As you descend ensure that you stop to admire the stunning views. With leaves on the trees in the foreground, the sun shining and the sea in - it provides one of the best vistas in the Island.

At the road turn left and proceed to the road junction in front of the church lychgate.

St. Brelade's Church. St. Brelade, a son of a Cornish King who lived in the 400s AD, is credited as founding the original Celtic religious community probably on the spot that he landed. The present beautiful stone church was begun in the late 1000s and by the 1100s most of the present nave and saddleback tower had been built. Substantial additions were made in the 12th and 14th centuries and a last one – being the north aisle and an extension to the nave – in 1537. At that time there was a ring of five bells in the bell-tower, but an Order of Council in 1550 ordered four of them to be removed and melted down (as similarly with other Island churches). The money raised was used to build up the Island's fortifications.

After more than 400 years, in the 16th century, this church, along with the others in the Channel Islands, changed governance from France to England and the Diocese of Winchester.

During the 18th century, as the population increased, several galleries were built within the church including one for the honorary police, and even a 'galerie des fumeurs' for men wishing to smoke during the sermon.

Substantial and much needed renovations were carried out by the Reverend Balleine in the late 1800s. In 1895 the plaster on the ceiling and walls was removed exposing the granite (from La Moye Quarry) and the beach pebbles. Through his careful work we have the buildings we see today.

Beauport and Les Creux
Walk Directions

The Fishermen's Chapel. The chapel became associated with the fishing guilds – giving rise to its present colloquial name – in the late medieval period. The building dates back to the 11th – 12th centuries and is believed to be on the site of the original timber and clay-floored church.

The wall paintings were completed in the 14th and 15th centuries shortly after the stone chapel was built.

During the reformation in the 16th century, like those in England, Jersey churches were ravished - extravagance and grandeur giving way to a new austerity. The chapel and, in particular its wall paintings, survived the Reformation only by its conversion in about 1550, into an armoury. It housed the parish cannon for some 300 years.

After the mid 19th century it had several different uses and disintegration continued.

Several major renovations in the 20th century restored the chapel to this present day austere and mystic place of prayer.

At the road junction turn left and proceed up the hill.

After the church office and hall to your right turn right into the car park and the start.

The Ultimate St. Brelade's

Parish	St. Brelade
Special Features	Spectacular scenery at Corbière and St. Ouen's Bay. World War II German Occupying Forces coastal defences. Sand dune climbing. Corbière section of the Railway Walk. (Good for striding it out!)
	CAUTION **This is a low-water walk. The beach on this walk should be attempted only if the tide is out or going out, otherwise use the coastal road as shown.**
Start	Car park, Corbière bus terminus, along side the Old Station House and public telephone box.
	From Red Houses, St. Brelade, traffic lights take A13 (Route Orange) signposted (sp.) Corbière. Keep straight on at sp. B44/B83 Petit Port, Beauport and Corbière. Turn left at B83 sp. Beauport, Corbière (Route de Sud). Keep straight on to Corbière (Rue de la Corbière). Pass the Highlands Hotel on your left. Then immediately in front of the small 'Corbière Scenic Car Park' sign on the right-hand side of the road, turn right and park in the small parking area behind the bus terminus and telephone box.
Map Reference	**Jersey Telephone Directory** Map 6 H4
	Official Leisure Map 55.6/47.9
	Jersey Street Guide Map 36 F7
Terrain	Predominately tracks but with coastal path, beach, sand dunes and road - all easy and straightforward, except some difficulty in the sand dunes.
Level of Difficulty	⬤ ⬤ ◯ **SOME DIFFICULTY**
Time (approx)	2 hours 50 minutes
Distance (approx)	9 kilometres (5½ miles)
Amenities	**Start and Finish (vicinity)** **En Route (St. Ouen's Bay)** Public toilets Public toilets Public telephone Public telephone Restaurant/bar Pub/food Ice-cream kiosk (summer) Café

The Ultimate St. Brelade's
Map Guide

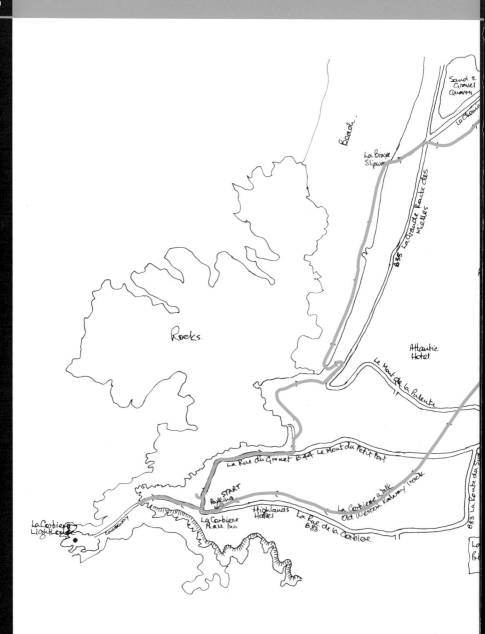

The Ultimate St. Brelade's
Map Guide

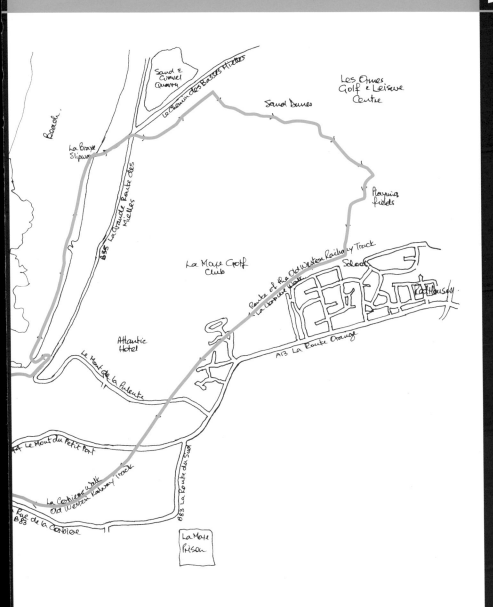

Sand & Gravel Quarry

La Chemin des Basses Mielles

Les Ormes Golf & Leisure Centre

Sand Dunes

Beach

La Braye Slipway

B35 La Grande Route des Mielles

Playing Fields

La Moye Golf Club

Route of the Old Western Railway Track

La Corbière Walk

School

Café/Houses

Atlantic Hotel

A13 La Route Orange

Le Mont de la Pulente

B44 Le Mont du Petit Port

La Corbière Walk Old Western Railway Track

B83 La Route du Sud

B83 Rue de la Corbière

La Moye Prison

The Ultimate St. Brelade's
Walk Directions

La Corbière – the place where ravens flock – is derived from 'Les Corbeaux'.

Descend the steps at the back of the car park and turn left onto the track (towards the lighthouse) and follow to the road.

The Germans occupied Jersey from 1st July 1940 to 9th May 1945.

Hitler was obsessed with the idea that the British would try to recapture the Channel Islands. On 20th October 1941 he issued an edict that the Islands be converted into an impregnable fortress 'the mailed fist of the Atlantic Wall'.

By 1945 there were 146 artillery guns in 37 battery sites in the Channel Islands. All were destined to see little action.

In Jersey a massive programme of defence works was ordered the magnitude of which is not generally recognised and belies belief.

Railways were constructed to transport materials – sand from Grouville Bay (estimated at over one million tons) and crushed stone from Ronez and other sites. 500,000 tons of concrete was laid in less than two years (one-fifth of all the concrete in mainland Europe's Atlantic Wall that stretched 2,700 kilometres from Norway to the Spanish border). There were up to 11,000 German troops and 6,000 foreign workers, mainly French and Spanish, but including 1,000-2,000 Russian and Polish slave workers. In the region of 300 concrete structures, 7,400 running metres of anti-tank wall and 23,500 square metres of floor space within tunnels on numerous sites, were built in the Island.

Despite all post-war attempts to dismantle and destroy, particularly by the British army in 1946 and the scrap-metal merchants in 1953, the local fortifications include some of the best surviving examples of their kind in Western Europe.

The fortifications must be viewed as part of the Island's heritage in the same light as the remaining fortifications, mainly castles and towers, of earlier centuries and treated as such for the benefit of future generations.

Corbière is the site of one of the Island's largest and well preserved World War II defensive positions ('Strongpoint Corbiere'). In the immediate area is a range of bunkers and casements which, during the Occupation, were surrounded by fences of concertina barbed wire.

Turn right onto the road and when possible - **very carefully** – cross over the road.

The prominent and impressive concrete tower to your left was a World War II German naval artillery direction and range - finding tower (Marine Peilstand und Meßstellung) MP2 and not part of 'Strongpoint Corbiere'.

It is 17.80 metres tall. Each floor was intended to control a separate artillery battery. In the event it was used for simple observation purposes and mounting radar and/or anti-aircraft guns. Of nine planned only three were built – the others being at Noirmont Point and Les Landes.

During the Occupation this tower was painted to resemble the random granite finish of an 18th century round tower.

Over recent times the tower housed the Radio Jersey Marine Coast Station. However, converted by Jersey Heritage, it is now a (certainly different) very popular holiday let, topped by a 360 degree panoramic lounge.

Proceed down the road. At the bend turn left towards the lighthouse.

As you descend, on your right-hand side, note the clasped-hand memorial to a near disaster on 17th April 1995.

As you proceed down you pass two German bunkers on your right-hand side. The first is a machine gun turret bunker which is connected by 37 steps, an 11 rung vertical ladder and a 40 metre tunnel (constructed by 'cut and cover') to the lower M19 Automatic Fortress Mortar Bunker included in which was storage for the 3,944 bombs that were available to be fired (exactly as stated in the training manual!). The bunker had an operational strength of 6/7 troops. These bunkers have been restored by the Channel Islands Occupation Society and are open to the public on occasions, mainly in the summer months.

The cottages to your right were originally built to house the now no longer required lighthouse keepers.

Stop at the Causeway at the bottom.

Corbière Lighthouse – now a symbol of Jersey - was built in 1874. With accounts of ships floundering since 1309 it was much needed. Imrie Bell the engineer chose an isolated rock 500 metres from shore. The base is a three metre high platform on which is a ten metre tower. The lighthouse was the first in the world to be built from moulded concrete. The materials for construction were carried from St. Helier by barge and winched onto the base area (at that time there was no road access to this then wild, desolate and remote area). To finance the construction, initially ships were charged for their safe passage. The lantern – some 36 metres above high water - was lit originally by oil. It was converted to electricity in 1965 and became automated in 1974. The light can be seen for some 30 kilometres (18 miles).

After checking the state of the tide and heeding the warning given on the commemoration plaque on your right-hand side at the causeway, you may wish to carry on across the causeway to the lighthouse. (Any time taken has not been allowed for in the timing of the walk.)

Re-trace your steps back towards the road.

As you turn to go back up to the road absorb the full information on the lighthouse on the two plaques on your now right-hand side.

The Ultimate St. Brelade's
Walk Directions

On your right-hand side are two further German emplacements. Nearest and most visible to you is a 60cm searchlight bunker. Behind, the roof of which is now a car park, is a 10.5cm coastal defence gun casement.

At the road, turn left and follow.

Initially the road has several bends. Stay on the left-hand side - it is safer around the bends and later enables you to use the grass verge and roadside.

½ mile off-shore to your left is La Rocco Tower (La Tour Rocque-Ho) - named Gordon's Tower in honour of Jersey's then Lieutenant-Governor - the last and biggest Jersey Round Tower, built 1796/1801 at a cost of £400.

It formed part of the Island defences against the threat of invasion from Revolutionary and the Napoleonic France.

Battered by the sea, it was restored in 1969 with eleventh hour help by the States of Jersey. Now used very much as a marker by pilots of small aircraft landing at the airport.

The small bay to your left is Petit Port.

After you leave the curve of Petit Port bay, and with the sea wall below you, turn left into the 'No-through' road (Chemin du Petit Port).

Once on the road, after 75 metres, at the end of the tarmac, turn right. Follow this path around ignoring all opportunities to turn off right.

After passing round the headland, just before you reach the road, take the path to the left climbing down five steps. Continue on this path as it runs alongside the road.

Opposite La Pulente public house turn down the steps to your left. At the bottom turn left again onto the slipway.

Slipways (or slips) are a common feature along the coastline. They act as a link between the beach road and the beach and were used mainly by farmers to collect seaweed (vraic – pronounced 'rack' or 'wrack') for use as fertiliser – the best natural replacement for the lack of chalk and lime in the local soil.

It is said that the vraic helped to give the Jersey Royal potato its unique flavour, thereby helping to establish it as 'the king of potatoes'.

Vraic was also dried to act as both fuel and bedding.

After spring tides the beaches swarmed with carts.

The importance of vraic can scarcely be comprehended today.

So popular was this free resource that collection had to be strongly controlled both as to timing and amount collected and policed by vraic officers. It is said that on one day on this slipway 250 carts and 17 boats were seen.

(PROCEED ALONG THE BEACH ONLY IF THE TIDE IS OUT OR GOING OUT. If you are in any doubt about the tide conditions follow the paths on the seaward side of the coast road until you reach the first road on the left-hand side leading to the café and Le Braye Slip.)

Go down the slipway and turn right onto the beach.

The sea wall was built by the Germans during the Occupation. It is one of seven anti-tank walls (Panzermauere) built. Their lengths totalled 7,400 metres.

Follow across the sand/pebbles.

Go round, or through, the rock outcrop (La Tête du Nièr Côti or La Carrière) and continue up the beach until you reach the first slipway.

(In an emergency there are steps to exit the beach adjacent to both sides of this rock outcrop.)

Proceed up the slipway (Le Braye).

Note the craftsmanship in the slipway masonry, in particular that the paving-stones are set at an angle – which helped horses' hooves to grip when pulling up the wet heavily laden vraic carts.

Pass the café, toilets and telephone and proceed to the main road.

Carefully cross over the main road. Take the sandy path to the right of the Chemin des Basses Mielles road sign on the right-hand side of the road as you look.

The overall aim is to climb the sand dunes in the far left-hand corner, to the right of the airport's revolving radar beacon (and a white painted house lower down to its left).

This area is known as Les Blanches Banques. The sand dunes are among the most important in Europe and were designated a Site of Special Interest in 1996 by the States of Jersey.

The lower-level sand dunes are up to 2,000 years old – dunes in the higher plateau are thought to be even older. The area is rich in archaeological evidence of the Neolithic Period (neo - new, lithic - stone), which lasted in Jersey from about 3000 BC to 1800 BC. Within the area are large Standing Stones ('menhirs') and a burial chamber - monuments to Jersey's early settlers.

'Menhir' is derived from the Breton words, men - stone, hir - long. We do not know whether the menhirs were intended for worship or ritualistic purposes, but we do know that they were erected by the 'Iberians' - Jersey's early settlers.

The Ultimate St. Brelade's
Walk Directions

Les Blanches Banques is part of a five kilometre stretch of dunes known as Les Mielles (Les Mielles being the Norman French word for sand dunes).

After fifteen metres there is a boundary stone in the ground, keep straight on, then follow round as the path veers left and heads in the direction of the airport's revolving radar beacon and the white painted house.

Continue with the path (do not be tempted to turn off right or left) passing a yellow topped horseshoe marker post on your right-hand side.

Keep with the path. Still continuing to resist the opportunities to turn off, head for the small copse of low trees to your left.

On the path you will walk over a small piece of concrete and start to see various small remnants of demolished walls and later, ground level concrete, pipes etc.

This is the site of a prisoner of war (POW) camp built during the 1914/18 World War. By 1917 the camp held 1,500 German prisoners as well as 150 guards and 20/30 officers. The camp closed in October 1919.

One of the German prisoners was an artist and helped with the restoration of the wall paintings at the Fishermen's Chapel, St. Brelade's Church.

Once past the piece of concrete carry straight on but, after some twenty metres take the sandy and very narrow path to brush past the small copse of low trees to your left.

Past the copse, keep straight on with the path to the next clump of trees.

Now the outline and full extent of the old POW camp starts to become apparent - in size 280 sq. metres, over 50 huts, sheds and infrastructure, all within a three metre high barbed wire perimeter fence.

Again brush past the trees on your left-hand side and continue with the path.

Aim for and go to another yellow topped horseshoe marker post straight ahead.

Carry on, passing the marker post to your left-hand side and still with the path, head straight on.

As you pass (again on your left) another very small cluster of low trees and shrubs, continue with the path as it turns to the right.

Keep following the path as it runs parallel with the sand dunes to your left.

Again, keep with the now more indistinct path ahead as it starts to climb up an apparent hollow/rift very slightly to your left, in the sand dunes ahead.

Continue climbing with the indistinct path straight ahead up through the hollow/rift and ignore all other possibilities, particularly to the right.

Look back and absorb the view of the Bay.

The Ultimate St. Brelade's
Walk Directions

Keep climbing up the hollow/rift through the bracken area until you reach a wooden fence.

At the fence turn right and continue to climb alongside it. After a few metres there is a stile in the fence. **Ignore it** - but immediately after, as the path forks, bear right continuing up a gradual incline.

Follow this path noting a row of boundary stones up ahead to your left. Keep with the sandy path as it bears left and takes you to the boundary stones.

Once through the boundary stones, stay on the path continuing to climb the dune.

Again look back at the view.

As you approach the top of the dune note a large pond to your right (often dry).

Continue following the path as it heads towards the houses (or their roofs!) and passes the end of the pond.

When, and only when, the last two roofs disappear, at the subsequent fork in the path veer right. Follow this path through the now wooded area.

Keep with this path, ignoring all temptations to turn off left or right, until you reach a small clearing.

Go through the small clearing keeping with the path back into the woods.

Once back in the woods keep with the path until meeting twelve stepping stones and thirteen railway sleeper steps. Use the stones and climb the steps. (If the area is too wet use the 'path' to the right-hand side to reach the top of the steps.)

At the top of the steps carry straight on up through the 'gully' to reach a wooden perimeter fence.

To your left is a stile in the fence. Go over the stile and immediately turn right onto the tarmac.

This is the cycle track of Les Quennevais Sports Centre.

Having turned right, follow the cycle track along the straight for 100 metres, still continue as it bears left and then passes a row of trees to your left.

After the trees continue down the straight to the far end. **As you proceed, count the stone benches to the right-hand side of the track.**

At the end of the straight, as the cycle track bears left, and adjacent to the 5th bench, turn off right and proceed the few metres to the perimeter fence.

Do **not** go through the fence but turn left in front of it into the long path canopied with pine trees.

Follow this long path through the trees to the end.

At the end, opposite Les Quennevais School, turn right onto a wide track. This is the Railway Walk.

A railway between St. Helier and St. Aubin had opened in 1870. In 1884 a line was built from St. Aubin's Hospital to the Corbière quarries to carry granite for export. In 1885 this line was linked to St. Aubin and in 1899 was extended by branch line to Corbière. (An eastern line from St. Helier to Gorey was started in 1872, but the final stage was not in place until 1891.) The railway's zenith was 1924/5, when for each of the two years over one million passengers were carried. (For comparison in 2010 some 3.2 million passenger journeys were made by (Connex) bus, Island wide). Numbers then declined. Rail-cars were substituted for trains, buses were started to link its stations, winter services were dropped, but all in vain - a fire at St. Aubin Station was the final straw and the lines closed in 1936 - a victim of the car and road transport.

Follow the sylvan track to the road. Cross over this golf club entrance road and continue along the track.

This spectacular golf course belongs to La Moye Golf Club.

Denied access to the prestigious 'toffs' Royal Jersey Golf Club (only the cream of local society were allowed to join at that time and certainly no tradesmen), in 1902 George Boomer, the new headmaster of the new La Moye School, created a rough and ready course on open dunes running down to the beach – the steep inclines to be called Cardiac Slopes. However, backed by local businessmen including a butcher, a hotelier, an ironmonger and a wine seller, further land was soon leased allowing the holes down to the beach to be eliminated.

The course was redesigned in the 1930s but, during World War II, was severely damaged and the clubhouse pulled down by the German Occupying Forces as part of their defensive plans for the Island. Four platoons (170 men) were billeted at the La Moye Golf Hotel. Along with trenches and other defensive constructions, tall timber posts, linked by wire and mined to prevent glider landings, were erected over the course and the area patrolled day and night.

Major alterations in the 1960s created a splendid championship course. Staging the Jersey Open since 1963, the club and course are now justifiably internationally recognised – a far cry from the humble 'tradesmen's entrance' start.

Shortly, cross straight over the housing estate road and again proceed along the track – marked 'Cycle Route 1 – Corbière'.

On the right-hand side, just before the main road, stood the last railway station before Corbière – a request stop called 'La Moie Halt' – certainly used by the golfers, often on the first train of the day arriving at 10.45 am.

At the main road **very carefully** cross over and continue along the track, again marked 'Cycle Route 1 – Corbière'.

Care again at the next, and last, road crossing. Keep straight on with the track.

Later as you proceed, ignore a turning to the left. Later again the track will fork. At that fork keep right staying with the main track 'Cycle Route 1 - Corbière'.

The fork to the left is the route of the original railway from St. Aubin to the Corbière quarries.

Continue on the path and proceed back towards the car park, which will be on your left-hand side, virtually opposite a large flat granite block.

This rectangular block of granite is called La Table des Marthes. It is the capstone of a prehistoric tomb built elsewhere in the area. Prehistoric objects were found underneath it.

When the railway was in operation the stone lay between two tracks used by the engine to change from one end of the train to the other.

Prior to the railway it is said that the stone was a real attraction to children – for playing their favourite game of knuckle-bones (like Jacks but using small bones). It became known as the knuckle-bone table (in French – la table des marthes).

Turn left into the car park.

As you turn, the building to the right is the renovated station house of the Corbière terminus of the old railway.

At the time of going to press, on the market for £1,750,000 (reduced from £2,450,000) - what price a view ?!

The old platform has been incorporated in the renovated terrace, but the old stone and brick retaining wall, with its tapered end, is still very clear to see.

Return to the start.

Val de la Mare Reservoir

Parish	St. Peter
Special Features	First half of the walk a flat wide hoggin path. (Good for striding it out!)
	Lovely views of St. Ouen's Bay and Corbière with the reservoir in the foreground.
Start	Val de la Mare Reservoir car park, La Grande Route de St. Pierre.
	From the airport/St. Helier direction, follow the A12 La Route de St. Beaumont and then La Grande Route de St. Pierre towards St. Ouen. Just before aMaizin! Adventure Park entrance turn left into car park.
	From St. Ouen direction follow the A12 La Grande Route de St. Ouen through the avenue of trees alongside St. Ouen's Manor, turning right into the car park just after aMaizin! Adventure Park entrance.
Map Reference	**Jersey Telephone Directory** Map 2 G4
	Official Leisure Map 58.9/52.5
	Jersey Street Guide Map 19 E1
Terrain	Path, undulating on the return half, with steps and a steep incline out of the base of the dam.
Level of Difficulty	◐◐○ **SOME DIFFICULTY**
Time (approx)	1 hour 10 minutes
Distance (approx)	3½ kilometres (2¼ miles)
Amenities	Portable toilet en-route, (on left-hand side, first half of the walk towards the dam.)

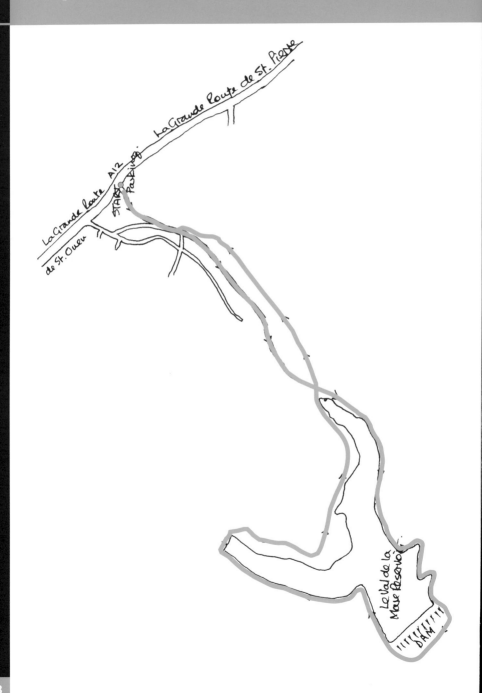

Val de la Mare Reservoir
Walk Directions

To add to the Island's water supply, construction work on the reservoir and the impressive dam commenced in the late 1950s. Water flowed from 1962.

Exit from the rear of the car park and enter onto the path by the side of the gate.

As you enter, on your right-hand side, read about Nigel Moores' inspiration and funding.

Proceed down the main path. Eventually keeping the reservoir to your right, follow the path's meandering to the dam.

A wonderful 1½ kilometres for striding it out, much to the sound and later also to the sight of water. Get those arms swinging as well!

When you reach the dam the halfway walkers should turn back and retrace their steps to the car park.

At the dam carry straight on, descending the path ahead until the path divides.

At this junction turn right, descend two steps and follow the path, initially alongside the dam, to the bottom.

At the bottom turn right and follow across, parallel with the dam, to the far right-hand corner crossing the bridge en route.

Climb the steps and the steep incline on the far side and turn right at the top.

Having seen both sides and the base of the dam you now have a better idea of its size (it is over 24 metres thick at the base) and the volume of water here.

The reservoir is Jersey's second largest, holding more than 900 million litres of water - enough to supply Jersey for five weeks. It links to all but one of the Island's other reservoirs, the core being a series of underground pipes which run from the desalination plant at Corbière to Queen's Valley in the east of the Island.

In 2011 the reservoir was emptied to undertake major works of repair and strengthening of the dam, costing £1.6 million. Although fundamentally maintenance work, it was also seen as a first stage of wider plans to enlarge the reservoir if future demand warranted.

Follow the now narrower path around the reservoir.

Keep with this path some distance, until you reach a short length of wooden fencing on your right-hand (reservoir) side.

Turn right through the gap in the wooden fencing, descend five steps and follow this lower path.

Val de la Mare Reservoir
Walk Directions

When you reach above the reservoir crossing, keep with the main path as it turns 90° to the right and descends twelve steps. After the steps cross over the reservoir.

After crossing, bear left, climb the twenty-two steps and proceed up the incline.

Keep with the path up to the highest point.

Make sure that you take in the lovely view of St. Ouen's Bay with Corbière lighthouse and La Rocco Tower.

Corbière Lighthouse – now a symbol of Jersey –was built in 1874 and was much needed. All ships coming to Jersey from the UK or the other Channel Islands must negotiate this treacherous rocky southwest corner of the Island, which faces the prevailing winds.

La Rocco tower was built in 1801 and formed part of the Island defences against the threat of invasion from Revolutionary and Napoleonic France. It was restored with the help of a 1969 public appeal and is now a navigation marker.

Follow the path down a small steep slope with steps to the right-hand side.

At the bottom of the slope ignore the turning to the right and carry on up the incline.

Keep with the path as it meanders and undulates, eventually descending to the main reservoir path.

Turn left onto that original main path and follow for some twenty-five metres.

At that point, in the middle of the wooden fence on the right-hand side, turn right and cross the bridge.

Bear around, initially right, with the path. Then, still with the path, bear left and climb ten steps, quickly followed by a further eight. Stay with this path and follow all the way back to the main path. (Do not be tempted to turn off left before the end.)

Rejoin the main path by turning right and follow the short distance to the gate, car park and the start.

Parish	St. Ouen
Special Features	Rural and open countryside. Lovely countryside paths, tracks and byways. Good historical interest.
	CAUTION **Because of vegetation growth, particularly in the summer, on sections of the paths that are not maintained, it is essential that you cover your legs.**
Start	Val de la Mare Reservoir car park, La Grande Route de St. Pierre.
	From the airport/St. Helier direction follow the A12 La Route de Beaumont and then La Grande Route de St. Pierre towards St. Ouen. Just before aMaizin! Adventure Park entrance turn left into the Reservoir car park.
	From St Ouen direction follow the A12 La Grande Route de St. Ouen through the avenue of trees alongside St. Ouen's Manor, then turning right into the car park just after aMaizin! Adventure Park entrance.
Map Reference	**Jersey Telephone Directory** Map 2 G4
	Official Leisure Map 58.9/52.5
	Jersey Street Guide Map 19 E1
Terrain	Byways, tracks and paths - including several reasonably steep climbs; occasional difficulties underfoot - possibly muddy in places.
Level of Difficulty	⬤⬤◯ SOME DIFFICULTY
Time (approx)	1 hour 30 minutes
Distance (approx)	5 kilometres (3 miles)
Amenities	None

Byways and Tracks - St. Ouen - *Map Guide*

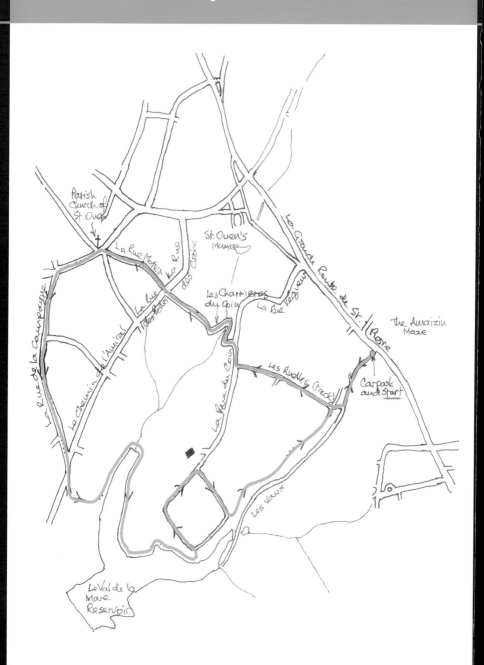

Parish Church of St. Ouen

St. Ouen's Manor

La Grande Route de St. | Rose

La Rue Motier

La Rue

Les Croix

Les Charrieres du Coin

La Rue Vegueux

The Amaizin Maze

Les Ruelles (Track)

Carpark and Start

Les Rue de la Campagne

La Chemin de l'Aumisal

La Rue Telesteria

La Rue du Coin

Les Vaux

Le Val de la Mare Reservoir

Byways and Tracks - St. Ouen - *Walk Directions*

Exit from the rear of the car park through the gateway by the side of the main locked gate onto the hoggin path.

As you enter, on your right-hand side, read about Nigel Moores inspiration and funding.

Proceed down this main path. After some 150 metres a wooden fence comes alongside on your right-hand side. Follow this fence for some 35 metres and then turn right, through a narrow gap in the fence, onto a path and immediately crossing a small stream.

Once over the stream turn left with the path. Keep following as it bears right up a short incline.

At the top of the incline keep straight on at the path/track junction. (You will come back to this junction later, by a different route.)

Keep straight ahead with this track, resisting all temptations to turn off right or left, until you reach the road.

At the junction with the road (La Rue du Coin) turn right and follow for 40 metres.

Eleven of the twelve Parishes are sub-divided into smaller areas called vingtaines' (i.e. originally based upon groupings of twenty or so properties - vingt being the french for twenty). However in St, Ouen vingtaines are known as 'cueillettes' (derived from the french verb 'cueiller - to gather) and refers to certain dues that were gathered from each district. 'Cueillette' was not always peculiar to St. Ouen, but it survives only in this parish.

This road serves the district known as Le Coin, which at one time had almost the standing of a cueillette and had its own Militia company, called Les Cracots du Coin - presumably dressed initially in black - 'cracot' being a well known species of black vraic (seaweed).

The Jersey Militia is recognised as having been first organised on a formal and parochial basis in 1337, based on orders of Edward III. In the 17th century the parochial bands were amalgamated into three regiments, the West, North and East and later in the century a troop of horse was added. In 1771 unpaid compulsory service for all able bodied males between 17 and 35 was introduced (and this was to last until 1924).

The distinctive red uniforms were introduced in 1778. Throughout our history the Militia played a most honourable part in defending the Island taking part in many battles.

Byways and Tracks - St. Ouen - *Walk Directions*

It was, in no small way, thanks to the Militia under the leadership of the brave, courageous and quick thinking Major Pierson that the French army was overcome in the Battle of Jersey in 1781. The Militia was mobilised at the outbreak of the First World War - over 6000 in number, of which nearly 900 were killed. It was remobilised again at the start of World War II.

After over 600 years, the Jersey Militia was disbanded in 1946. It was reformed as the Royal Militia Island of Jersey in the 1980s in very different circumstances.

On the right-hand side of the road, just before the turning to the left, is what is believed to be an unfinished fountain. The inscription includes the names of the Constable and the Roads Committee, with a date of 1898. We can only speculate that the flow of water expected from the field did not materialise!

Permanent parish works, of which this is an example, provided ample opportunity for local tributes to those who gave honorary service to the community.

Take the turning left virtually opposite the unfinished fountain. Follow the road (Les Charrières), first descending and then ascending the valley. Then carry straight on to the end of the road.

When you reach the road (Rue des Pelles) turn right and immediately left into Rue Motier and follow this track.

Near the end this track has a tarmac base that will take you to the road in front of St. Ouen's Parish Church.

The exact age of the church is unknown but it is certain that it pre-dates 1066. It is as old, if not older, than St. Brelade's Church and was initially a little thatched chapel. It is said to have been consecrated on 4 September 1130, with the altar containing a tiny bone splinter of Saint Ouen, the famous 7th century Archbishop of Rouen (in those days a relic was required to consecrate an altar). Additions were made particularly in the 13th and 15th centuries. Also there was a great restoration carried out between 1865 and 1870 (which included the ousting of the Militia cannon that had been stored in the south aisle for centuries), so the church has no predominant architectural style.

At the main road turn left past the church and follow the road along.

The tower to your right is all that remains of the last St. Ouen's (or Grantez) windmill (Le Moulin de la Campagne).

Sites of 12 windmills (and 38 watermills) in the Island are known, some of them dating from the 11th century. All of them would have been rebuilt many times.

A map of 1563 shows this windmill site to be one of only three at that time. Such windmills were built on high ground to serve areas away from the flowing streams and watermills. Their main function was grinding corn.

Only four windmills survive today - the others being Rozel, St. Peter and Grouville.

During the World War II Occupation, the Germans capped the tower with an observation platform (Batterie Ludendorff). The ranging chart still survives above the observation slits.

The tower is now a navigation marker with the site used as a headquarters by a local scout troop.

At the first road junction, virtually a crossroads, turn left into Rue de la Campagne and follow to the end of the road.

On the left-hand side notice that the cultivation here is done in strips of land separated by grass banks and low dry-stone granite walls. This is an ancient form of farming. The strips of land were called campes and groups of campes were called riages or reages - hence the area is shown on certain maps as Les Riages.

On the right-hand side ensure that you take in the lovely panorama of St. Ouen's Bay with La Rocco tower and Corbière lighthouse in the background.

At the end of the road turn right and follow the road for 50 metres. Then turn left into Jersey Water's Val de la Mare reservoir area. Enter through the two concrete gate posts.

During the German Occupation in World War II this site was an AA battery, the only one built to fortress standard and believed to be named Batterie Metz. The battery had a total of nine guns - 6 x 8.8cm Flak and 3 x 2cm Flak.

All the underground shelters have been filled in and with the area widely used by Jersey Water during the construction of the Val de la Mare Reservoir in the 1950s (completed in 1962), care must be taken to differentiate between the concrete put down by Jersey Water and that of German origin.

After ten metres bear left at the main track's 'Y'- junction and follow the track around.

The track opens out into a small car park, keep to the left-hand side. Ten metres after entering the car park turn left onto a short grassy track. Again after ten metres go through the Jersey Water small gate in the wooden fencing.

Descend a total of 63 steps to the bottom.

As you descend note the main expanse of the reservoir to your right.

The reservoir is Jersey's second largest, holding more than 900 million litres of water - enough to supply the Island for five weeks. It links to all but one of the Island's other reservoirs, the core being a series of underground pipes which run from the desalination plant at Corbière to Queen's Valley in the east of the Island.

In 2011 the reservoir was emptied to undertake major works of repair and strengthening of the dam, costing £1.6 million. Although fundamentally maintenance work, it was also seen as a first stage of wider plans to enlarge the reservoir if future demand warranted.

Near the bottom you reach a wooden fence on your left-hand side. Turn left, through a gap in that fencing, descend the last five steps and then follow the reservoir-side path.

When you reach above the reservoir crossing, keep with the main path as it turns 90° to the right and descends twelve steps. After the steps follow across the reservoir.

After crossing, keep with the path, climb 22 steps and proceed up the incline.

Keep with the path to the highest point.

Make sure that you take in the lovely view of St. Ouen's Bay with Corbière lighthouse and La Rocco Tower.

Corbière lighthouse - now a symbol of Jersey - was built in 1874 and was much needed. All ships coming to Jersey from the UK or the other Channel Islands must negotiate this treacherous rocky south-west corner of the Island, which faces the prevailing winds.

La Rocco tower was built in 1801 and formed part of the Island defences against the threat of invasion from Revolutionary and Napoleonic France. The tower was restored with the help of a 1969 public appeal and is now a navigation marker.

Follow the path down a small steep slope with steps to the right-hand side.

At the bottom of the slope ignore the path off to the right and carry on up the incline and follow round to the right.

Still follow the path as it meanders, passing two benches on the left-hand side, then passes through a canopy of pine trees and continues up a slight incline.

Then follows a long, straight, flat section. At the end of that section, in the left-hand corner as the path bears right and starts to descend, is a small wooden gate supported by a little fencing and a low granite pillar to the left-hand side. (On the other side of the gate is a Jersey Water sign.) Go through that gate (but perhaps easiest to go round it to the left) and follow a now narrow path protected by trees and bushes (mind your head as you go along, and at certain times of the year plough through lush vegetation!).

Follow the path all the way, staying with it as eventually it veers right, becomes a track and passes a large house on your left-hand side.

At the driveway entrance to the house, and where the track becomes a tarmac based byway, turn 90° right through a field-opening, onto a grassy track that follows the right-hand side of the field. Keeping a row of young trees to your right follow this sometimes rather indistinct track along the right-hand edge of the field and into the next one.

Keeping with the track, bear left and follow along the right-hand edge of several fields, now with woodland to your immediate right.

Carry straight on with the track as it drops down below the level of the fields.

At the track/pathway crossroads (the same junction as earlier in the Walk - Page 153) turn right and proceed down into the trees.

As you near the Val de La Mare Reservoir main path turn right, cross over the stream, go through the gap in the wooden fencing and turn left onto the main path.

Proceed the short way back to the start car park.

The Ultimate St. Ouen's

Parish	St. Ouen
Special Features	Lovely beach, country and reservoir walking. World War II German Occupying Forces coastal defences. Spectacular views. **CAUTION** **This is a low-water walk. The beach section of this walk should be attempted only if the tide is low enough and going out. There is the easy alternative of the promenade.** **Because of vegetation, growth in the summer on sections of the paths and because some sections of the paths/tracks are not maintained, when walking at that time, it is <u>essential</u> that you cover your legs.**
Start	Public car park, Kempt Tower, St. Ouen's Bay. Follow the B35 La Grande Route des Mielles (Five Mile Road) towards L'Étacq. Pass the Watersplash on your left-hand side and continue along, leaving a road, signposted C106 St. Ouen's Church, on your right-hand side. Kempt Tower (Les Mielles Visitor Centre) is the first tower on your left-hand side. Carry on past the first 'Kempt Tower Les Mielles Visitor Centre' sign on your left-hand side. 100 metres further on, and past the Tower, turn left following the 'Kempt Tower Visitor Centre' parking/information sign. Park in the car park.
Map Reference	**Jersey Telephone Directory** Map 1 C4 **Official Leisure Map** 56.2/52.5 **Jersey Street Guide** Map 18 B2
Terrain	Byways, paths and beach with several climbs. At times, some sections of the paths can be 'enjoyably' somewhat overgrown!
Level of Difficulty	⬤ ⬤ ◯ SOME DIFFICULTY
Time (approx)	2 hours 50 minutes
Distance (approx)	8½ kilometres (5¼ miles)

Amenities	**Start and Finish**
	    None
	 En Route (St. Ouen's Bay, near start)
	    Public telephones
	    Restaurants / bar / summer food trailer

The Ultimate St. Ouen's
Map Guide

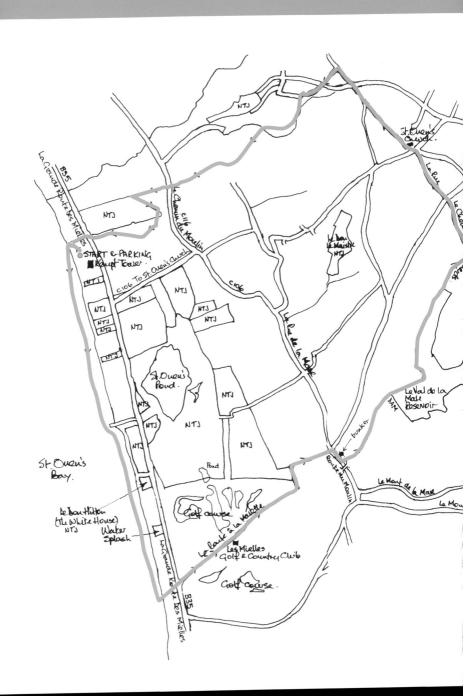

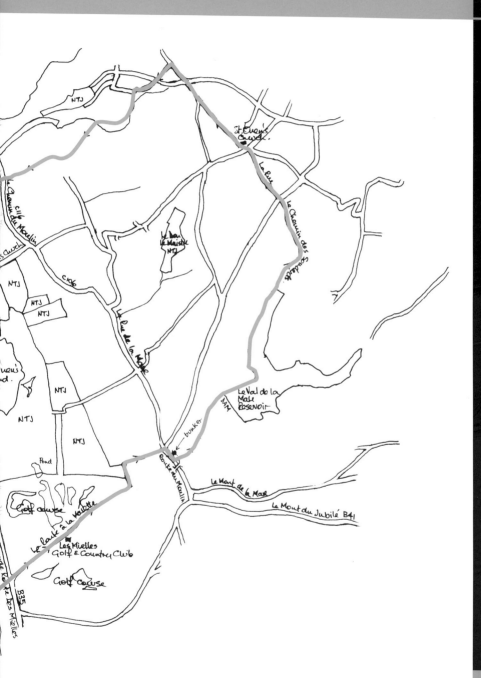

The Ultimate St. Ouen's
Walk Directions

Leave the car park by turning towards the concrete bunker and following the 'Kempt Tower Visitor Centre Entry this Way' sign, up three concrete steps.

IF LOW TIDE OR THE TIDE IS GOING OUT – turn right and take the steps to the beach. Once on the sand turn left and head for the first slipway.

Turn over the page for your next instructions.

(IF YOU ARE IN DOUBT IN ANY WAY WHATSOEVER ABOUT THE TIDE – carry on along the promenade, first passing the house (Cutty Sark), then Big Vern's Café, then The Watersplash and then a pair of steps down to the beach. At the next pair of steps to the beach (virtually directly in line with the airport runway **rejoin the walk, as shown over the page.)**

The sea wall was built by the Germans during the Occupation. It is one of seven anti-tank walls (Panzermaurs) built. Their lengths totalled 7,400 metres.

At that time the beach was studded with steel rails, then came the anti-tank wall of steel and concrete. Behind were the minefields, the masses of barbed wire and the cunningly placed and camouflaged guns.

To the right, looking towards the lighthouse, is the La Rocco Tower (Gordon's Tower) – the only Jersey Round Tower remaining in the bay and the last of an original five. All the other four were close to the shore, three have disappeared with the sands of time, one at least caused by the force of the sea. The fourth, sited at the head of Les Laveurs slip (adjacent to Big Vern's), was destroyed by the Germans as part of their World War II defence strategy for the bay.

La Rocco was built 1796/1801 and formed part of the Island defences against the threat of invasion from Revolutionary and then Napoleonic France. The tower was restored with the help of a public appeal launched in 1969 and eleventh hour help by the States of Jersey. Now it is used very much as a marker for small aircraft by pilots landing at the airport.

Slipways (or slips) are a common feature along the coastline. They act as a link between the coast road and the beach and were used mainly by farmers to collect seaweed (vraic – pronounced 'rack' or 'wrack') for use as fertiliser – the best natural replacement for the lack of chalk and lime in the local soil. It is said that the vraic helped to give the Jersey Royal potato its unique flavour thereby helping to establish it as 'the king of potatoes'.

Vraic was also dried to act as both fuel and bedding. The importance of vraic can scarcely be comprehended today. After spring tides the beaches swarmed with carts. So popular was this free resource that collection had to be strongly controlled both as to timing and amount collected and was policed by vraic officers.

Carry on past the first slipway (L'Ousière - Big Vern's) and the nearby steps on each side up to the promenade.

Carry on past the small white National Trust for Jersey building - Le Don Hilton (La Caumine à Marie Best / The White House).

The white building, and the surrounding four vergees of land, were given to the Trust in 1975, by Mrs Marie Genevieve Hilton (née Hind), the widow of Lt. Col. John Aston Hilton.

The stone-roofed building was originally St. Peter's Guardhouse and Magazine. It was built in 1765 being a replacement for a guardhouse and magazine which had been blown up. The guardhouse was called La Caumine à Marie Best, named after a lady who lived there following the departure of the military.

It was altered after World War I to serve as a seaside bungalow. Seaside huts were both fashionable and numerous at that time and concrete platforms, on which huts stood, can still be seen on the site.

At high tide the land around the guardhouse is frequently drenched with seawater, so salt-marsh plants thrive including the rare Alderney Sea-lavender.

Carry on past the pair of beach steps, virtually in front of Le Don Hilton, then pass another pair of beach-to-promenade steps virtually in front of the Watersplash complex.

Take the next pair of steps up to the promenade. These are situated some 200 metres further on - usually with a food trailer in the car park above and with the end of the airport runway in the background.

Cross over the promenade, up and over the low retaining wall and into the car park.

THOSE WHO TOOK THE PROMENADE ROUTE RE-JOIN HERE.

The Ultimate St. Ouen's
Walk Directions

Cross over the car park and out of the exit to the main coastal road (Five Mile Road).

Cross over the Five Mile Road into Route de la Marette signposted 'Les Mielles Golf and Country Club'. **Take care – this road has a sign 'Beware flying golf balls' for very good reason!** Continue along the road, passing Fun Zone and the Driving Range to your left and then Les Mielles Golf Clubhouse to your right. Proceed to the 'S' bend.

> *As you proceed out of the 'S' bend, a sign on the left-hand side confirms that the area to the left is a National Trust for Jersey Nature Reserve - La Mare au Seigneur (St Ouen's Pond). The Reserve covers 280 vergees (50 hectares) and contains a rich mixture of wetland habitats including open water, reed-bed, fen, wet-meadows, dune grasslands, rank grassland and scrub land. The pond is the largest area of natural open water in Jersey and dates back to 1309.*

> *In the wetlands, back to your left, you should see three large standing stones. The three stones are known as Les Trais Rocques Standing Stones. Such large upright stones are called menhirs (from the Breton words, men –stone, hir – long). They date from the Neolithic period (neo – new, lithic - stone), which lasted in Jersey from about 3000 BC to 1800 BC and were erected by the 'Iberians'. We do not know whether they were intended for worship or ritualistic purpose but at some other sites it is clear that burials have been marked.*

> *For ornithological and safety reasons the National Trust for Jersey does not permit the crossing of the wetlands, so sorry it's the closest you are going to get to the stones.*

Stay with the road until the end. At the road junction turn right into La Route du Moulin and follow for 25 metres.

At the electrical sub-station, on your left-hand side, turn left and enter the car park area of the Val de la Mare Reservoir.

At the back of the car park, where the car park becomes a track leading to a gate, take the rather narrow grassy uphill path to the left.

Climb up, bearing left and then right, with the path until you reach the German bunker.

> *This German World War II 'Resistance Nest' ('La Mare Mill') is a very rare type of heavy machine-gun turret bunker with a six-loopholed turret (two were blocked off because of the sloping terrain into which it was built).*

Follow right into the gully, leaving the concrete bunker to your left, proceed to the end and the bunker entrance.

> *Sense the foreboding and sinister atmosphere.*

Return to the end of the bunker and turn right out of the gully onto a small winding path heading for the top and front of the bunker ('Resistance Nest'). Turn left at the top and walk around the heavily camouflaged and disguised front.

Stand on the top of the bunker.

It is still camouflaged with stone and, even today, remains difficult to discern on the hillside into which it is emplaced. What a unique view of the whole of St. Ouen's Bay. Can you imagine a more inconspicuous placement or a better sited defensive position?

Come off the top and walk right around the front of the bunker.

Note the four shooting apertures.

Return down the path to the car park.

At the car park turn left and proceed down the lane to the gate at the back of the car park.

Go past the gate and, keeping with the track, head for the dam of the Val de La Mare Reservoir.

On the right-hand side of your path notice the water tap. It cannot be to drain the reservoir surely!

As you near the dam keep going straight on and head for the path upwards in the top left-hand corner.

The impressive dam is over 24 metres thick at the base.

Climb with the now narrow path. At the top turn right and continue with the path alongside the reservoir.

The reservoir, built in 1962, is Jersey's second largest, holding more than 900 million litres of water - enough to supply the Island for five weeks. It links to all but one of the Island's other reservoirs, the core being a series of underground pipes that run from the desalination plant at Corbière to Queen's Valley in the east of the Island.

In 2011 the reservoir was emptied to undertake major works of repair and strengthening of the dam, costing £1.6 m. Although fundamentally maintenence work, it was also seen as a first stage of wider plans to enlarge the reservoir if future demand warranted.

Keep with this main path some distance, until you reach a short length of wooden fencing on your right-hand (reservoir) side.

The Ultimate St. Ouen's
Walk Directions

Turn right through the gap in the fencing, descend five steps and follow this lower path.

When you are above the reservoir crossing, keep with the main path as it turns 90° to the right. Descend twelve steps and then immediately turn left and follow the grassy track.

Keep with the track through the gateway as it starts to climb and follow it all the way to the road (Rue des Pelles) at the top.

On reaching the road, cross over into La Rue and proceed to the end.

At the end of the road cross over the main road and go through the church gates.

> *St. Ouen's Church. The exact age of the church is unknown, but it is certain that it pre-dates 1066. It is as old, if not older, than St. Brelade's Church and started as a little thatched chapel. It is said to have been consecrated on 4th September 1130, with the altar containing a tiny bone splinter (in those days a relic was required to consecrate an altar) of Saint Ouen, the famous 7th century Archbishop of Rouen. The church has no predominant architectural style - additions were made particularly in the 13th and 15th centuries. There was a great restoration carried out between 1865 and 1870, which included the ousting of the Militia cannon that had been stored in the south aisle for centuries.*

Bear left, leaving the church on your right-hand side, and then take the churchyard path on your left to bring you to the seaward extremity of the churchyard.

Follow to the gates.

Go through the gates and follow the path to the road. Join the road (Rue du Couvent) by bearing right.

> *The tower on your left-hand side is all that remains of the last St. Ouen's (or Grantez) windmill (Le Moulin de la Campagne). Sites of twelve windmills (and thirty-eight watermills) are known, some of them amongst the earliest occupied sites dating from the 11th century. All of them would have been rebuilt many times.*

> *A map of 1563 shows this windmill site as one of only three in the Island at that time. Such windmills were built on high ground to serve areas situated away from flowing streams and the watermills. Their main function was to grind corn. Only four windmills survive today – the others being Rozel, St. Peter and Grouville.*

> *During The Occupation of World War II the Germans capped the tower with an observation post for a nearby battery (Batterie Ludendorff). The ranging chart still survives above the observation slits.*

> *It is now a navigation marker with the site used as headquarters by a local scout group.*

Carry on down the road, now Rue de Grantez, turning first left into Rue de la Ville au Bas. Follow the road to the end. At the farmhouse, La Ville au Bas, bear left with the last part of the road and then join the narrow path to the left and follow down the hill for 30 metres.

After 30 metres, at the path 'Y' junction, bear right through the gap in the path barrier posts and follow down (carefully minding both your head and your feet!).

As you proceed down, stop at the first turning left, indicated by a green-topped path marker post and read The Rotary Club de la Manche sign.

Continue to follow the path down, later to run alongside a long garden to your right.

At the end of the path turn right onto a track, leaving a marker post (sometimes missing!) at the corner on your right-hand side. Follow this track straight down to the road.

Go straight across the road picking up the left-hand (higher) footpath.

At the first path junction turn left and again follow. At the 'T'-junction, where the path joins a wider one, turn left. After 30 metres, and keeping the green gate to your left, bear right with the path.

Follow the path round and, where it opens out, go into the grassy area bearing round to the right to join a path on your right.

Follow the path, ignoring turnings off both right and left, until you reach a short wicket fence to your right-hand side with the sign headed ' Bird Refuge'. Proceed up the short path within the fence and enter the bird hide.

Inside read about 'The Sand Dunes' and 'The Need for Sand Dune Management'.

Return to the path, turn right and follow to the gate before the road. At that gate bear right and follow the path a short way until it comes alongside the road.

With great care, cross over the busy main road to the signpost to the 'Kempt Tower Visitor Centre' and its car park. Follow track into the car park and the start.

Tracks and Paths over St. Ouen's Bay

Parish	St. Ouen
Special Features	Superb views over St. Ouen's Bay. Lovely open countryside.
	CAUTION
	Because of vegetation growth in the summer on sections of the paths and because some sections of the paths/tracks are not maintained, when walking at that time, it is <u>essential</u> that you cover your legs.
Start	Car park, St. Ouen's Church.
	Turn off the A12, Le Grande Route de St. Ouen, onto C117 La Rue du Manoir. Turn right – (well) before the Church – into La Rue de la Cour signposted to 'St. Ouen's Parish Church Car Park' then turn first left and follow the road into the car park.
Map Reference	**Jersey Telephone Directory** Map 2 F4
	Official Leisure Map 57.9/52.9
	Jersey Street Guide Map 10 A9
Terrain	Hillside tracks and paths - with one long climb - occasionally difficult under foot. At times, some sections of the paths can be 'enjoyably' somewhat overgrown!
Level of Difficulty	⬤ ⬤ ◯ **SOME DIFFICULTY**
Time (approx)	1 hour 15 minutes
Distance (approx)	3¼ kilometres (2 miles)
Amenities	**Start and Finish**
	Toilet (by churchyard entry gate)

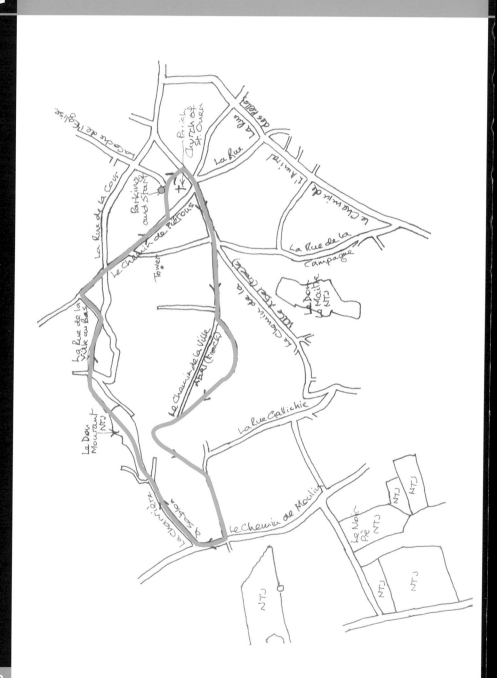

Pass through the churchyard leaving the church to your right. Go through the iron gates. Turn right onto the road (heading towards the sea) and follow.

St. Ouen's Church. The exact age of the church is unknown, but it is certain that it pre-dates 1066. It is as old, if not older, than St. Brelade's Church and started as a little thatched chapel. It is said to have been consecrated on 4th September 1130, with the altar containing a tiny bone splinter (in those days a relic was required to consecrate an altar) of Saint Ouen, the famous 7th century Archbishop of Rouen. The church has no predominant architectural style – additions were made particularly in the 13th and 15th centuries. There was a great restoration carried out between 1865 and 1870, which included the ousting of the Militia cannon stored in the south aisle for centuries.

When you reach the first road junction take the unmarked track ahead of you through the field, keeping the old windmill tower to your right. Head towards the sea for some 240 metres.

The tower to your right is all that remains of the last St. Ouen's (Grantez) windmill (Le Moulin de la Campagne).

Sites of 12 windmills (and 38 watermills) are known, some of them amongst the earliest occupied sites dating from the 11th century. All of them would have been rebuilt many times.

A map of 1563 shows this windmill site as one of only three in the Island at that time. Such windmills were built on high ground to serve areas situated away from the flowing streams and the watermills. Their main function was grinding corn.

Only four windmills survive today – the others being Rozel, St. Peter and Grouville.

During the World War II Occupation the Germans capped the tower with an observation post for a nearby battery (Batterie Ludendorff). The ranging chart still survives above the observation slits.

It is now a navigation marker with the site used as a local scout group headquarters.

After 240 metres, opposite a very small line of shrubs to the left, ignore a track off to the right and carry on for another 30 metres.

Notice that the cultivation on the right-hand side is done in strips (campes) of land separated by grass banks. Groups of campes were called riages or reages. This is a survival of an ancient form of farming.

After those 30 metres turn left onto a somewhat indistinct track and follow alongside the fairly tall evergreen shrubs and around the seaward edge of the field.

Tracks and Paths over
St. Ouen's Bay - *Walk Directions*

This track is not maintained so, as it veers to the right, in the summer, it can start to become quite overgrown. Do not be put off, it clears later and the lovely views make it **so** worthwhile! The basic rule is keep to the seaward edges of the fields as you follow the further directions below.

Follow the track as it continues to circle the field on the seaward side.

Later, still keeping to the edge, continue to follow around the field as the track turns into more of a path, veers right and leaves gorse land to the left-hand side.

As you approach the gorse on the seaward side, stop and soak up the wonderful vista of St. Ouen's Bay. As you pass the gorse, L'Étacq comes more into view. Again a superb vista.

The whole panorama of St. Ouen below, from the distant sand dunes of Les Blanche Banques to the water and surrounding areas of St. Ouen's Pond, has been designated as various Sites of Special Interest for ecological, zoological, botanical and archaeological interest that attaches to them, with all the protection that this offers. The protection covers the high value wildlife and landscape, particularly the sand dunes, archaeological artefacts, 19th century coastal towers and the fortifications built by the German Occupying Forces during World War II.

L'Étacq. The north point of St. Ouen's Bay is a high rock called Le Grand Étacquerel. South of this are some small channels between reefs that enable fishermen to use the area, aided by a slipway and a breakwater. Hence it became known as Le Port de l'Étacq.

At really low tide peat beds and tree stumps of predominantly oak, beech and hazel are revealed, thereby confirming that, when the Island was once joined to the Continent, it was covered with forest. This forest can be dated at 5000 BC.

The World War II German bunker on the tip of the headland – Le Petit Étacquerel - now houses a vivier.

Continue along the seaward edge and as the path returns to track and starts to veer to the right carry on to the track junction. At the track 'T'-junction (or perhaps more of a 'Y'), turn sharp left and join a track for just ten metres before continuing straight on with the then very narrow and awkward path on the left that drops down towards the bay.

Shortly, in front of the rather makeshift wire fence, bear right keeping with the main path. As the path turns right, immediately step over the remnants of a low dry stone wall and follow down.

Stop again to admire the vista, which this time includes Corbière lighthouse.

Corbière lighthouse – now a symbol of Jersey – was built in 1874 and was much needed. All ships coming to Jersey from the UK or the other Channel Islands must negotiate this treacherous rocky southwestern corner, which faces the prevailing winds.

Keep with the path, later including steps, to the small stream.

Listen to the soulful sound of the water.

Cross over the bridge and up the other side 20 metres to another path.

Note the sign of The Rotary Club de la Manche.

At the new path turn left, proceeding down-hill, passing a long garden to your right-hand side.

At the end of the path turn right onto a track, leaving a marker post (often lost or hidden) at the corner on your right-hand side. Follow this track straight on to the road.

At the road turn right and follow for some 100 metres. Then turn right (the first turning) into Les Charrières à Sablon.

At the top of the road carry straight on into the narrow path that climbs up alongside the left-hand side of the property 'Willorn'.

Climb to the top.

Do not forget to look back at the view.

Where several paths/tracks meet ignore the path coming in at 45º from the right, but take the next right, at 90º to you.

This track, with properties to the right, will convert to more of a lane and eventual tarmac. Proceed to the end.

At the 'T'-junction turn left into the road and proceed again to the end.

At this 'T'-junction turn right and continue straight on into Rue du Couvent.

Rue du Couvent bears to the right where it nears the old mill tower (on your right-hand side). At that point bear left up the 'No-through' road (towards the church).

Proceed through the church gates and turn left into the churchyard.

It is probably one of the best-maintained churchyards in Jersey!

Leaving the church to your right, return to the car park and the start.

Remote St. Ouen's

Parish	St. Ouen
Special Features	Bracing open countryside walking. Wonderful vistas and magnificent coastal panoramas. Dolmen site. Often horses, donkeys and sheep can be seen.
Start	Public car park at Le Val ès Reux, Le Chemin des Monts. Opposite the St. Ouen Parish Hall take the B64 Route du Marais (the straight road with the hydrangeas). Take the fifth turning left (some 200 metres past the end of the hydrangeas, as the road starts to descend) into Rue de Grantez. Take the third turning right into Chemin des Monts. Follow the road to the end and then keep going straight-on as it turns into a track - the car park is at the end. **(Take care with the track, particularly with low- slung cars.)**
Map Reference	**Jersey Telephone Directory** Map 1 D3 **Official Tourist Map** 56.5/53.7 **Jersey Street Guide** Map 9 B6
Terrain	Plateau byroads, tracks and country paths, can be wet and muddy in places.
Level of Difficulty	⬤ ◯ ◯ **EASY**
Time (approx)	1 hour 15 minutes
Distance (approx)	3¼ kilometres (2 miles)
Amenities	None

Remote St. Ouen's
Map Guide

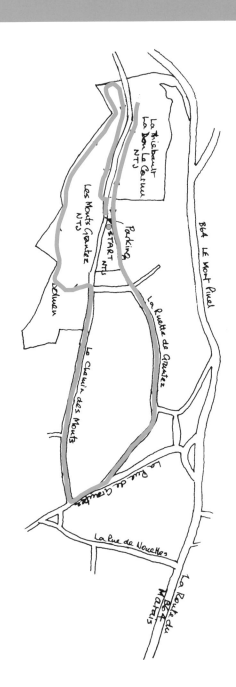

Exit the car park at the far side to the entrance.

Turn left onto the track and follow down to the National Trust for Jersey gate - La Grande Thiébault - Le Don Le Cornu.

> *Le Don translates from the French as 'the gift' and, as a mark of gratitude, precedes the name of the donor of land or property to the National Trust for Jersey - In this case the headland, La Grande Thiébault (and two other adjoining/adjacent pieces of land) was gifted by Miss E. M. Le Cornu, in 1966 in memory of Thomas Le Cornu.*

> *In 1978 the Trust bought two further areas of adjacent land, thus reuniting to one owner, land that once belonged to the Le Cornu family.*

> *The National Trust now owns the whole of this headland right over to the far northwest corner.*

Go through the small gate to the left-hand side of the main gate.

Follow the grassy rather indistinct path for 25 metres. Then, at the path 'Y'- junction, take the right-hand path and follow down the length of the headland to reach a stile in the fencing in front of you.

> *(As part of the National Trust for Jersey land management programme at certain times of the year sheep grazing takes place here. Therefore if the central areas are fenced off proceed to the stile down the path on the left-hand side of the path 'Y'- junction.)*

Climb over the stile and follow a narrow awkward meandering path to the rocky outcrop (La Rocque à l'Aigle).

> *At the outcrop admire the spectacular and stunning vistas and panoramas encapsulating L'Étacq.*

> **L'Étacq.** *The north point of St. Ouen's Bay is a high rock called L'Étacquerel in front of which is Le Petit Étacquerel. This side (south) of the promontory are channels between the reefs that enabled fishermen, aided by a slipway and a small breakwater, to use the area. Hence it became known as Le Port de L'Étacq.*

> *At really low tide peat beds and tree stumps of predominantly oak, beech and hazel are revealed, thereby confirming that, when the Island was once joined to the Continent, it was covered with forest. This forest can be dated at 5000 BC.*

> *The World War II German emplacement on the tip of the headland - Le Petit Étacquerel - now houses a vivier.*

Return and climb back over the stile into the field.

Note the memorial stone on the now left-hand side recording the gift to the National Trust for Jersey by Miss E. M. Le Cornu in memory of Thomas Le Cornu.

The objective now is to return to the same gate as you entered.

Once back in the field, and with your back to the memorial stone, turn right and follow back with the path <u>but</u> for only ten metres. Then take the grassy path to your right and follow, initially with the post and wire fencing to your immediate seaward side.

Continue through the gorse area and then proceed to the entry gate still with the same path, keeping the post and wire fencing to your immediate right.

Bracken and gorse are still allowed to grow here. In bygone days bracken was used for bedding and with gorse for fuel. Now, in this very windy spot, they help to keep the light sandy soil from blowing away.

Exit the National Trust for Jersey land at the gate and follow the track - this time continuing past the car park now on your right-hand side.

Keep with this track for 500 metres ignoring opportunities to turn off right.

In due course you will reach some agricultural buildings on your left-hand side (where the track becomes a road) - keep straight on.

When you reach the next road junction (Le Viér Mont) bear right and follow the road.

At the next 'T'- junction, again proceed right and then take the first turning right into Chemin des Monts.

Keep with this long straight road for some 650 metres.

Often there are horses to be seen along this road and usually donkeys in the paddocks of the donkey sanctuary on the left-hand side.

After some 650 metres, opposite the road off to the right (Ruette de Grantez), take the granite steps over the wall and proceed up to the Dolmen.

Dolmen des Monts Grantez. (Dolmen is derived from two Breton words, dol – table, men – stone.)

Although within the National Trust for Jersey land, this Neolithic (New Stone Age) passage grave dated around 4000 – 3250 BC, is owned by The Société Jersiaise. It is also known as La Pouquelaye des Monts, and anciently was called Le Trou les Faîtiaux.

Great ignorance and superstition prevailed in the Island over centuries and folklore was believed as true. The reality of witchcraft, the notion of the devil, and the belief in a fairy race, both good and evil, remained widespread.

Superstitious people believed that the dolmen had been built by fairies or dwarfs ('pouquelaye' – puck or fairy stones, 'les petits faîtiaux' – little people). For example when the Société Jersiaise were superintending the excavation in 1912 a local man in his eighties was horrified, screaming 'idiots …if you disturb the fairies you will bring trouble…'.

The land Les Monts Grantez comprises some 60 vergees (25 acres) and was purchased by the Trust in 1976.

Climb over the protecting wall of the Dolmen using the stone steps provided.

As you look into the dolmen and the dark covered foreboding chamber, feel the emotion of this Neolithic passage grave built 6000 years ago!

Within the oval chamber is a small side cell. In the main chamber a skeleton was found plus evidence of seven burials. There was also evidence of a burial in the side cell. The bodies were crouched on their sides with offerings laid on their tombs including limpet shells and coloured beach pebbles.

After exiting keep to the path behind the dolmen heading towards the bay and the seaward perimeter fence. Keep with the path as it veers right and runs parallel to the bay.

At the extremity, look out over the fence and absorb the magnificent panorama of St. Ouen's Bay and Les Mielles.

Les Mielles is the hinterland of St. Ouen's Bay. It was designated a 'Special Place' by the States of Jersey in 1978 and comprises land, including the slopes of the plateau, totalling some 8% of Jersey. It is special for a number of reasons – the high value wildlife and landscape, particularly the sand dunes, archaeological artefacts, 19th century coastal towers and the fortifications built by the German Occupying Forces during World War II.

Continue with the path straight on, leaving the line of fir trees (or what is left of them after the great storm of October 1987) to your left-hand side.

When you reach the large fir trees in front of you, at the path 'Y'-junction, bear left and follow the path into the trees.

Now it becomes a somewhat eerie interior abetted by fallen trees and crows.

Carry straight on through the trees picking a route to the seaward side, keeping close to the post and wire fencing, to emerge onto the headland.

Proceed down onto the tree-stumped promontory.

Remote St. Ouen's
Walk Directions

Go forward and admire the incredible vistas.

This area forms a natural amphitheatre for the National Trust for Jersey's highly successful summer sunset concerts.

Return by taking the path on the left-hand side, and follow up. After the copse keep with the trees and the fence to your left-hand side.

30 metres after passing the old water trough and water pump, exit to your left-hand side and proceed into the car park and the start.

Les Landes

Parish	St. Ouen
Special Features	Wonderful vistas of headland, rugged coastline and cliff formations. Excellent views of other Channel Islands. World War II German Occupying Forces coastal fortifications 14th century castle and other historical interest as far back as 125,000 BC. Public racecourse.
Start	Public car park Grosnez Castle. Join the B55, from St. Ouen's Village - Route de Vinchelez and La Rue du Val Bachelier - or from the West B55, (La Route du Ouest), Rue de la Mare and La Route de Grosnez. On the bend of La Route de Grosnez and Rue du Val Bachelier turn into the road to the race course and Grosnez Castle. Proceed down to the car park at the end in front of the castle.
Map Reference	**Jersey Telephone Directory** Map 1 B1 **Official Leisure Map** 54.9/56.4 **Jersey Street Guide** Map 1 C4
Terrain	Plateau, coastal and headland paths and tracks.
Level of Difficulty	◉ ◯ ◯ **EASY**
Time (approx)	1 hour 30 minutes
Distance (approx)	5 kilometres (3 miles)
Amenities	None

Les Landes
Map Guide

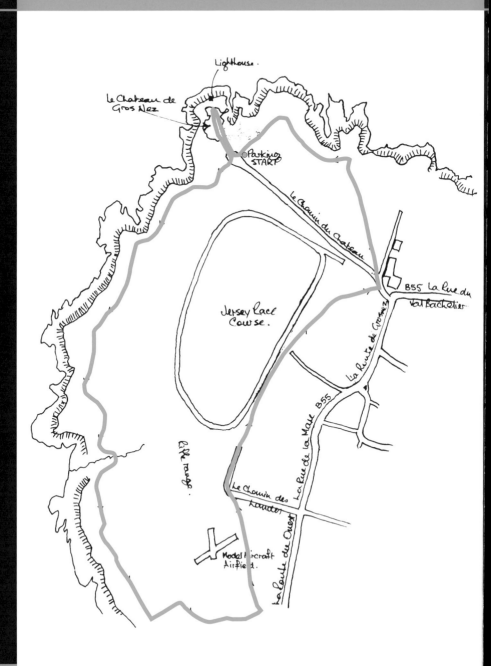

Lighthouse.

Le Chateau de
Gros Nez

Parking
START

Le Chemin du Chateau

B55 La Rue du
Val Bachelier

La Route de Grosnez

Jersey Race
Course.

La Rue de la Maue B55

Rifle range.

Le Chemin des
Landes

Model Aircraft
Airfield.

La Route du Ouest

Les Landes
Walk Directions

First explore the castle. Walk from the car park to the castle ruins entering by climbing up the eight steps to the right of the arch.

Grosnez Castle (Le Chateâu de Gros Nez) was built around 1330. It was not so much a defensive fortification as a place of refuge where the civilian population, with their cattle and their valuables, were able to obtain some protection from wars and pestilence, particularly by French sea-raiders during the Hundred Years War of the 14th century. Life for the islanders could be appalling. In 1339 the Island was effectively razed to the ground three times by the invading French.

The castle space, of almost an acre, was enclosed by a wall. With its back secured by steep cliffs, the landward side was protected by a broad ditch cut through solid rock and also a massive wall - much higher than the current five metres. The gatehouse had a portcullis and a roof. Flanking the gatehouse were two massive two-storey towers with arrow slits, enabling defenders to cover the drawbridge. A third tower on the west wall provided back-up. Inside were six small stone buildings.

It served its purpose but who finally destroyed the castle is not known.

Just inside, on the right-hand side, read also the information board.

Once inside proceed straight ahead and walk to the top of the lighthouse steps on the far right-hand side.

Admire the fabulous view of the other Islands ahead of you, Guernsey, Herm, Jethou and Sark, Sark being the closest to Jersey – some sixteen kilometres (ten miles). To the far right is the coast of France - The Cherbourg Peninsular.

In between Sark and France, some 56 kilometres (30 miles) away, is Alderney, visible only in the best of weather conditions. The lighthouse was built to help guide ships around this dangerous north-west corner and in particular the Paternoster reef.

The group of rocks (reef) out to sea called Les Pierres de Lecq or Paternosters are notorious. In 1565, during the reign of Elizabeth I, permission was given to colonise the then uninhabited Sark. Five Guernsey and thirty-five Jersey families were selected, many with young children. One of the ships taking the Jersey families foundered on Les Pierres de Lecq, drowning many, including women and children.

Whenever there is a storm it is said that terrified screams and ghostly cries of the children can still be heard.

The name Paternosters came about because sailors and fishermen were accustomed to reciting the Lord's Prayer (from Latin pater noster 'our father') whenever they passed this reef by way of remembrance of those who drowned and fears for their own safety.

If you feel adventurous walk down to the lighthouse (not allowed for in the timing).

Retrace your steps and exit by the same steps.

Les Landes coastal heath-land was designated an ecological Site of Special Interest in 1996. It is the most distinctive and spectacular aspect of Jersey's wild environment. Bound seaward by three kilometres of the exposed, dramatic and rugged granite cliffs of the north-west coast, it is Jersey's largest single expanse of maritime heathland. It covers an area of 160 hectares and contains a variety of habitats with over 200 species of flora and much wildlife.

There is evidence that Man has used Les Landes for at least 5,500 years.

The next objective is to reach the inland side of the five storey World War II German observation tower on the headland over to your right. There are several paths across. However, the following directions will give you the best route.

After leaving the castle head for the first green-topped wooden path-marker post somewhat straight ahead, adjacent to the road and near the end of the overhead wires. Follow the main path right. After approx 170 metres, at the next green-topped wooden path-marker post, take the narrow path to the right-hand side and follow to the headland.

At the next marker post bear left, still with the same path, and follow.

When you reach the next marker post the path divides, continue left with the higher path. Again keep heading for the Tower. After 120 metres you reach a fork in the path take the right-hand lower path and follow.

At the junction with the main path (at the next marker post) turn left still heading for the tower.

The Germans occupied Jersey from 1st July 1940 to 9th May 1945.

Hitler was obsessed with the idea that the British would try to recapture the Channel Islands. On 20th October 1941 he issued an edict that the Islands be converted into an impregnable fortress - 'the mailed fist of the Atlantic Wall'.

By 1945 there were 146 artillery guns in 37 battery sites in the Channel Islands. All were destined to see little action.

In Jersey a massive programme of defence works was ordered the magnitude of which is not generally recognised and defies belief.

Railways were constructed to transport materials – sand from Grouville Bay (estimated at over one million tons) and crushed stone from Ronez and other sites. About 500,000 tons of concrete was laid in less than two years (one-fifth of all the concrete used in mainland Europe's Atlantic Wall stretching 2,700 kilometres from Norway to the Spanish border).

There were up to 11,000 German troops and 6,000 foreign workers, mainly French and Spanish, but including between 1000/2000 Russian and Polish slave workers. In the region of 300 concrete structures, 7,400 running metres of anti-tank wall and 23,500 square metres of floor space within tunnels on numerous sites were built in the Island.

Despite all post-war attempts to dismantle and destroy, particularly by the British army in 1946 and the scrap-metal merchants in 1953, the local fortifications include some of the best surviving examples of their kind in Western Europe.

The fortifications must be viewed as part of the Island's heritage in the same light as the remaining fortifications, mainly castles and towers, of earlier centuries and treated as such for the benefit of future generations.

Les Landes is one of the biggest and most well-preserved sites of the Island.

After 40 metres (at the next marker post) bear right and continue on this path towards the tower.

The prominent and impressive structure to your left was a naval artillery direction and range-finding tower (Marine Peilstand und Meßstellung), MP3.

Each floor was intended to control a separate artillery battery. In the event it was used for simple observation purposes and mounting radar. Of nine planned, only three were built – the others being at Corbière and Noirmont Point.

This tower was unique in that it has slightly tapering sides.

The radar was protected by two nearby anti-aircraft installations.

The tower was under navy control – separate to the army controlled 'Batterie Molkte' (see later).

Stop opposite the lower, semi-underground concrete bunker adjacent to the tower to your right-hand side.

Now proceed to the actual tower - which you cannot enter - by turning right, off this main path and proceeding down through the cutting with the concrete bunker to your left-hand side.

The concrete bunker, which is largely buried, was the unique large combined generator and personnel bunker for the tower.

At the tower, to gain the best perspective, **carefully** go to the front. **You must return the same way (to attempt to come up the other side of the tower is too dangerous).**

However, as you return and come back up to the concrete bunker, this time turn right and climb up the narrow path seaward side of the bunker. At the top, turn onto its roof.

Now you have a better idea not only of its size, but also, even after so long, of the lengths the Germans went to camouflage their installations.

From the roof, return to the main path. Bear right, taking the diagonal path to the right and head for and pass in between the next two World War II concrete structures.

The small bay immediately to your right, adjacent to the tower, is known as 'gun graveyard'. In February 1946 the British army collected all the German heavy artillery, 25 pieces, from across the Island and simply dumped them over the cliffs into the sea. Subsequently, seven have been rescued and restored. Two went to Guernsey, two are now displayed at Noirmont and three are displayed further down this headland (see later).

The first gun salvaged took two summers to raise, moving two metres at a time using a specially designed twenty-ton hydraulic ram. During the winter it was held in place by six steel cables and it still moved with the force of the tides despite weighing six and a half tons. The heaviest gun lifted was nine tons.

The heavy recovery vehicle used to transport the guns - Ward La France - was purchased from The States by the late Don Pallot and can be seen today at the Pallot Steam, Motor and General Museum in Trinity.

The remaining guns can still be seen at very low tide.

Continue with this headland path.

The impressive crag that you see to your right is called aptly Le Pinacle and is over 60 metres high. The site at the foot (Le Pinacle Settlement) was occupied by the farming Iberians during the Neolithic period - some 2000/3000 years BC. Excavations also found evidence of civilisation from the Copper, Bronze and Iron Ages. A coin and earthworks gave further evidence of probable shrine worship in Roman times, around 200 AD.

Particularly, as the site was barren and exposed to the fiercest gales, the attraction must have been the awe-inspiring crag and its seemingly mystical and symbolic presence and stature, but you wonder the real effect on a sparse, ignorant and illiterate community in the Dark and Middle ages.

Continue with this headland path leaving the next marker post to your left, taking the right-hand lower and narrower path.

At the next marker post turn right, proceed down and cross the decking bridge.

This boggy part of the heath-land is called Le Canne de Squez.

On the other side of the bridge climb the 24 steps, at the top of which keep right with the narrower headland path.

Stop at the next marker post. Carefully move forward, slightly to your right.

I make no apology to mention again Le Pinnacle. The view from here only re-enforces what a massive and impressive crag it is. Imagine those Iberians looking up with awe from that grassy base area.

Return to rejoin the coastal path to the right and following seaward.

As you climb the gentle incline take the opportunity to climb onto the concrete base to your left-hand side to take in the view of Corbière lighthouse and the far end of St. Ouen's Bay.

The next objective is to arrive at the big gun ahead of you in the distance to the left.

Carry on with the path keeping the next marker post to your left.

Now the bay really starts to emerge and you get the first glimpses of L'Étacq in the foreground below.

Also becoming more and more apparent are the ruins of the German fortifications that lie semi-concealed everywhere.

Keep following the headland path across the various promontories.

Keep on admiring the seaward views, particularly of L'Étacq below.

Continue on the path, turning off only to reach the big gun on your left-hand side.

The German emplacements spread across the headland were 'Batterie Moltke', part of Army Coastal Battery 356.

Les Landes was one of the earliest sites chosen by the Germans in Jersey. The Battery arrived in 1941 with four French 15.5cm guns of First World War vintage, recently captured in France. They were intended as a stopgap pending the arrival of new German guns. These never arrived due to the Allied bombing of the factory. However, such was the German efficiency that, in anticipation of the new guns, every appropriate emplacement in the Island was duplicated (the new guns required a differently designed emplacement) and here is perhaps the best example - look at the adjacent structure!

Surrounding the renovated gun emplacement and support bunkers were the other defences of the battery – three French machine guns in tank turrets, two heavy machine guns, one light machine gun, fourteen flame throwers and one 150cm searchlight (codenamed 'Arthur').

Les Landes
Walk Directions

There were three other emplacements on the common and nearby were three anti- aircraft guns.

Walk up to the gun emplacement and it is a must to stand on the renovated platform immediately behind it, in the firing position.

The gun is one of the original 15.5cm French field guns of the battery and was recovered from the 'gun graveyard', mentioned earlier, in the 1990s.

It is awesome simply to stand there and, as you look down the barrel out to sea, reflect for a minute, imagining that you are on duty.

The emplacement was supported by two ammunition bunkers and a personnel bunker with inter-connecting tunnels up to 54 metres long.

This section of 'Batterie Moltke' has been restored by the Channel Islands Occupation Society and is open to the public on certain days – an incredible experience.

With your back to the gun, and leaving the sentry box to your left-hand side, proceed across the facing car park.

Note the green tank obstacles on the left-hand side.

Also on that side, next to the locked green gate, read the plaque on the stone block relating to Les Landes.

Exit and follow the car park exit track for 100 metres.

Over the heathland gorse and heather are predominant. You will recognise that the gorse is controlled to prevent it dominating the thick carpet of heather and to provide niches for other plants to thrive.

It was the collection of gorse and bracken by the local community for fuel and bedding, and the grazing areas for sheep and cattle, that helped shape the habitat we see today.

After 100 metres, on the left-hand side next to a locked green gate, you will come to a bridle path (yellow marker) and a footpath (green marker), follow the left-hand footpath.

As you proceed, note the model aircraft runways to your left-hand side used by the Jersey Model Aero Club since the 1970s.

Keep on this path until you reach another locked green gate. Go straight across into the track leaving the wire fence to your right-hand side.

The track to your left was the entrance road to Batterie Moltke. Imagine the road lined by concertina barbed wire and protected by a gun emplacement, with it and the whole Batterie surrounded by minefields, further barbed wire and automatic flame throwers strategically placed across the headland.

Note the earth mound to your left. It is the butts of the old rifle range. The current range is located at Crabbé but it is only long enough for shooting up to 600 yards. Accordingly the heathland is closed about four times a year to enable the Jersey Rifle Club to continue 900 and 1000 yard shooting here.

Keep with this track all the way – do not be tempted to turn off at the next locked green gate on your left-hand side.

Continue to follow the track keeping the racetrack to your left-hand side.

Race meetings are conducted here on a regular basis under the auspices of The Jersey Race Club.

There has been horse racing in Jersey continuously since 1789.

Racing has been conducted at numerous sites in the Island, including Les Landes, and The Jersey Race Club returned here, to this new course, in 1962.

As one of the only social events in earlier days, racing was hugely popular – large numbers attended, often requiring a strong police presence. On one occasion they closed down 40 gaming tables.

The meeting at Noirmont on 18th September 1872 was a very windy occasion requiring Monsieur Felix, a coiffeur in Queen's Street, to attend the ladies' toilette!

Lillie Langtry attended on 21st September 1876. On the day, a local evening paper apologised to its readers for not printing the results of the day's last two races – the carrier pigeon with the information had not landed on their office windowsill in time!

Introduced by Bertie, King Edward VII, Lillie Langtry was heavily into racing, owning a number of racehorses including one called Merman. This horse was highly successful in England winning at least one of the classics and after which she named a house she owned in Jersey. The house still has that name today.

At the road turn left and after some thirty metres, in front of the three big stones, cross over the road onto the grass, keeping to the left extremity.

Proceed out of the grass area by taking the path on your left-hand side set at an angle of some 45° and in a straight line facing towards Sark.

At a path 'crossroads' keep straight on, still facing Sark.

Note again the views of France, the Paternosters and, if you are lucky, Alderney.

Still facing Sark carry on into the small open area and proceed down the short path, on the other side, to the coastal path.

Les Landes
Walk Directions

To your right see the lovely beach and bay of Plémont but sadly still with the iniquitous derelict holiday camp on the headland. May the long outstanding decision about the future of the site be resolved without further delay, hopefully agreeing to restore it to nature.

At the time of going to press yet another Planning Application had been submitted, this time for 28 properties, and a Public Enquiry had been ordered by the Minister for Planning and Environment.

At the coastal path turn left and follow.

Below you as you turn is the cave La Cotte à la Chevre. It is world famous, being one of the few remaining Middle Palaeolithic (the very earliest Mousterian period) sites in north-west Europe. Neanderthal man was living here around 125,000 years BC - a time when Jersey would have been joined to France and the sea level (at 18 metres) was higher than today.

Man then was short in stature with jaws of brutal strength and ferocity and walked with a bend at the knee. He was, purely and simply, a cave dweller with a mentality of little more than a basic brute.

Keep with the coastal path and follow around the headland back to Grosnez Castle, the car park and the start.

The Soul of St. Ouen

Parish	St. Ouen
Special Features	Coastal path with wonderful vistas. Expanses of open countryside. Quiet lanes and byways. Backwater tracks and paths. Good historical interest. The blight of Plémont.
Start	Free public car park, Grève de Lecq.
	Follow the B40 Mont de Ste. Marie from St. Mary's Village, or the B55 and then the B65 (Le Mont de Grève de Lecq) from St. Ouen's Village.
	The car park surrounds the 'martello' tower and the entrance is on the main road as you start to climb towards St. Ouen.
Map Reference	**Jersey Telephone Directory** Map 2 F2
	Official Leisure Map 58.2/55.2
	Jersey Street Guide Map 3 C9
Terrain	A long, difficult first coastal path section. Straight forward tarmac byways and lanes. Stretches of grassy, in places muddy and difficult underfoot, footpaths and tracks. One short awkward path section sometimes somewhat overgrown.
Level of Difficulty	● ● ● **VERY HARD**
Time (approx)	3 hours 20 minutes
Distance (approx)	11 kilometres (7 miles)
Amenities	**Near the Start** Bay amenities - public toilets, public telephone, two beach-style cafes and pub/restaurant.
	Plémont (nearby) Beach café and public toilets Five minutes additional walking to the Bay, on RHS from the bus terminus - (see page 196)
	Route de Vinchelez North Point Bistro & Tea Room - (see page 196)

The Soul of St. Ouen
Map Guide

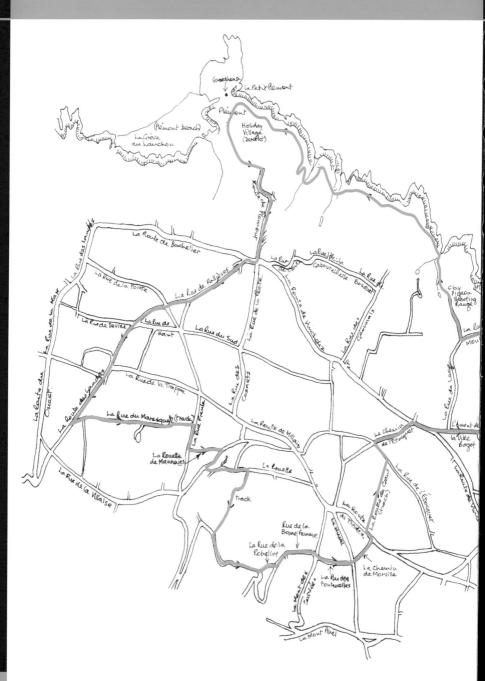

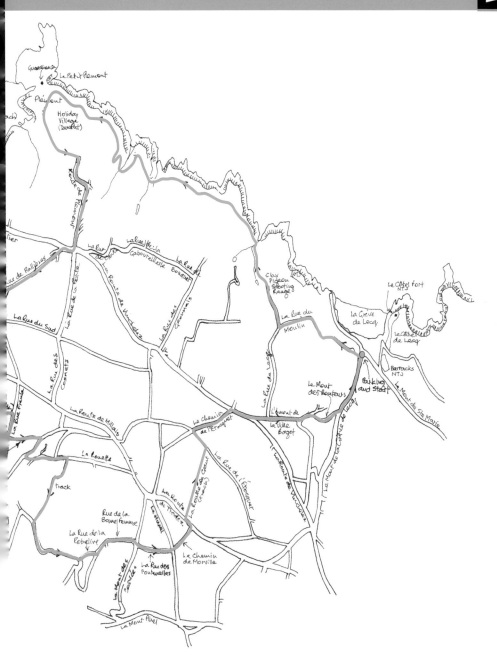

Exit the car park by the way you came in.

Stranded in the car park is a Jersey Round Tower. It was built in 1780, is 22 metres high and has walls over two metres thick. On the top it had an 18-pounder carronade on a traversing platform. Such towers were usually occupied by twelve or so soldiers.

The towers are usually known by the inaccurate name 'Martello'. Martello arises from Cape Mortella in Corsica where a round coastal tower caused the defeat of the British warships in 1794. The name has become very much generic for all round towers.

In fact Jersey Round Towers began to appear some 15 years earlier based upon a plan to erect 32 around the coast. The plan called for beaches that were deemed vulnerable to attack from Napoleonic France to be protected, with corresponding batteries in all accessible parts of the coast. But only 22 were built, in the period 1780 - 1800, a number of which can still be seen around the coast. Their design was quite different to the English Martello - taller, tapering, more elegant and of granite. They also had machicolations - those protrusions at the top through which hot liquids or burning objects could be dropped on the attackers.

At the car park exit turn right, immediately cross over the road and then immediately turn left to take the 'Cliffpath to Plémont'. Go past the 'No-through' road sign and proceed up the incline by the side of the Guest House.

Keep climbing as the tarmac disappears - to be replaced by a path and steps.

As the view of Grève de Lecq becomes clearer and more expansive stop to admire the picturesque bay. 'Grève' means a sandy beach scooped out from the foot of cliffs and 'Lecq', probably derived from the old Norse word 'La Wik' meaning creek (first mentioned in St. Mary's parish register in 1215) - obviously referring to the stream that runs onto the beach. Both beach and stream can be seen clearly from here.

The promontory backdrop on the far side of the bay is interesting. The top of the promontory is the earliest known fortification to be built around Grève de Lecq - an Iron Age hill-fort known as Le Câtel (Castel) de Lecq, bounded to the east by a large earth mound 270 feet high. Like Le Câtel de Rozel, the other Island Iron Age promontory fort, it was used as a place of refuge in the late medieval period. Again, like Rozel, the site has never been excavated.

Below, nestling in the cliff-side, is Le Câtel Fort. The fort was built in 1779 as a guardhouse and magazine (La Vielle Garde). By 1789 it had been upgraded to a fort and armed with three heavy 32-pounder guns mounted on traversing platforms. The fort is leased from the States of Jersey and looked after by the National Trust for Jersey.

The Soul of St. Ouen
Walk Directions

Down the hill from the fort are The Barracks. As a further part of fortification of vulnerable bays, construction started in 1810 to accommodate up to 250 garrison troops. The officers, their horses and their families (in that priority order!) lived in adjacent accommodation. The Barracks remained in use until 1926, when the last regiment, the 2nd Battalion of the East Surreys, departed. The Barracks were purchased by the National Trust for Jersey in 1972 and underwent a sympathetic programme of restoration.

Further up, the path becomes a track and then the track becomes a tarmac byway - keep following.

At the first road junction turn right (Rue du Moulin) following the 'Cliffpath' arrow and, passing the interesting poultry farm on the left-hand side, keep straight on.

If you hear sounds of gunshot the Lecq Clay Target Club sign on your right-hand side should allay your fears, but don't go through the gate!

Keep with the tarmac as the road bears left.

Pass Le Lecq Farm on your right-hand side and keep straight on to join the hoggin path and continue.

Reach the next Lecq Clay Target Club gate. In front of the gate turn left and follow the 'Footpath' sign onto the narrow path.

Follow the path down the steps, through the valley and up the other side. You are now firmly set on the coastal path that will take you to Plémont, some 3000 metres (two miles) away.

As you traverse the higher ground ensure you take time to capture the wonderful views and vistas - Guernsey, Herm and Sark - the Paternosters - France, the Cherbourg Peninsular - our lovely Island coastline.

Later on, of course - the blight on the landscape - the ubiquitous dilapidated and deteriorating Plémont Holiday Camp.

In 2007 the National Trust for Jersey obtained over 10,000 signatures supporting the return of the headland to natural beauty. Despite States of Jersey support, strongly backed by the Constable of St. Ouen and the rising indignation of islanders over the lack of a definitive outcome, at the time of going to press in 2011, matters still remained unresolved with processes still rumbling (or stumbling) on. With yet another Planning Application submitted, this time for 28 houses, a Public Enquiry had been ordered by the Minister for Planning and Environment.

As you approach the underbelly of the old holiday camp look out for the small granite plaque, in the retaining wall on your left-hand side, relating to the path construction.

The Soul of St. Ouen
Walk Directions

The plaque records the path construction in 1981 and the names of the surveyor and foreman.

As the coastal path bears inland and climbs up out of the underbelly of the old holiday camp, stop at the top of the steps to absorb the information on the board to your right-hand side relating to Plémont Guardhouse, down to your right.

The guardhouse was originally built in the 19th century and was linked with a battery which in 1812 housed one 18-pounder cannon. During the Occupation the Germans converted it into a Re-enforced Gun Position, to which they added alongside a twin machine gun emplacement, an observation post, mortar emplacement and a searchlight shelter with railway lines and twin operating platforms. The position also had a Tobruk mounting topped with a tank turret.

Continue to climb up and go through the pathway entrance gateway. Cross the small car parking area and exit ahead via the tarmac track.

Keep with the tarmac as it becomes a byway. Ignore all opportunities to turn off right and leave paths, car park and bus terminus to your right-hand side.

Keep with the road - Rue de Petit Plémont - to reach the main road.

As you walk, reflect on the total unsuitability of this area for a housing enclave and the desecration it would bring to the soul of this whole area of St. Ouen.

At the main road (Route de Vinchelez) - **CARE!** - turn right and follow for 30 metres, then turning left into Rue des Pallières and follow.

Shortly, on your left, you will pass La Ferme Vinchelez.

At the time of renovations a square bottle, probably a Dutch gin bottle, was found embedded in the wall with some stones, two at least of which were artefacts. There were also fragments of pots and some seaweed. These objects indicated 'insurance' against witchcraft and lightning. There is also a recess in the east bedroom wall, quite straight, extending the full length of one's arm into the thickness of the wall. More than imagination leads to the view that this could be a 'paùte' - a traditional secret hiding place. What stories could the original old property tell?

Keep with this road all the way, virtually straight on for some distance, until you reach the main road.

At the main road carry straight on following that main road, to your right, shortly to pass a red postbox on your left-hand side to confirm that you are on the right road.

Keep with this road for 300 metres and then stop at a 'Disabled people' sign on your left-hand side.

Ten metres past the sign, and at the house name Les Landes Cottage, turn left (hairpin back on yourself) onto the grassy, often muddy and difficult underfoot, track and follow straight on, keeping with the track.

As you near the houses on your left-hand side at the other end, still keep with the main hoggin-based track, turn initially left into, then complete an 'S' bend. Carry straight on to the road, still with the track.

At the road turn right and follow.

Take the first turning left into Ruette des Mannaies and follow.

At the 'T'-junction at the end of the road turn right and follow.

Take the first turning left (after 200 metres) into La Ruette and follow.

Past the property 'Le Mont' (on the right-hand side) look out for the wonderful examples of ivy and lichen covered, very old roadside dry-stone granite walling, particularly on the right-hand side.

Carry straight on to reach Maison de la Ruette on your right-hand side. At the end of the boundary wall of the farm turn right into the track (you will think that you are going into the farmyard - but, no). However do stop!

The house is an important property of at least the late 18th century. (Parts of the property suggest an older house as far back as the late 16th century).

As you turn onto the track immediately look to your left.

On the left are two unusual (probably unique) pigsties hollowed out under the field bank. They have rectangular openings about 30 x 60 cms (1ft x 2ft) and are circular inside with a large flat stone forming the roof. They cannot have been convenient either for the farmer or the pigs.

As you start to follow the track, stop again and look to the property, on your right-hand side, to see the marriage stone above the door.

Granite carved marriage stones appeared in the 18th century, attaining maximum popularity between 1720 and 1880. They were usually rectangular lintels above the front door. They consisted of the initials of the husband and wife (the husband's on the left and the wife's on the right, using her maiden name), with one, two or entwined hearts, usually all within the date. The date recorded would be of significance to the couple, often the date of marriage or the construction of the property.

Here, over the south façade door, the stone shows - 17 PMG SLF 90 - interestingly using MG for Mauger and LF for Le Feuvre. (Probably consistency was sacrificed here for symmetry.)

Follow the track, virtually straight, all the way to the road.

At the road turn left and follow.

Keep on following as the road becomes Rue de la Robeline (road name on right-hand side).

Still keep with the road, with all its bends and twists and finally a severe 'S' bend, then to become Rue de la Bonne Femme. Continue to the main road.

At the main road cross over into Rue des Fontenelles and follow to the crossroads.

Again admire the high roadside dry-stone walling - a feature all the way down to the properties. Also, look out for the road-side spring on the left-hand side, opposite Les Papillons.

At the next crossroads go straight across into Chemin de Morville and proceed the short way to the main road.

At the main road (B34 La Route de Trodez) turn left and follow for 50 metres to reach the entrance gates of Morville House on the left-hand side.

In front of the gates cross over the road to the other side and take the single file path virtually in front of you, to carry on across the fields at 90° to the road. (The path is along the left-hand side the field as you look at the field from the road and it is protected by a line of trees to its left-hand side.)

Follow the narrow, awkward, and sometimes somewhat overgrown path, straight across along the edges of the fields, to reach the road on the far side.

At the road turn left and follow.

Take the first turning right - Chemin de L'Etocquet- and proceed to the main road.

At the main road (B55 - La Route de Vinchelez) - **CARE!** - turn right and follow. When possible cross over the road. After100 metres take the road that veers off to the left - La Petite Rue - and follow.

At the road junctions keep straight on into L'Amont de la Ville Bagot and follow straight on.

Continue with the road - L'Amont de la Ville Bagot - and, as it starts to descend, still keep straight on downhill until the tarmac finishes. At that point, ignore the left-hand grassy track ahead that starts to climb up, carry straight on downhill into the now narrow (and dark) concrete and stone-based byway.

Follow this steep and slippery byway (Le Mont des Routeurs), probably with flowing water, carefully down to the main road.

Care at the main road, cautiously turn left and proceed back to the car park on the right-hand side and the start.

Parish	St. John and St. Mary
Special Features	Lovely countryside and open headland walking. Spectacular and stunning views. Lovely coastal paths and country byways. Much historical interest. **Optional visit to the eerie and spectacular Devil's Hole.** (Now a National Trust for Jersey property with free admission.)
Start	Public car park, opposite Les Fontaines Tavern, La Route du Nord (C100), St. John's. From St. John's Church follow La Route du Nord, the C101. At the 'T'-junction (when it becomes more the coast road and the C100), turn left and follow round until you see Les Fontaines Tavern on the inland side of the road. Park in the car park on the seaward side of the road, just before the tavern, immediately opposite a '200 yds' and picnic road-sign on the left-hand side.
Map Reference	**Jersey Telephone Directory** Map 3 A1 **Official Leisure Map** 62.1/56.2 **Jersey Street Guide** Map 5 D4
Terrain	Byways and lanes, undulating tracks and paths, including the coastal path, and one steep incline.
Level of Difficulty	●●○ **SOME DIFFICULTY**
Time (approx)	3 hours (+ 20/25 minutes to visit Devil's Hole)
Distance (approx)	9 kilometres (5½ miles)

Amenities	**Start and Finish**
	    Pub/restaurant
	
	En Route
	    Restaurant/shop (La Mare Wine Estate)
	    Pub/food (The Priory, Devil's Hole)

The Ultimate St. John's/St. Mary's
Map Guide

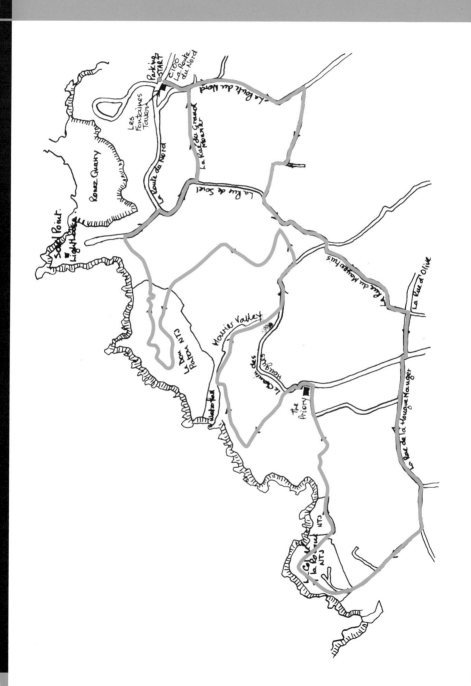

Exit the car park by crossing over the coast road and proceeding up the road that runs alongside Les Fontaines Tavern (La Rue de l'Étocquet).

Ignore the first turning right and, after 250 metres when the road appears to fork, keep with the same road veering right and follow to the end.

At the 'T'-junction turn right into Le Canibut and follow the road.

> *On your right is Le Mottais Farm. Initialled stones on the property place its earliest history in the 17th century.*

> *In 1668 Jean Marche married Jeanne Le mot Motey and in 1750 another Jean married Esther Le Mottais. The name of the property could originate from either of these two marriages but, whichever, it is a good example of how a property came to be named after a family.*

At the next road junction keep left with the road, which is now called La Rue de Sorel, and follow round.

Continue straight on as La Rue de Sorel becomes Le Mont de la Barcelone.

Proceed down the hill.

At the crossroads at the bottom of the hill carry straight on into La Rue de Maupertuis.

> *Stop and listen to the lovely sound of the babbling water.*

Proceed all the way to the top of the gradual incline.

> *On your way up, notice the old unnamed small cottage on your right-hand side (opposite the property, Fern Valley) dated 1725. In the yard in front is a white door and covered wellhead. It is unusual in that it has, roughly carved, on its side, a marriage stone dated 1765.*

Granite carved marriage stones appeared in the 18th century, attaining maximum popularity between 1720 and 1880. They were usually rectangular lintels above the front door. They consisted of the initials of the husband and wife (the husband's on the left and the wife's on the right, using her maiden name), with one, two or entwined hearts, usually all within the date.

The date recorded would be of significance to the couple, often the date of marriage or construction of the property.

In this case we can speculate that because the 1725 lintel was already in place, the later marriage stone, of perhaps the next generation, was put on the granite wellhead. Also, because of the crudity, could it have been carved in situ?

Proceed up the road.

As you approach the next road junction, on your right-hand side, are two granite gate-posts inscribed 'Clos des Pauvres' and 'Don Gruchy'.

Land would be given or bequeathed to the parish, or bought by the parish from monies given or bequeathed, to bring in an income for the parish poor. The fields (Clos des Pauvres) were rented to the highest bidder at parish meetings.

The poor ('pauvre' in French) were cared for in this manner in Jersey since mediaeval times.

The name of the donor of the Clos des Pauvres was occasionally remembered in granite at the site.

In this case 'Jeanne Gruchy' is the most recognisable of the names so inscribed. In her lifetime thought more thrifty than wealthy, she died in 1848 somewhat surprisingly leaving a substantial sum for the relief of the parish poor. Her will required each parish to purchase a plot of land at her bequest and apply the income generated to help the needy parishioners. However, her remembrance was usually more potent than simply her surname on a granite gatepost as here.

At the crossroads turn right, signposted La Mare Wine Estate and Vineyard Restaurant, and follow the road.

At the next road junction turn right and then immediately left (La Rue de la Hougue Mauger) and past La Mare Wine Estate (La Mare Vineyards and Distillery) to your right.

La Mare Wine Estate. The earliest buildings date from the 17th century, but the main house, previously known as The Elms, with the lovely pink granite, is dated 1797 – the date of the marriage stone over the front door. The exquisite house is more than set off by the lovely and immaculate gardens.

The original family owned the property until 1968. The new owners, the Blayney family, restored the then very dilapidated property, planted Jersey's first commercial vineyard in 1972 and later developed the distillery and a range of farmhouse provisions. After the sale in 1997, further progress has been made by the new owner Trevor Owen and his professional team. La Mare now has seven and a half hectares of vineyards with some 17,000 vines. Within a 25 acre working estate there are 12 acres of grapes and 11 acres of apples. La Mare Wine Estate is a major tourist attraction and with its restaurant, is a busy events centre and by far the most popular wedding venue on the Island - an absolutely delightful setting.

Stay with the road all the way to the end and continue straight into La Rue des Touettes.

After 200 metres from the start of La Rue des Touettes (say 260/280 paces) turn right onto a track. **(Care to ensure the distance because there are no markers to assist.)** To help identification, an extra half-metre of road tarmac starts to direct you forward into the grass centred track and sometimes there is a scaffold structure each side of the road (which supports field-watering pipes over the road).

As you proceed ensure you take in the wonderful panoramas of open countryside, the sea, distant France (Cherbourg Peninsular) and the Islands of Sark, Herm and Guernsey.

Proceed down the track. Particularly as you approach the coast do not be tempted to turn off left or right - keep straight on until you reach the National Trust for Jersey sign 'Le Don Mourant'.

Le Don translates from the French as 'the gift' and, as a mark of gratitude, precedes the family name of the donor of land or property.

In this instance this extensive area of coastal land (referred to again later) was donated to the Trust in 1946 by Oliver Mourant in memory of his wife , Lilian, née Le Brocq.

Immediately you pass the National Trust sign ignore the main track to the right and keep straight on, down the narrower path, for **just** 45 metres.

After 45 metres, (before the path veers right and opens out to bramble and gorse-land) turn left into a small, cleverly disguised, path opening. Go through the opening, down three steps and turn right onto the coastal path. (To your left is a granite signpost in the ground, which directs you to 'Devil's Hole 1½'.)

Proceed down through the now gorse-lined path and follow round.

In due course you will go down ten steps. Stop some ten metres past these steps and look seaward.

The small islet rising up out of the sea to your left is called L'Île Agois. It is some 450 metres square, separated from the mainland by a narrow gorge, has cliffs some 75 metres high and reputedly was used for sheep grazing. Remains of fourteen ancient hut-circles can be traced and amongst artefacts found have been Neolithic pottery and seven coins of Charles the Bald, who died in AD 877. All this indicates that it must have been lived on both BC and AD. What a place to have lived – perhaps it was not an island then and perhaps it was used only as a refuge. Even so... the raging tide and howling wind! Interestingly too, the site might well have derived its name from the breton-french 'gois', meaning causeway.

Continue with the path. Ahead of you an outcrop of rock looms large. Proceed to the base of that outcrop on your left-hand side and **stop** (just before the path turns right and descends by steps).

You have reached Le Col de la Rocque - perhaps the finest viewpoint anywhere in the Island.

Dependent on how adventurous you want to be, climb all or part of the Col for stunning panoramas from Sorel Point in the east (RHS) to Plemont in the West (LHS).

In the background is Guernsey and Sark. In the foreground is a group of rocks (reef) called Les Pierres de Lecq or The Paternosters.

In 1565, during the reign of Elizabeth I, permission was given to colonise the then uninhabited Sark. Five Guernsey and thirty-five Jersey families were selected many with young children. One of the ships taking the Jersey families foundered on Les Pierres de Lecq, drowning many including women and children. Whenever there is a storm it is said that terrified screams and ghostly cries of the children can still be heard.

The name Paternosters came about because sailors and fishermen were accustomed to reciting the Lord's Prayer (from Latin pater noster 'our father') whenever they passed this reef by way of remembrance of those who drowned and fears for their own safety.

In 2005 the Paternosters - a haven for wildlife - together with the Ecréhous and the Minquiers, was named alongside the Island's east coast as a United Nations Ramsar - protected site.

Continue on the path and descend nine wooden steps. Stop at the bottom and take time to look over to your left.

The cliffs along this coast were formed over 600 million years ago. With tempestuous tides fuelled by gales over such a long period of time, you can see why many of the Island's 300 caves have been formed along this coast.

Across the other side of the inlet you will see the renovated steps (and viewing platform) that lead down to a natural cavernous hole – The Devil's Hole – a great opening behind the cliff eroded by the sea which enters by means of a blow-hole or channel. It measures 30 metres across and plunges 60 metres down.

The cave's proper name is Le Creux de la Touraille or Le Creux de Vis.

In 1851 the French vessel La Josephine foundered offshore and began to break up. The ship's figurehead became firmly wedged in the cavernous hole. Local people saw the opportunity and commissioned the addition of arms, horns, a tail and a trident.

With horse-drawn excursion cars and wagonettes just starting at that time, and later the motorisation of the stables, it is said that the name Devil's Hole was created to attract visitors to the area - it certainly became a major tourist attraction!

Are you going to add to the numbers? (see later)

In 2009 the Clarke family gifted the land Le Creux de Vis to the National Trust for Jersey in memory of Fred Clarke - a previous constable of St. Helier.

With the original 'devil' destroyed somewhat appropriately by fire, the current replica (see later) originated in 1957.

Keeping with the path you pass on your right-hand side the National Trust for Jersey sign 'Le Col de la Rocque Le Don Mourant'.

This second sign is at the other extremity of the land gifted by Oliver Mourant. When you add that the gift included not only the coastal land you have walked through but also the steep slopes leading down to the shore and the islet L' Île Agois, what a wonderful and unique gift in memory of his wife.

Continuing with the path you pass on your left-hand side the National Trust for Jersey sign 'Les Falaizes Le Don Lesbirel'.

This area of coastal land covered with gorse and dense bracken was gifted to the Trust in 1970 by Miss E. A. Lesbirel.

With further adjoining land purchased by the Trust in 1953, also abutting Le Don Mourant, how good to feel that this whole wonderful area is under the guardianship of the Trust in perpetuity.

In earlier times this extensive area was used for sheep grazing.

The Ultimate St. John's/St. Mary's
Walk Directions

On this walk, as with others where coastal paths are involved, you will pass low stonewalls on the landward side of the paths. These were built to keep the sheep out of the fields and remain on the cliff tops and tricky and spartan ledges and edges of the coast.

Continue past the bridle path to your right. When you come to a path junction, turn left signposted 'Cliff Path' (low stone signpost). Keep with the path.

After 60 metres turn left with the path.

Continue on the cliff path until just after passing a house and buildings on your left-hand side. Turn right as the path opens out into a lane (which has tarmac for a few metres) and bears left. Immediately after the bend turn left, signposted 'Cliff Path'.

Continue to follow the path finally descending eleven granite steps to The Priory and Devil's Hole.

> **YOU MAY WISH TO (IN FACT IT IS A MUST) TAKE TIME OUT HERE TO DESCEND THE RENOVATED PATHWAY TO DEVIL'S HOLE ITSELF AND THE VIEWING PLATFORM.**
>
> **Eerie, spectacular, disturbing, even sinister - raw unspoiled nature at its amazing best - not to be missed!**
>
> **Allow 20/25 minutes - 104 shallow steps and a good pathway.**
>
> **If time does not allow, proceed just a few metres to see the 'Devil' in the pond on your right-hand side!**

Cross over the car park in front of The Priory and then immediately (at the end of the building) turn left onto the road.

Follow the road around as it bends. After a few metres, and as it starts to rise, turn left onto the path signposted 'Cliff Path'.

On the right-hand side as you turn is the Parish of St. Mary's Millennium Standing Stone.

The Société Jersiaise and Ronez Quarries jointly gave each parish a standing, undressed granite stone to commemorate the Millennium. The stone acknowledges earlier paganism. Note the plaque giving the names of the benefactors involved.

Additionally the States of Jersey presented each parish with a round section granite cross 2.475 metres high on a simple stepped plinth. The cross symbolises and is in recognition and celebration of the second millennium of the Christian faith.

Go through the gate reading carefully in relation to the sheep grazing.

In 2009 a flock of some 30 Manx Loaghtan sheep were released by the National Trust for Jersey onto this stretch of coastline where they have free access to 30 hectares of coastline between Devil's Hole and Sorel Point. The sheep, hailing from the Isle of Man, are a hardy and primitive breed predating the Vikings and perhaps the nearest today to the breed that used to cover Jersey in the olden days. Their often four horned and brownish coloured lambs make them instantly recognisable and they fit exactly the sheep grazing part of the Trust's land management programme. They thrive on these marginal areas of rugged cliff and coastline habitat, eating poor vegetation including gorse, brambles and ivy.

A shepherd looks after the flock and a group of Trust volunteers assist in the sheep's overall well-being.

Once on the path keep to this main path, bearing left, all the way to the headland.

On the headland ignore the paths immediately to your right and do not veer right until directed by the small stone sign 'Cliff Path'. Follow this path.

Continue to follow this path all the way and descend into the valley (La Vallée des Mouriers - Mourier Valley).

The cave that you can see across to your left is called La Cave de la Vielle Église.

At the valley bottom turn right, head for the pumping station and exit the sheep grazing headland.

The stream in this valley was powerful enough to turn three mills. Today, it is dammed close by the pumping station and the water pumped over the hills to Handois Reservoir in St. Lawrence.

Keep straight on up the valley track to the top.

When you reach the road turn left and follow – the road starts to climb and a water gully appears on the left-hand side.

This gully is in fact a stream and the stream acts as the boundary between the parishes of St. John and St. Mary.

Just after the low concrete wall of the gully/stream finishes, turn left in front of the wellhead, as if you were heading up the front garden of the property (London House). Yes, it **is** a public right of way – but keep right and respect the property owner's privacy.

London House. Note the 1842 marriage stone above the door. In this case Edouard Ahier and Ester D' Auvergne were married in 1806 so the date is probably that of the building. The stone - Ed. AH 1842 E.DVG - is also of unusual design in that the date is between the initials of the husband and wife and also for the abbreviation 'Ed' rather than simply the initial.

The Ultimate St. John's/St. Mary's
Walk Directions

Follow the narrow path immediately to the right of the property uphill. It climbs steeply and then follows the edge of a field. Climb to the top keeping straight on for a few metres when the path becomes a track.

This path is known as Petticoat Lane – probably inspired by the property's name!

The initial short stretch of original cobblestone was unearthed in 2005 at the time of the renovation of London House.

At the top turn left onto the tarmac lane. Follow this lane to the signpost 'Private – No Through Road' and continue. Later it becomes an unmade track.

Carry on down the track (do not be tempted to turn off either right or left). As the track starts to near the coast keep with it as it veers right and follow to the end.

At the end of the track opposite you is a National Trust for Jersey gate Le Don Paton.

Le Don Paton comprises a large area of coastal land with agricultural fields (78 vergees/14 hectares) between Les Mouriers Valley and Sorel Point. It was gifted to the Trust in 1995 by Sir Angus Paton.

Now very much the sheep's domain.

That gate is usually open. Go through and carry on to the 'sheep' gate 35 metres further on.

Pay attention to the sheep warning and ensure the small gate is properly fastened once you are through.

Proceed through the gateway and follow the track keeping the main gorse, bracken and brambles immediately to your right.

In bygone days gorse and bracken were collected by the local inhabitants and used for fuel and bedding.

As the track opens out into headland it becomes more of a path. Follow the path keeping to the right-hand side of the headland.

When possible join the coastal path ahead of you, by turning right.

This section of the coastal path is one of the oldest. The path was constructed by the prisoners of the States prison (now La Moye) during the 1960s.

Turn right onto the cliff path and follow all the way to the end of this section of the coastal path, exiting the sheep grazing area through the gate on the way.

The shipping light to your left is at Sorel Point.

Sorel is the northernmost tip of the Island.

When you reach the end exit through the path barriers and then immediately turn right up the three steps into the car park.

To your left notice the Millennium Standing Stone for St. John.

Cross over the car park exiting via the tarmac on the far side. Turn right out of the car park and follow the road to the end.

To the left-hand side is the moto-cross track where events are run under the auspices of The Jersey Motor Cycle and Light Car Club.

At the main road turn right and follow the road round.

At the point the road loses its white lines turn left into La Rue du Grand Mourier.

Proceed to the end of the road.

Towards the end of the road on your left-hand side is the property Le Grand Mourier.

The property was built in the mid 18th century. There is evidence of an earlier property of the 16th century.

The main house gives good examples of stone ledges on the chimneys. Such stones are sometimes referred to as 'witches' seats' (in folklore they had to sit somewhere). Originally the property would have had a thatched roof and these stones were so placed to deflect rainwater at the vulnerable point where the thatch joined the chimney stack.

At the 'T'-junction turn left and follow the road to Les Fontaines Tavern (on your left-hand side) and the coast road, La Route du Nord.

La Route du Nord is known as a 'war' road.

There was much unemployment during the German Occupation of the Island in World War II and there was no wish for the unemployed to do good works for their oppressors. Therefore local men were found work by the States of Jersey to widen and construct new roads and to take their time about it! One of their main tasks was to construct a road from Les Mouriers to La Saline. However, the road could not go past Sorel because beyond to Les Mouriers was a German military zone. The road around Saline was completed and the foundations laid for the remainder to Sorel - eventually finished in 1953.

Cross over the coast road to the car park and the start.

Read the plaque in the middle of the car park dedicated to the men and women of Jersey who suffered during World War II.

Byways and Paths – St. John's

Parish	St. John
Special Features	Lovely coastal and cliff-top paths. Stunning views over Bonne Nuit Bay. A leg-stretching climb out of Bonne Nuit. Good historical and folklore interest.
Start	Very limited roadside parking at the end of La Rue de Frémont (ex Wolf's Caves and Abundant Life Church Centre). From St. John's (Church) take the main A9 towards Trinity. Turn left sign-posted (sp.) B52 (C99) Bonne Nuit and Wolf's Caves. Turn left again sp. C99 Wolf's Caves and Bonne Nuit. From Hautes Croix (Trinity) follow the sp. A9 St. John's Church. Turn right sp. B52 Bonne Nuit. Turn left sp. C99 Wolf's Caves and Bonne Nuit. Then follow sign to Wolf's Caves into La Rue de Frémont and proceed to the end of the road. At the end of the road turn around to come back the way you came and park 'prettily' and considerately and at your own risk, perhaps on the left-hand side where the road is widest some 40 metres down the road.
Map Reference	**Jersey Telephone Directory** Map 3 C1 **Official Leisure Map** 63.5/55.8 **Jersey Street Guide** Map 6 C6
Terrain	Undulating lanes, paths and tracks, to include a long and hard climb involving coastal-path steps.
Level of Difficulty	⬤ ⬤ ⬤ **VERY HARD**
Time (approx)	1 hour 30 minutes
Distance (approx)	4½ kilometres (2¾ miles)

Amenities	**Start and Finish**
	    None
	
	En Route (within adjacent Bonne Nuit Harbour)
	    Public toilets
	    Public telephone
	    Beach café

Byways and Paths - St. John's
Map Guide

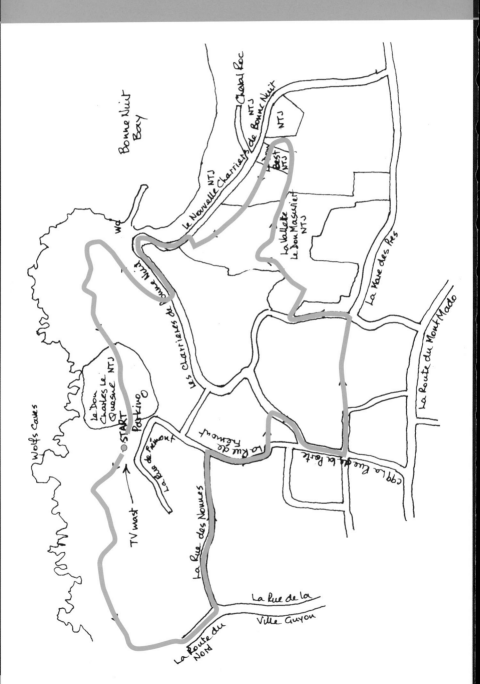

Bonne Nuit Bay

Chapel Roc

NTJ

Le Nouvelle Charriere de Bonne Nuit

NTJ

NTJ

PB8T
NTJ

La Vallette
Le Dou Masurier
NTJ

La Mare des Pres

La Route du Mont Mado

WC

Les Charrieres de Bonne Nuit

Wolfs Caves

Le Dou
Charles Le
Quesne NTJ

START
Patino

La Rue de Frémont

La Rue de Frémont

La Rue de Frémont

TV mast

egg la Rue de la Porte

La Rue des Nouves

La Rue de la
Ville Guyon

La Route du Nord

The name Wolf's Caves has never been explained satisfactorily though one suggestion is that it had to do with a sea-wolf or pirate. The main cave is impressive - over 100 metres long, 18 metres high and up to 15 metres wide.

The caves are only accessible by sea.

Walk back to the end of the road and straight ahead join ten metres of grassy track to reach a five-bar gate (to the right of which there is usually a small National Trust for Jersey sign relating to sheep). At the gate take the narrow path on the left side as indicated by the marker post.

Follow that path the short way to the coastal path.

Turn left onto the coastal path and follow along the coast.

The tall mast, on your left-hand side, is the Independent Broadcasting Authority's Transmitting Station.

Enjoy the view to the right. Ahead are the islands of Sark, Herm and Guernsey with the reef in the foreground, Les Pierres de Lecq or Paternosters.

In 1565, during the reign of Elizabeth I, permission was given to colonise the then uninhabited Sark. Five Guernsey and thirty-five Jersey families were selected many with young children. One of the ships taking the Jersey families foundered on Les Pierres de Lecq, drowning many, including women and children. Whenever there is a storm it is said that terrified screams and ghostly cries can still be heard.

The name Paternosters came about because sailors and fishermen were accustomed to reciting the Lord's Prayer (from Latin pater noster 'our father') whenever they passed the reef by way of remembrance of those who drowned and fears for their own safety.

In 2005 the Paternosters - a haven for wildlife - together with the Ecréhous and the Minquiers, was named alongside the Island's east coast as a United Nations Ramsar - protected site.

To the right is the coast of France.

After some distance you will pass a 'Danger. Blasting in progress when the siren sounds' warning sign. Be aware!

The gates to the right below the sign, protect the Island's old refuse dump when straight into the sea was the order of the day and the site was open to the public for just four hours a week - on a Wednesday. (A far cry from today's green and protective environment with the new £100 million La Collette energy-from-waste plant, capable of processing 105,000 tonnes of waste a year and complete with a generating capability to produce an estimated 7% of the Island's electricity from its waste).

Continue to the road, bearing left with the path that will have a tarmac surface as you approach the road.

At the road turn left and follow.

La Route du Nord is known as a 'war' road.

There was much unemployment during the German Occupation of the Island in World War II and there was no wish for the unemployed to do good works for their oppressors. Therefore local men were found work by the States of Jersey to widen and construct new roads and to take their time about it! One of their main tasks was to construct a road from Les Mouriers to La Saline. However, the road could not go past Sorel because beyond to Les Mouriers was a German military zone. The road around Saline was completed and the foundations laid for the remainder to Sorel - eventually finished in 1953.

At the top of the incline keep straight on into La Rue és Nonnes, which is a green lane, and follow this road to the end.

At the 'T'-junction turn right (La Rue de Fremont) and continue up the road until it turns 90° to the left. Follow round that bend but, where the road then turns immediately 90° right, leave the road and carry straight on down the very narrow path to your left.

At the end of this short path turn right and proceed up the hill.

At the 'T'-junction turn left into La Rue de la Porte and then take the first turning left into La Ruette de la Carrière. Where the road takes a 90° turn to the right carry straight on up the track that faces you on the left-hand side – Mont Mado Lane (Cycle Route 1).

On each side, but particularly to the left, were the old individually-owned quarries - the famous prized stone Mont Mado Quarries - where quarrying of the beautiful pink coloured stone was carried out from very early days until well into the 20th century. The finest houses and the States buildings were at least faced with the stone. There is evidence to show quarrying as far back as 5,000 years ago - the Neolithic period - but commercially not until the late 18th century. By the mid 19th century there was employment for over 25 men.

In the earliest days the area rose to a 400 foot rocky peak, on which a windmill was built in 1826. With increasingly high demand for the prized stone, the upsurge in quarrying took its toll. First to go were the wooden sails of the windmill - lost to the strong updrafts caused by the changing landscape - then, after only some 50 years of use, followed the slow collapse of the stone windmill itself. Things did not stop there. With persistent quarrying the 400 foot peak then disappeared and finally a large chasm created.

After quarrying had ceased the chasm was poorly infilled causing water pollution in the vicinity. However, all ended happily - cows now graze healthily upon it.

On reaching the crossroads turn left (La Rue des Barracques) and follow until, on your right-hand side, you see the National Trust for Jersey plaque for La Vallette. Stop to view the gate, gate posts and stile.

La Vallette. The line of probable owners has been traced back to Thomas Pinel who married Elizabeth Arthur in 1665. Their house would have been the standard four-roomed thatched cottage.

It was his great great great granddaughter Elizabeth, who married Charles Le Masurier in 1790, (so many generations in such a relatively short period - such was life expectancy in those days). They rebuilt the house to its present form in 1796. The rebuilding of the property is marked by their marriage stone above the front door.

Granite carved marriage stones appeared in the 18th century, attaining maximum popularity between 1720 and 1880. They were usually rectangular lintels above the front door. They consisted of the initials of the husband and wife (the husband's on the left and the wife's on the right, using her maiden name), with one, two or entwined hearts, usually all within the date.

The date recorded would be of significance to the couple, often the date of marriage or construction of the property.

However, note the unusual marriage stone on the entrance gateposts. 1812 was the year of the birth of Elizabeth and Charles' last child. They put their initials and the date on the gateposts and beside it constructed a neat stile - also note the excellent example of a traditional Jersey gate.

The property stayed for a number of generations in the Le Masurier family and it was Philip who generously bequeathed the property to the National Trust for Jersey in 1965.

Byways and Paths - St. John's
Walk Directions

Proceed down the road for a further 35 metres to reach a field gateway on the right-hand side. Turn into the field and join a grassy rather indistinct path to the left-hand side. Follow this path to the far side of the field, keeping the tree line to your immediate left.

At the gap on the far side of the field turn left into the trees and, almost immediately, turn left again onto the path between the two path signs.

Follow down to cross over the low wooden 'bridge' and continue straight on through the overgrown côtil until you reach the end.

At the path 'T'-junction turn right and follow that path across the top for 400 metres.

While traversing, admire the wonderful views to your left of Bonne Nuit Bay and the distant coastline of France.

The rock in the middle of Bonne Nuit Bay is called Le Cheval Guillaume. In pagan times, and over the following centuries, on midsummer's day, crowds from all over the Island came to the bay to be rowed around the rock – an action that supposedly guaranteed them good luck throughout the coming year!

Deemed a probable place for insurgents to land, Bonne Nuit Bay's defences were always being strengthened – cannon, guard-house powder magazine and then, by 1835, the building on the right-hand side of the Bay – a small fort 'La Crête' armed with six 32 pounder guns. With no attack ever made, La Crêté was later converted into a retreat for the Lieutenant-Governor of the Island. Of recent times it has become a Jersey Heritage holiday-let. It is a beautiful piece of military architecture – note the granite roof and guttering.

The breakwater was built in 1872 as a shelter for inshore fishing boats as well as a facility for exporting the high quality granite from Mont Mado quarry.

After 400 metres, just after ignoring a path upward to the right-hand side, the path turns left descending steeply. With the help of steps and stones descend all the way to the road.

At the road turn left and follow the short way down. When you reach the road junction ignore the turning to the right signposted to Bonne Nuit Harbour, instead proceed up the hill (Les Charrières de Bonne Nuit).

There is a theory as to how it became named Bonne Nuit. This relates to the sea outside the bay, which was called 'of ill repose'. In contrast, the shelter of the harbour offered a good night's sleep (bonne nuit being French for good night). It may be correct, but what is certain is that Bonne Nuit was a smugglers' haven in the 19th century.

Smuggling was a very lucrative business in the late 17th-19th centuries. Smuggling wine, spirits and tobacco to England was nearly as profitable as into France. The English customs awoke to the fact that the Island was importing much more tobacco than it could possibly smoke.

Enterprising merchants were buying it in Southampton, getting a rebate on the duty, bringing it to the Island and then landing it on moonless nights in remote Devon coves. When a customs officer arrived in 1681 he complained that the whole Island was in conspiracy against him and that, whenever he tried to do his duty, he was affronted and beaten and could get no help from the jurats and constables!

The Jersey smugglers defied all efforts to outwit them.

After the apartment building on your right-hand side turn right onto the cliff path signposted 'Cliff Path to La Saline'.

Proceed up the steep and long climb to the top.

As you climb ensure you take in the views to your right. In the background is the French coast. The reef in the middle of the sea (about half-way to France) is called Les Ecréhous.

The reef comprises a group of islets and rocks and is administered by the parish of St. Martin. There are three main islets Maître Île, Marmotière and Blanche Île. They were inhabited in prehistoric times, however, the first mention in historic times is 1203 when permission was granted for the building of a small chapel, the remains of which exist today.

In 1848 Philip Pinel a Jersey fisherman built himself a little cottage on Blanche Île and lived there for almost 50 years. He was nicknamed 'King of the Ecréhous' and when Queen Victoria visited Jersey in 1859 they exchanged gifts - he gave a basket woven out of dried vraic (seaweed) filled with different kinds of fish, she a blue coat.

Small houses exist on the islets that have predominately remained in the possession of and been visited by Jersey families over many generations.

In 1953 an age-old unresolved dispute as to the ownership of the reef was taken to the International Court at The Hague by France and Great Britain. The Court ruled that sovereignty belonged to Great Britain.

In 2005 the Ecréhous, together with the Paternosters and the Minquiers, was named alongside the Island's east coast as a United Nations Ramsar - protected site.

In the foreground are Bonne Nuit Bay and the harbour.

Byways and Paths - St. John's
Walk Directions

To the right-hand side, at the top of the steps, note the National Trust for Jersey sign 'Le Don Band' (sign often goes walkabout!) and round the corner of the path another sign 'Le Don Charles le Quesne'.

Le Don translates as 'the gift' and, as a mark of gratitude, precedes the name of the donor. In these two cases areas of headland were donated to the National Trust for Jersey in 2003.

This area of headland is known as Frémont Point - Frémont means 'cold hill'. In 1160 it was known as Frigidus Mons and is believed to be the site of an early Iron Age promontory fort.

Continue to follow the cliff path.

Ahead of you notice the buildings on the furthest promontory. They form part of the Ronez quarry complex. A siren sounds to warn of imminent blasting.

Ronez Ltd is a long established UK owned Jersey quarrying company. Prior to the 1960s it was named the Jersey Granite and Concrete Company. Its business is obtaining raw rock, crushing it into aggregate and making stone-based products – ready-mixed concrete and building blocks. It also has a road resurfacing division.

The business grew from humble beginnings in the late 19th century when it started to export granite setts (cobble stones) to the UK. This grew into the shipping of 3,000-5,000 tons of stone a week to a London base. Starting from their own jetty the ships would do round trips returning with cement to St. Helier harbour. Exporting ceased in the 1960s and the jetty is no longer in use.

The start of the 21st century has seen the company re-confirm its core business as quarrying aggregate and delivering related products.

Keep with the coastal path until you reach the barrier to the 'old' path ahead of you and the new path diverted right. At that point turn left onto a narrow path, keeping the wire fencing to your immediate left. Emerge from the path onto the road and carry straight on to return to the start.

Égypte

Parish	Trinity
Special Features	Lovely woodland path. Incredible views of the north coast with distant panoramas of France. Walking up (virtually) to the highest point in Jersey.
Start	Roadside parking at the end of La Rue D'Égypte. From the C97 La Rue des Platons turn into the 'No-through' road, La Rue D'Égypte. After 500 metres turn 90° right, still with the road, and follow down. Where the road next turns 90° to the right park 'prettily' on the road side.
Map Reference	**Jersey Telephone Directory** Map 4 F2 **Official Leisure Map** 65.9/55.7 **Jersey Street Guide** Map 7 E7
Terrain	Virtually all headland and cliff paths and tracks, with steep climbs, including some steps. A short byway section to finish.
Level of Difficulty	⬤ ⬤ ⬤ **VERY HARD**
Time (approx)	2 hours
Distance (approx)	5 kilometres (3 miles)
Amenities	None

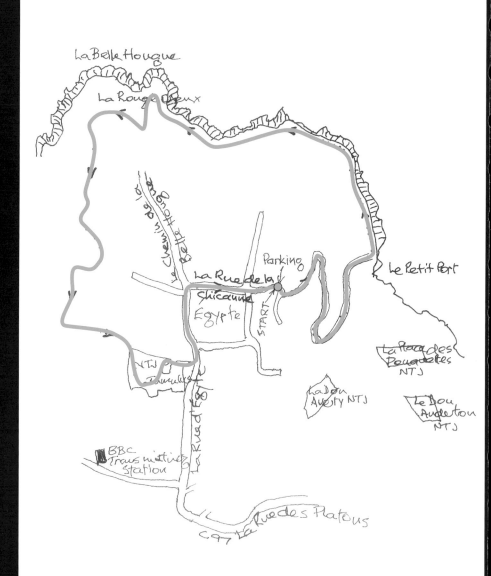

Head down the road towards the property entrance gates.

After twenty metres take the track in the left-corner and follow.

As you proceed, take in the lovely views of the coast and France.

The reef of rocks and islets half-way to France is called Les Ecréhous and is considered to be part of the parish of St. Martin.

There are three main islets, the biggest Maître Île (some 300 metres long and 150 metres broad), Marmotière and Blanche Île. They were inhabited in prehistoric times, when part of the mainland, but the first mention in historic times is 1203, when permission was granted for the building of a small chapel, the remains of which still exist today.

Small cottages exist on the two main islands and have predominately remained in the possession of and been visited by Jersey families over many generations.

In 1848 Philip Pinel, a Jersey fisherman, built himself a little cottage on Blanche Île and lived there for almost fifty years. He was nicknamed 'King of the Ecréhous' and, when Queen Victoria visited Jersey in 1859, they exchanged gifts - he gave a basket woven out of dried vraic (seaweed) filled with different kinds of fish, and she a blue coat.

In 1953 an age-old unresolved issue as to the ownership of the reef was taken to the International Court at The Hague by France and Great Britain. The Court ruled that sovereignty belonged to Britain.

In 2005 Les Ecréhous, together with Les Dirouilles, the Paternosters (Les Pierres de Lecq) and Les Minquiers, was named alongside the Island's south east coast as a United Nations Ramsar protected site - a Wetland of International Importance.

Keep with the main track and follow as it takes a hairpin to the right.

Crossing several small trickles of water, follow to where the stream crosses the path, with the small waterfall to the left (adjacent to the footpath signs).

Stop and listen to the water and, to the right, admire nature's carpet surrounding the tumbling water.

Cross over the stream and continue to the left, following the path signposted 'Cliff Path to Bonne Nuit 1982'.

Keep with the path, re-crossing the stream, down to the small building on your right-hand side – 'Wolf's Lair'.

There is a bench on the left-hand side close to Wolf's Lair. Read the memorial plaque of obviously two Jersey characters, plus the more recently added Sophie.

Égypte
Walk Directions

Wolf's Lair is an old Napoleonic guardhouse. Currently it is rented by The Canoe Club, whose kayaks are often seen rock-hopping and exploring the many bays, inlets and caves along the north coast.

Also on your right-hand side, read the Memorial to the ill-fated British and French commandos on Christmas Day in 1943. Captain Ayton was just 22 years old when he was fatally wounded. A memorial service is conducted every year at this site to remember him.

On your left-hand side notice the newer bench in appreciation of Members of The Special Boat Service.

Follow round to your left with the now narrow path as it climbs upwards and continue for some 550 metres.

After the 550 metres, as the path rises a little more steeply, you reach a small outcrop of rock on your right-hand side. Here the original path has been closed - it was dangerous - but before you follow the new path to the left, relax on the bench.

Whilst sitting on the bench, starting with the right-hand side, absorb the wonderful panorama of France (Cherbourg Peninsular) and the north coast of Jersey. Then turning left, absorb the incredible vista of the more immediate - rather bleak - Jersey coastline - with Sark in the background.

Resume along the new path, crossing over a small trickle of water, aided by four stepping stones.

After rejoining the old coastal path climb nine steps and continue.

Stay with the path until the next headland and it starts to turn inland. Then, turning with the path, climb 14 steps, a further 25 and than another 6.

Bear left, again with the path, and continue to climb.

After 35 metres take the path to the right, initially by climbing 15 steps, then another 6, then another 2 and so on, to the 'top'.

Looking out to sea to your right you are now getting a real feeling of height!

Start to descend with an initial 7 steps.

Make sure that you admire the lovely view of Bonne Nuit Bay.

After 35 metres, as shown by the ground-level signpost, take the 'Upper Path' and climb up the new path.

Égypte
Walk Directions

Carry on until you reach a green-topped marker post to your left-hand side. (This is some 800 metres (½ mile) ahead, some 15 metres before a large flat piece of rock makes the path base in front of you with the airport revolving radar beacon in the background.)

Turn left up this new path, initially climbing eight steps to reach the top.

At the field carry straight on, keeping to the right-hand edge of the field on a rather understated or often indistinct pathway for 70 metres.

After 70 metres, at the green-topped marker post (**care**- this post often 'disappears'!) turn right. (If the post is missing look for the narrow worn pathway through the hedge and follow.) Go straight across the narrow field.

On the opposite side of the narrow field continue up the hill on a narrow path through the scrub for some 50 metres.

After climbing approximately 50 metres (say around 90 paces) take a rather undefined grassy path to the left that heads to a tall evergreen tree ahead and with a house to the right-hand side.

Follow the path all the way to the tree(s).

Ensure you take the time to look at the view - a real panorama, from Guernsey and Sark to your left as you look seaward, then following the distant long line of the Cherbourg Peninsular, to the Island's lovely landscape in front of you and to your right.

In front of the trees bear left and then, almost immediately turn right, and follow a rather secondary indistinct path straight on across what appears to be the bottom of a garden, ensuring the 'garden' trees and shrubs remain just to your right. (Do **not** take the perhaps more obvious path to the left into the field which has the derelict farm equipment.)

Once across, turn right, around the last tree and follow up the grassy edge of the National Trust for Jersey scrubland, but <u>definitely</u> keeping the house garden trees and shrubs to your right-hand side.

The National Trust for Jersey own approx. 14 vergees of heath-land located in this highest part of the Island (452 feet). The land was donated to the Trust in 1988 by Rediffusion Channel Islands Ltd.

The adjoining land houses two BBC masts - one also fitted with antennas for mobile phones - and a Transmitting Station.

Égypte
Walk Directions

Further up on your left-hand side is a large dense clump of taller gorse bushes and scrub. Continue to climb past the gorse clump and continue upwards along the rather indistinct grassy path to reach the information board of La Hougue des Platons - a late Neolithic/Chalcolithic cist-in-circle - owned by the Société Jersiaise, but set in land owned by the National Trust for Jersey.

The cist was built some 5000 years ago (2820 - 2250 BC).

It consists of a low circular mound which originally covered a small square stone cist (box) and surrounded by a circle of upright stones and dry-stone walling.

The cist was removed from the centre in 1914, during excavations and investigations and was re-erected in the grounds of La Hougue Bie Museum.

Two pottery vessels were found in the cist, one contained the cremated remains, apparently of an adult and a child. The cist and vessels can be seen at Hougue Bie.

Exit the site, straight down the grassy path through the gorse to your left as you face the information board.

Keep with the path as it drops down, turns to the right (below a property boundary), and then passes a green-topped marker post. (**Care** - again, this post too goes missing!)

Join and follow the track/driveway straight ahead to the road.

At the road turn left and follow.

After 200 metres turn right with the tarmac road and follow down to the start.

The Alternative Boulay Bay Hill Climb

Parish	Trinity
Special Features	Beautiful open valley countryside vistas. Incredible views of the north coast and France. Lovely woodland and coastal paths. One piece of real historical interest.
Start	Public car park – Le Parc de la Petite Falaise, La Rue de la Petite Falaise (at the top of Bouley Bay).
	Turn into La Rue de la Petite Falaise (C96) from either, La Rue du Bouley, or from A8, La Rue des Croix. Signposted 'Bouley Bay' at the five-road junction approaching Trinity Parish Hall.
	The turning into the car park is on the seaward (north) side of the road, marked only at the entrance.
	The car park is 200 and 400 metres respectively along La Rue de la Petite Falaise.
Map Reference	**Jersey Telephone Directory** Map 4 G3
	Official Leisure Map 66.4/54.2
	Jersey Street Guide Map 15 A4
Terrain	Country roads and byways, coastal path with one very steep long climb with steps, country paths with one climb and one very steep difficult descent (poor and slippery terrain in one part, sometimes muddy in places).
Level of Difficulty	⬤ ⬤ ⬤ **VERY HARD**
Time (approx)	2 hours 15 minutes
Distance (approx)	6½ kilometres (4 miles)
Amenities	**Start and Finish** None **En Route (in adjacent Bouley Bay)** Public toilets Public telephone Hotel, bar and restaurant Beach café

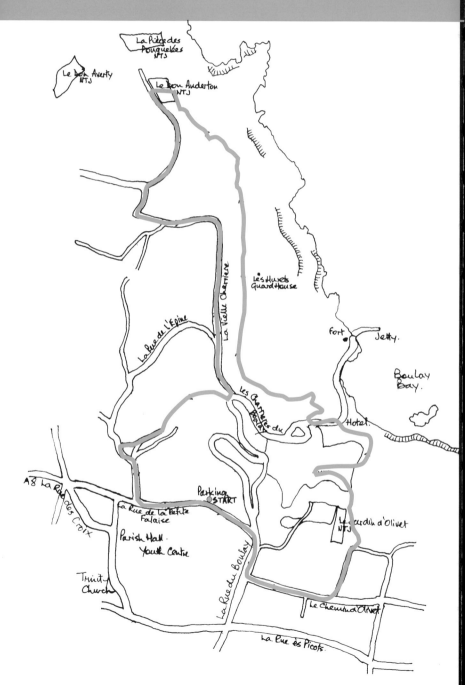

Exit out of the front of the car park. Turn left onto the road. Keep to the **left-hand side** of this difficult road and follow.

At the junction, as the main road turns left, **carefully** turn right into La Route du Boulay.

After approx 150 metres turn left (arrowed Cycle Route 1, Chemin D'Olivet) and follow this road.

After approx 200 metres, take the first turning left and follow this road down to a car park.

Proceed to the back left-hand side of the car park and take the very narrow path to the left into the woods.

This woodland area above Bouley Bay known as Le Jardin d'Olivet (Le Don Micheli) was donated to the National Trust for Jersey in 1999 by Mme. C Micheli (née Chappuis). This area formed part of the adjoining Rockmount de Moustiers gardens. Within the then extensive gardens were certain follies. The gardens have sadly long since gone, replaced over time by woods.

Below this area Jersey Trees for Life have co-ordinated and undertaken not insignificant remedial works to the path that you will use which will bring you down to the cliff path at Rozel. That area will be managed as amenity woodland with special concern for wildlife. They plan to research the wood's history, being particularly interested in the numerous species of pine and the fine retaining walls which border the path. They see it as a 'fairy tale' like woodland.

In 1549 this area was the scene of a little remembered but bloody battle - The Battle of Jardin d'Olivet. At this time of the Reformation, Henry II King of France attacked the Channel Islands. With Sark captured and having been repulsed in Guernsey the invaders sailed to Jersey, landed in Bouley Bay and met the Jersey Militia at Jardin d'Olivet. Jersey's Lieutenant-Bailiff was among those killed in the ensuing battle but the French were routed and retired to St. Malo with their dead and wounded (some accounts report their dead as many as 1000). Certainly following news of the defeat Henry II forbad his courtiers ever to mention Jersey again in his presence.

Bearing right, proceed down through the trees by a difficult (very steep and slippery) indistinct path. Ensure you go <u>straight down</u> for 70 metres, keeping parallel with the right-hand side of the wood. **(It is very steep and slippery - take special care as you walk down, particularly if it is muddy and/or with fallen leaves.)**

On the left-hand side you will pass one of the follies mentioned above (the one within the gifted land), in the shape and outline of a miniature castle. The National Trust for Jersey has already undertaken structural repairs to consolidate the walls and when funds permit would like to complete the project by making the building wind and water tight with the addition of roof, door and windows.

The Alternative Boulay Bay Hill Climb - *Walk Directions*

After 70 metres you will reach a bridle path, which crosses your path, identified by two yellow-topped marker posts, one to the right and one to the left. (Also there is a large fallen oak tree by the path to your right.)

Turn left onto the bridle path initially passing the left-hand yellow-topped marker post to your left-hand side. Follow this path keeping the undergrowth covered low dry-stone granite wall to your left-hand side.

> *Be warned this whole area is thought to be haunted! An enormous black dog, big as a man, with bright yellow eyes the size of saucers was believed to have prowled up and down these cliffs in the dead of night.*

> *Most likely this is a tale invented by smugglers as a deterrent!*

> *Have you seen and heard the replica in the Jersey Maritime Museum at the St. Helier waterfront?*

> *Smuggling was a very lucrative business in the late 17th - 19th centuries. Smuggling wines, spirits and tobacco to England was nearly as profitable as into France. The English customs awoke to the fact that the Island was importing much more tobacco than it could possibly smoke. Enterprising merchants were buying it in Southampton, getting a rebate on the duty, bringing it into the Island and then landing it on moonless nights in remote Devon coves. When a customs officer arrived in 1681 he complained that the whole Island was in conspiracy against him as whenever he tried to do his duty, he was affronted and beaten and could get no help from the jurats and constables!*

> *The Jersey smugglers defied all efforts to outwit them.*

When you reach a path junction hairpin right (very much back on yourself) go through the gap in the path gateway, (arrowed to Bouley Bay and Rozel Bay on the small sign to your right-hand side aligned to the (new) path gateway barriers) and proceed down.

At the next hairpin bend, turn left down four steps and continue left.

At the next sharp turn bear right, initially down six steps and continue downhill with the path.

Shortly after having gone down a further six steps, turn off sharp left and proceed down another six steps. You are now on the coastal path to Bouley Bay as a small sign on the corner confirms.

At the end of the path descend a number of flights of steps, through a gateway and then the concrete steps, to go through the tarmac area to reach the road.

Note the new self-catering chalets to your right.

At the road turn left and proceed up the hill.

After some 40 metres turn right onto the path signposted 'Footpath' and with a stone marker 'Cliff Path to Bonne Nuit, 4 miles, 1982'.

Go through the gap in the entrance barrier and climb up this long steep path.

Take in the views of the beach and bay to the right.

Bouley Bay has a good anchorage of at least six fathoms close to shore –obviously therefore it was another bay to be guarded. The first defences appeared in 1596.

The Fort, on the far right-hand side of the bay (not on the extreme promontory but the next lower one), is L'Étaquerel. The fort, magazine and quartermaster's stores, guardroom and other buildings were built around 1835.

These days very basic holiday lets are available at the fort from Jersey Heritage for upto 60 guests during daylight hours and 30 overnight in sleeping bags.

After you have climbed the many steps, and the path has turned inland, continue with the path as it now becomes less of a climb, more of a track and runs above the steeply sloped early potato côtils to the left-hand side.

Côtil is a Jèrriais (Jersey Norman French) word meaning a small hillside slope which is wooded or cultivated for crops such as the Jersey Royal potato.

Sloping in a sheltered sunny situation these potato growing côtils to the left yield Jersey Royals early - a great market advantage.

Jèrriais was the language used in the Island from medieval times until the mid-20th century and now spoken by very few.

Near the end of the côtils take care to notice the sunken stone path signpost on the right-hand side directing you to turn right following the 'Cliff Path'. Follow this path climbing up to the top with the help of 49 wooden steps.

Continue to follow the path across the top with the valley to your left-hand side.

Once on the headland still continue to follow the path.

Ensure you stop to absorb the views.

To your right the far promontory is White Rock (the start of another lovely walk – Walk 29 Rozel Bay - Coast and Hinterland).

In the far distance is the coast of France. The reef of rocks and islets in the foreground halfway to France is called Les Ecréhous and is part of the parish of St. Martin.

There are three main islets, Maître Île, Marmotière and Blanc Île. They were inhabited in prehistoric times but the first mention in historic times is 1203 when permission was granted for the building of a small chapel, the remains of which still exist today.

In 1848 Philip Pinel a Jersey fisherman built himself a little cottage on Blanc Île and lived there for almost 50 years. He was nicknamed 'King of the Ecréhous' and when Queen Victoria visited Jersey in 1859 they exchanged gifts - he gave a basket woven out of dried vraic (seaweed) filled with different kinds of fish, she a blue coat.

Small houses exist on the islets that have predominately remained in the possession of and been visited by Jersey families over many generations.

In 1953 an age-old unresolved dispute as to the ownership of the reef finally was taken by France and Great Britain to the International Court at The Hague. The Court ruled that sovereignty belonged to Great Britain.

In 2005 the Ecréhous, together with the Paternosters and the Minquiers, was named alongside the Island's east coast as a United Nations Ramsar - protected site.

The objective now is to follow the coastal path to reach the National Trust for Jersey land, Le Don Anderton on your left-hand side. The National Trust sign is difficult to see and the little path to take you up onto the land comes slightly ahead of seeing the sign.

So! Continue along the coastal path looking out on your left-hand side for the early warning of two green painted 'chalets/sheds' on the land of a nearby private house.

Leaving the chalets/sheds behind follow down with the path, then to climb again. As you climb you will be helped initially by 27 railway sleeper steps and, virtually at the top, by a further 3.

Still with the path, descend the steps and traverse across with a small headland below you to the right.

The path then starts to descend. Then, a few metres later you will need to climb up onto the Trust land (alongside the left-hand side of the coastal path) by an unmarked very short pathway (just a few steps) on the left-hand side that runs off at 45°. Then aim to reach the Trust sign which is behind the first big tree to your right.

This area of coastal land Le Don Anderton was purchased in 1966 by the National Trust for Jersey with funds donated by Brigadier W. D. Anderton, a former President of the Trust. A bungalow which stood on the site burned down in 1969.

Le Don translates from the French as 'the gift' and, as a mark of gratitude, precedes the name, usually the family name, of the donor.

Continue by exiting the land along a short row of mature pine trees adjacent to the Trust sign, with the remnants of a tarmac drive to the previous bungalow under foot. At the end of which turn left and follow the track up the incline.

Follow the track to the road and then turn left.

Proceed all the way down the long hill to the bottom.

At the 'T'-junction (Les Charrières du Boulay) turn right and then immediately turn right again through the entrance and into The National Trust for Jersey land, Le Grand Côtil du Bouley.

> *This large wooded area behind Bouley Bay Hill, Le Grand Cotil du Bouley, Le Don Ferey, was donated to the Trust in 1965 by Mr Francis Philip Ferey.*

Proceed up this fern-fringed path.

> *As the stream appears on your right-hand side, stop and listen to the water as it breaks the complete stillness.*

Exit the land.

> *Immediately stop! With a little imagination you have entered a time capsule of early Jersey rural life. The place is called Le Puchot – which means a rough fountain or water source in the form of a pool.*

> *On the left is the wellhead (dated 1788) and nearby the lavoir - a communal place for washing clothes and linen, constructed in 1834. Note the stone sides of the lavoir, the central trough and the stone 'ford' allowing the water to continue to run across the path – no doubt allowing animals to drink as well.*

> *There are two other paths leading to this communal spot giving access ('droit au douet' - the right to use) to the immediate surrounding community. People, animals, water, washing - what a gathering spot, what a focal point - the social hub. Imagine!*

Carry on up to the top.

> *Near the top, on the left-hand side, note a second well.*

At the road turn left, follow the road round and proceed to the end.

> *On the left-hand side, as you approach the top, there is a small single storey cottage (Maison de Haut on the gate).*

> *There is a 1741 marriage stone above the door.*

> *Granite carved marriage stones appeared in the 18th century, attaining maximum popularity between 1720 and 1880. They were usually rectangular lintels above the front door. They consisted of the initials of the husband and wife (the husband's on the left and the wife's on the right, using her maiden name), with one, two or entwined hearts, usually all within the date. The date recorded would be of significance to the couple, often the date of marriage or construction of the property.*

Additionally note the protruding flat stones (dripstones), on the central chimney. In folklore such stones were referred to as 'witches' seats' (they had to sit somewhere!). Originally the property would have had a thatched roof. At the level of the original thatch, these stones were used to deflect the rainwater at the vulnerable point where the thatch joined the chimney stack.

At the 'T'-junction turn left (following Cycle Route 1) and, keeping to the left-hand side, follow the road for approx 200 metres.

Turn left into the car park and the start.

Parish	Trinity and St. Martin
Special Features	Extensive views of France. Open and expansive countryside. Beautiful and stunning north coast vistas including Les Ecréhous and other Channel Islands.
Start	Headland public car park, White Rock (La Tour de Rozel). Approach Rozel from Durrell (Jersey Zoo). Turn left opposite Durrell into Rue du Pot du Rocher then carry on into Route des Côtes du Nord (C93). After 1½ kilometres (1 mile) take the turning left, (Rue de Câtel) which is more of a filter, (an impractical turn from the other direction) signposted 'Footpath and Parking'. Immediately before the first property on your left and, signposted 'Footpath', turn left into the track (yes, it is a public track). Keep left and follow the track. Continue with the track as it turns 90º to the right and later 90º to the left and proceed into the car park.
Map Reference	**Jersey Telephone Directory** Map 4 J3 **Official Leisure Map** 68.9/54.7 **Jersey Street Guide** Map 16 D2
Terrain	Undulating country and coastal paths, country roads and byways, with one steep and very long climb.
Level of Difficulty	⬤ ⬤ ◯ **SOME DIFFICULTY**
Time (approx)	2 hours
Distance (approx)	6½ kilometres (4 miles)
Amenities	**Start and Finish** 　　None **En Route (Rozel environs)** 　　Public toilets 　　Public telephone 　　Hotel 　　Bar-restaurant 　　Restaurant, tea-room and food shack

Rozel Bay - Coast and Hinterland
Map Guide

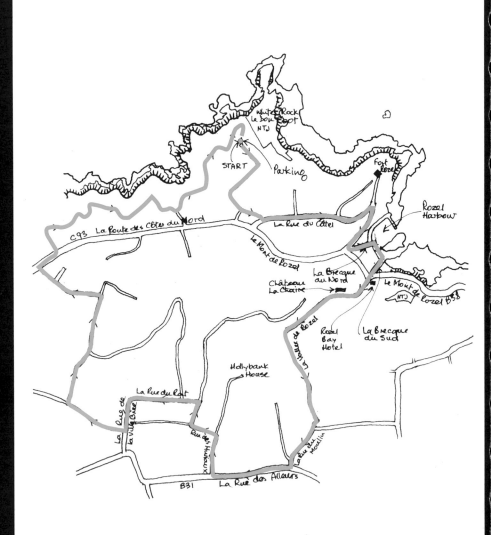

Leave the car park by the route that you came in and start following the track back to the road. Stop as you come up to the second 90° bend.

> *Across the field in front of you there is a backdrop of an earth bank some 200 metres long, 6 metres high and 8 metres thick at the base, except a narrow gap in the middle with a pathway. This is all that is left of a great rampart of an Iron Age Settlement (or promontory fort) 'Le Câtel de Rozel' that stretched over this whole cliff top area (1600 metres long and up to 800 metres wide), some 2000 years ago.*

> *The Earthworks stretched in a north-west/south-east direction from this cliff top on the east side of Bouley Bay towards the steep-sided valley running down to Rozel Harbour. Thus the Settlement/Fort was protected by three things - the sea, a steep-sided valley and the Earthworks.*

> *The site has never been excavated but several large hoards of Gaulish (circa 50/100 BC) and a few Roman Republic coins have been found from within the defended area. Those finds with those dates support the long held view that Le Câtel may have been a camp of refuge for Gauls from the continent - hopefully all will be revealed if an excavation takes place in the future.*

Proceed down the track to reach the road.

At the road turn left and follow it down to the bottom as it twists and turns.

> *Take the opportunity to enjoy the views of the French coast in the distance and the picturesque Rozel Bay and harbour below to your right.*

> *The harbour was built in 1829 to shelter the overflow of oyster boats that could not anchor in the overcrowded Gorey harbour at a time when the oyster industry was in its heyday. Other subsidiary harbours were Boulay Bay and La Rocque.*

> *Oyster beds have been in the bays of St. Catherine and Grouville since time immemorial. But in 1797 important oyster beds were found between Jersey and France (near Chaussey) and, to the chagrin of the French, the export of oysters really began. A great number of fishermen came over from England during the fishing season.*

> *The trade grew and grew so much so that, in the early 19th century, up to 300 boats and over 3,000 people were involved. 1,000 were on land, a large proportion being the sorters, women and girls, for the 12,000 oysters per boat per day that were being ruthlessly and recklessly dredged. At Gorey, the local old and decaying pier was rebuilt in 1817, then followed buildings like, the now known as, Moorings, Seascale and Dolphin, built to provide essential services to the fleets - hotels, inns, lodging houses, chandlers, grocers and bakeries. Rows of workers cottages were also built and in 1832 Gouray Church, to provide spiritual needs and English services.*

> *The bubble eventually burst – disputes with France, the beds over-trawled and conservation ignored, the oyster beds were exhausted and by 1864 the industry had died.*

Rozel Bay – Coast and Hinterland
Walk Directions

At the bottom of the hill turn sharp left into La Brecque du Nord and proceed down towards the beach.

Look out for the ducks and geese.

At the beach proceed partway down the slipway and turn right, walking across the pebbles and keeping to the top part of the beach.

(Should the tide conditions be wrong for the beach crossing, turn back to the main road. At the main road turn left and very carefully follow until the turning right into the road of the gastro-pub and hotel shown below.)

On your right-hand side a granite wall runs along the beach and turns to form the corner of the road. Now part of a new development of apartments, the wall was formerly part of the Rozel Barracks built in about 1810, as part of the Island fortifications (note the gun slits now blocked up). The barracks accommodated 68 men. It was last garrisoned in the late 19th century.

British troops were garrisoned in the Island from the 18th century until 1924.

After 100 metres, at the concrete culvert, turn right and proceed up the road.

At the top of the road, **very carefully**, cross over the main road and head up past The Rozel Bar Restaurant and Chateau La Chaire Hotel (on the left and right respectively).

Just around the corner of the first 90° turning to the left, notice the large upright granite stone against the wall of the property. Such stones, usually more rounded and much smaller, are called 'heurteurs'. Positioned around exterior walls their purpose was to prevent carriage wheels, often of heavy carts, from hitting the wall. These days one often sees granite stones similarly placed to stop damage by cars and lorries.

Also on the same property (Cintra) notice the 1797 marriage stone above the door.

Granite carved marriage stones appeared in the 18th century, attaining maximum popularity between 1720 and 1880. They were usually rectangular lintels above the front door. They consisted of the initials of the husband and wife (the husband's on the left and the wife's on the right, using her maiden name), with one, two or entwined hearts, usually all within the date. The date recorded would be of significance to the couple, often the date of marriage or construction of the property.

After some twenty metres, on the right-hand side, notice a small fountain set into the garden wall.

Make the long and steep climb up, where necessary keeping right with the road, and eventually following Cycle Route 1 to the top (Rue du Moulin).

Near the top note Rozel Windmill on your right-hand side.

Sites of 12 windmills (and 38 watermills) are known, some of them amongst the earliest occupied sites, dating from the 11th century. All of them would have been rebuilt many times.

A Rozel Mill existed in 1219 and a map of 1563 shows Rozel to be one of only three windmills at that time. Such windmills catered for areas remote from streams and for the summer when the flow of water might be inadequate to turn the water wheels. Their main function was grinding corn.

Only four windmills survive today – the others being in St. Ouen, Grouville and St. Peter.

During World War II the German Occupying Forces built an Observation Post (M6) on the top.

When you reach the 'T'-junction at the top turn right and follow the road for approx. 400 metres.

Take the first turning right into Rue des Huriaux.

Where the road takes a 90° turn to the left - stop. On your right-hand side read the sign 'caution - racehorses in training'.

Detour off the road by walking a few metres straight ahead to the gates of Hollybank House.

Hollybank House is a substantial property, difficult to see, but dates from around 1680 and first enlarged around 1715. The lovely grounds fall to a small valley that leads down to Rozel; and yes, on the left-hand side it is a race track for horse training and it is supported by racing stables.

Return to the road and follow right, later keeping left as necessary, still with the road.

Again keeping with the road, continue along the long straight section for some 400 metres.

Then again turn left 90° with the road and proceed uphill.

On the right-hand side, just after turning the corner, on the ground in front of the retaining wall and near the entrance gate, is a classic example of a heurteur (mentioned earlier).

Keep on past La Chaumiere on your right-hand side.

Notice the thatched roof on La Chaumiere, one of the few thatched roofs in the Island.

On early properties the normal roofing material was thatch, which was, of course, highly inflammable so by-laws were introduced in 1715 to curtail its use. For example in the towns of St. Helier and St. Aubin all houses had to be roofed in slate or tile within ten years.

Rozel Bay - Coast and Hinterland
Walk Directions

This thatch is relatively recent with the top somewhat lower than the original would have been. The cement filling at the bottom and the raised protruding stones – dripstones – on the end chimney are likely clues.

Dripstones are often referred to as witches' seats or stones – in local superstition they were believed to be resting places for witches – they had to sit somewhere! In fact, the stones were so placed as to prevent rainwater seeping in at the vulnerable point where the thatch adjoined the chimney.

At the end of their garden wall, and opposite the far end of La Ville Bree on the left-hand side, turn right into the track that follows the side wall of another property.

Keep on this track until the first opportunity to turn right. At that point turn right following a line of very mature trees.

Follow this track down the hill.

As you approach the farm keep left with the track that now has a concrete base. Then bear right, still with the track, and pass in front of the agricultural buildings. Briefly bear right again remaining with the concrete track. Leave the farmhouse very much to your right and then turn left again to exit the complex.

Follow the lane downhill and continue until you reach the main road.

At the main road turn right and cross over to the other side of the road.

After some 100 metres, on the left-hand side, you will see a track heading towards the sea, with an open field to its right and a high hedgerow to its left. Follow this track down through the field.

After the field and a small parking area to the right, the track bears left, (sign-posted on the ground to your right 'L'Etacquerel Fort'). Keep with the track, that immediately becomes a path, as it now turns right and heads towards the sea.

Follow the path until it joins the coastal path where you turn right (in line with the direction shown on the signpost).

In due course on the seaward side you will see the National Trust for Jersey sign 'La Tourelle'. This area of coastal land was donated to the Trust by The Directors of P.B. Properties Limited, in 2003.

Continue along the coastal path ignoring the turning right marked 'Main Road 84 yards'. Instead follow the granite marker on the opposite (left-hand) side of the path at that point, showing 'White Rock - ½ Mile'.

As you continue to follow the path along the coastline do not be tempted to follow any path or track to the right.

Also do not forget to stop and take time to admire the stunning views seaward to include looking back to Sark, Herm and Guernsey.

At the signpost to Rozel on the left-hand side, and adjacent to the starting car park, keep left onto the headland. Wander as much or as little as you want but certainly repose on the benches.

Imperative, though, is that you go far enough onto the headland to ensure the most stupendous views of the north coast and France are seen.

The islets, reefs and rocks in the sea halfway to France are called Les Ecréhous and are administered by the parish of St. Martin.

There are three main islets Maître Île, Marmotière and Blanc Île. They were inhabited in prehistoric times, however, the first mention in historic times is 1203 when permission was granted for the building of a chapel, the remains of which still exist today.

In 1848 Philip Pinel, a Jersey fisherman, built himself a little cottage on Blanche Île. He lived there for almost 50 years and became known as the 'King of the Ecréhous' and when Queen Victoria visited Jersey in 1859 they exchanged gifts - he gave a basket woven out of dried vraic (seaweed) filled with different kinds of fish, she a blue coat.

Small houses exist on the islets that have predominately remained in the possession of and been visited by Jersey families over many generations.

In 1953 an age-old unresolved dispute as to the ownership of the reef was taken to the International Court at The Hague by France and Great Britain. The Court ruled that sovereignty belonged to Great Britain.

In 2005 the Ecréhous was named as a United Nations Ramsar - protected site.

Return to the car park and the starting point.

Byways of St. Martin

Parish	St. Martin
Special Features	Easy straight-forward countryside walking. Interesting and entertaining history.
Start	Public car park opposite St. Martin's School and St. Martins's Parish Hall. Situated central village on the main road (B30 Rue de la Croix au Maître) adjacent to the road traffic calming measures. Entrance opposite the school playground. Park towards the far end of the car park. Although a free car park, you are asked to display the time of your arrival.
Map Reference	**Jersey Telephone Directory** Map 4 J4 **Official Leisure Map** 68.8/52.3 **Jersey Street Guide** Map 25 D2
Terrain	Undulating tarmac byways, with one short stretch of grassy country footpath (sometimes muddy in places).
Level of Difficulty	● ○ ○ **EASY**
Time (approx)	2 hours 15 minutes
Distance (approx)	7 kilometres (4¼ miles)

Amenities	**Village amenities near the start**
	    Public telephone
	    Tea room
	    Pub/restaurant
	    Shop

Byways of St. Martin
Map Guide

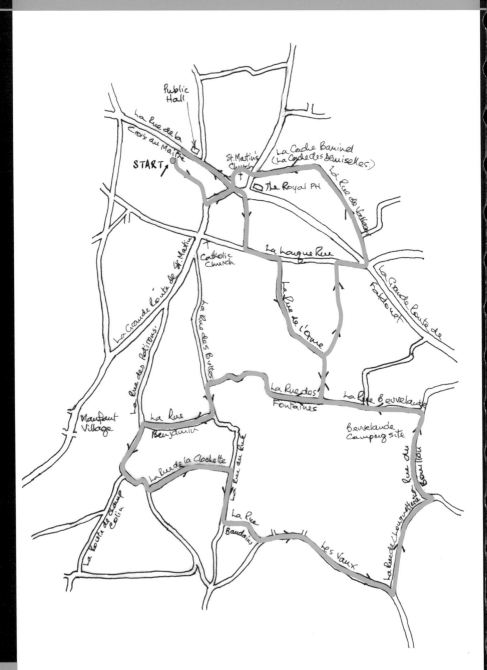

Byways of St. Martin
Walk Directions

With your back to the main road, school and parish hall, leave the car park by the exit in the middle, into the Parish Village Green area.

Once through the gap, turn left and follow the hoggin path. Proceed through a 90° bend to the right and on past the boules area (to your right).

Exit the Green by keeping straight on.

As you leave the path keep straight on, keeping the St. John's Ambulance building to your left, to reach a 'T'-junction.

At the 'T'-junction turn left to reach the main road.

At the main road, **very carefully**, cross over onto the pavement on the other side of the road. Turn left and follow the pavement down to the road junction in front of the church.

At the road junction, keeping on the pavement, turn right and follow the few metres to the first turning right (opposite The Royal public house).

Take that first turning right, Rue de Payn, and follow this road past the 'No-entry' sign to the end.

At the 'T'-junction at the end of the road turn left and follow.

In front of the 'No-entry' signs turn right into Rue de l'Orme and follow to the end, passing Surville Farm to your left.

At the end of the road turn left into Rue de Beuvelande passing Beuvelande Camp Site to your right.

There are three camp sites in Jersey. Beuvelande is the only one to have the AA 5 Pennants. It opened in 1965 and was in the same family ownership for 45 years. Now in new family hands, it has all the usual facilities including a shop. Also there is a café, bistro, bar and takeaway open in the summer and at weekends in the 'shoulder' months.

Camping in Jersey is subject to stringent rules and regulations. Visitor caravans/motor homes require Campsite Permits and States of Jersey Planning and Environment Letters of Authority. They are allowed to stay for up to one month, (each night to be spent on a registered campsite) and must meet length and width restrictions. Caravans are allowed only one journey to and from the campsite to the port. Special dispensation allows motor homes to circulate the Island during the day but they must return to the designated site each night.

Byways of St. Martin
Walk Directions

At the 'T'-junction at the end of the road turn right into Rue du Bouillon and follow.

Take the first turning right into Rue de la Chouquetterie and follow.

The property that makes the right-hand corner as you turn is called La Chouquetterie. The house takes its name, as often is the case, from the family that lived there. The Chouquets were French refugees who were first recorded on the Island in 1701.

As you turn the corner what a peaceful meadow setting for this lovely house.

Again take the first turning right leaving Les Vaux Farm to your left and proceed up the incline.

Take the first turning right (after 600 metres) into Rue de Baudains and proceed up the incline.

Reaching the 'T'-junction at the top of the road, turn right and follow past Haut de la Rue Farm on the left-hand side.

After the farm take the first turning left and follow up the slight incline to the end of the road.

At the 'T'-junction turn right, follow round the 'S' bend and keep with the road.

Ignore Rue du Champ Colin to your left, after which take the next turning right. (Check you are on the right road by passing the Rue Potirons electrical sub-station after 20 metres to your left-hand side.)

After 125 metres turn right into Rue du Benjamin and follow to the end.

At the 'T'-junction turn left and follow.

After 110 metres turn right into Rue des Fontaines and follow.

After passing the yard entrance to Les Fontaines Farm on the left-hand side, follow round the next bend to reach the front of the property and the apple-crusher in the garden behind the wrought-iron gates.

In 1795 over 20% of the Island's arable land was under orchard. In the 1830s cider was still the main source of the farmer's wealth and every farm had cider-making equipment. In 1839, 270,000 gallons were exported to England, but much was drunk locally - it was the main drink. The cider making process took place inside the farm buildings. The apples were poured into the crusher and a horse would circle round pulling the large round granite stone on view, to crush the apples. The resultant mulch then would be shovelled into the cider press and squeezed to make the final liquid for the barrels. Needless to say quality was varied!

Continue up the road as it bends and twists, to reach the property Beauchamp on the left-hand side. Above the name over the front door note the marriage stone EGD.FNC.1753.

> *Granite carved marriage stones appeared in the 18th century, attaining maximum popularity between 1720 and 1880. Usually they were - as this one - with the initials of the husband on the left and the wife's on the right, with a heart (or entwined hearts), all within the date. The date would be of significance to the couple, often the date of marriage or construction of the property.*

Continue with the road and where it leads into Rue de Beuvelande (see road signs on your right-hand side), turn left (Rue de L'Orme) and proceed to Surville Farm on your right-hand side.

At the big oak tree standing proud on its own, take the footpath to the right as shown by the sign 'Public Footpath to St Martin' initially heading for the farmyard and then bearing left, literally across the fields.

At the end of the track turn right onto the tarmac lane and follow to the main road.

At the main road - **CARE!** - Cross over into the less important left-hand road of the two roads on the other side (Rue des Vallées, marked 'Start of Green Lane') and follow.

In due course, just as you start to see the church at the end of the road, stop at the entrance to Bandinel Farm, on the right-hand side.

> *The farm is associated by name to the Bandinel family and is a very important early house, dated above the arch as 1619. The Bandinels were a family of Italian origin who came to the island early in the 17th century. It was David Bandinel who bought the house and he became Jersey's first Anglican Dean. Because of anti-Royalist support he was imprisoned in Mont Orgueil Castle along with his son, the Rector of St Mary, where they both died, he in 1645, of injuries sustained whilst trying to escape. There is a legend of a secret tunnel leading from the house to the Castle, which is of course impossible.*

> *The road you are in now is called La Chasse des Demoiselles Bandinel and leads from the church to the farm. One theory is that this shows that the Misses Bandinel (Douce who died in 1829 and Elizabeth who died in 1844) descendants of the Dean, did actually live there. An alternative theory is that the road was a favourite promenade for the girls of the village after attending Church, where they would stroll and hope to meet their beaux.*

> *It is rather pleasing to associate the second theory with the farm after the stormy scenes it must have witnessed during the Dean's ownership and as you walk down the road towards the church it is easy to picture pretty parasols promenading, particularly on a sunny Sunday!*

At the main road - **again carefully** - cross over into the churchyard.

There has been a church on this site for over 1000 years - the first record being in 1042 with a Charter in which William, Duke of Normandy (later 'William the Conqueror') granted to Cerisy Abbey in France, this church, its lands and a third of its corn-tithe.

Slowly over the next five centuries the original small church, on the site of the present chancel, grew into the building we have today - the oldest building in the Parish.

The original spire (first heard of in 1582) did not have a long life. In 1616 one Sunday morning, as people - naïve, superstitious - were going to church, the spire was hit by lightning, breaking off in the middle, causing widespread panic, a dread of evil doings and a foreboding of some kind of retribution - in short, an omen of impending disaster. It was rebuilt two years later, but imagine the minds and fear of the people when it happened again, being destroyed by lightning in 1837. (The subsequent rebuild has the appropriate lightening conductor!)

In 1794 permission was given to block up two of the Church's four doors. With only two almoners, monies/dues at the end of the service could only be collected at two doors - the congregation had become very adept at slipping out through the other two!

Renovations cost money, but with the 1877 works, the problem of finance was partly solved - by the churchwardens printing bank notes. (The printing plates are still in the safe at the Parish Hall.)

Cross over the churchyard keeping the church to your left-hand side.

Emerge from the churchyard on the far-side, having walked under the light, and continue along the pink granite church footpath to reach the main road.

At the main road turn right and stay on the pavement on this side of the road, passing the Parish Hall, until time to cross over to the middle entrance of the car park and the start.

Schedules of Walks

Walks by Time

UP TO ONE HOUR

Time (approx)	Degree of Difficulty	Walk	Walk Name	Parish
45 mins	EASY	3	Queen's Valley Reservoir	Grouville
45 mins	SOME DIFFICULTY	9	Fern Valley	St. Helier
45 mins	EASY	14	Portelet Nature Reserve and Common	St. Brelade

ONE TO TWO HOURS

Time (approx)	Degree of Difficulty	Walk	Walk Name	Parish
1 hour	SOME DIFFICULTY	2	Rozel Woods – Henry's Walk	St. Martin
1 hour 10 mins	SOME DIFFICULTY	16	Beauport and Les Creux	St. Brelade
1 hour 10 mins	SOME DIFFICULTY	18	Val de La Mare Reservoir	St. Peter
1 hour 15 mins	SOME DIFFICULTY	21	Tracks and Paths over St. Ouen's Bay	St. Ouen
1 hour 15 mins	EASY	22	Remote St. Ouen's	St. Ouen
1 hour 25 mins	EASY	15	L'Ouaisné and St. Brelade	St. Brelade
1 hour 30 mins	EASY	12	West St. Lawrence	St. Lawrence
1 hour 30 mins	SOME DIFFICULTY	19	Byways and Tracks - St. Ouen	St. Ouen
1 hour 30 mins	EASY	23	Les Landes	St. Ouen
1 hour 30 mins	VERY HARD	26	Byways and Paths – St. John's	St. John
1 hour 40 mins	SOME DIFFICULTY	4	The Ultimate Inner Grouville	Grouville
1 hour 45 mins	SOME DIFFICULTY	5	The Ultimate St Clement's/ Grouville	St. Cl./Gr

Walks by Time

ONE TO TWO HOURS

Time (approx)	Degree of Difficulty	Walk	Walk Name	Parish
1 hour 50 mins	SOME DIFFICULTY	7	Byways, Tracks and Paths - St Saviour and Grouville	St.S./Gr

OVER TWO HOURS

Time (approx)	Degree of Difficulty	Walk	Walk Name	Parish
2 hours	VERY HARD	27	Égypte	Trinity
2 hours	SOME DIFFICULTY	29	Rozel Bay – Coast and Hinterland	Tr./St.M
2 hours 10 mins	SOME DIFFICULTY	1	The Ultimate St. Martin's	St. Martin
2 hours 10 mins	SOME DIFFICULTY	13	St. Aubin to Noirmont and return	St. Brelade
2 hours 15 mins	VERY HARD	28	The Alternative Boulay Bay Hill Climb	Trinity
2 hours 15 mins	EASY	30	Byways of St. Martin	St. Martin
2 hours 20 mins	SOME DIFFICULTY	10	Sights and Sounds of Water	St. Lawrence
2 hours 20 mins	VERY HARD	11	Two Valleys	St. Lawrence
2 hours 30 mins	SOME DIFFICULTY	8	A Quirky Sunday Town Stroll	St. Helier
2 hours 45 mins	SOME DIFFICULTY	6	Byways of St. Saviour and Trinity	St.S./Tr
2 hours 50 mins	SOME DIFFICULTY	17	The Ultimate St. Brelade's	St. Brelade
2 hours 50 mins	SOME DIFFICULTY	20	The Ultimate St. Ouen's	St. Ouen
3 hours	SOME DIFFICULTY	25	The Ultimate St. John's/St. Mary's	St.J./St.M
3 hours 20 mins	VERY HARD	24	The Soul of St Ouen	St. Ouen

Walks by Degree of Difficulty

⬤ ◯ ◯ EASY

Walk		Walk Name	Parish	Time
3	⬤ ◯ ◯	Queen's Valley Reservoir	Grouville	45 mins
12	⬤ ◯ ◯	West St. Lawrence	St. Lawrence	1 hour 30 mins
14	⬤ ◯ ◯	Portelet Nature Reserve and Common	St. Brelade	45 mins
15	⬤ ◯ ◯	L'Ouaisné and St. Brelade	St. Brelade	1 hour 25 mins
22	⬤ ◯ ◯	Remote St. Ouen's	St. Ouen	1 hour 15 mins
23	⬤ ◯ ◯	Les Landes	St. Ouen	1 hour 30 mins
30	⬤ ◯ ◯	Byways of St. Martin	St. Martin	2 hours 15 mins

⬤ ⬤ ◯ SOME DIFFICULTY

Walk		Walk Name	Parish	Time
2	⬤ ◖ ◯	Rozel Woods – Henry's Walk	St. Martin	1 hour
8	⬤ ◖ ◯	A Quirky Sunday Town Stroll	St. Helier	2 hours 30 mins
9	⬤ ◖ ◯	Fern Valley	St. Helier	45 mins
16	⬤ ◖ ◯	Beauport and Les Creux	St. Brelade	1 hour 10 mins
18	⬤ ◖ ◯	Val de la Mare Reservoir	St. Peter	1 hour 10 mins
1	⬤ ⬤ ◯	The Ultimate St. Martin's	St. Martin	2 hours 10 mins
4	⬤ ⬤ ◯	The Ultimate Inner Grouville	Grouville	1 hour 40 mins
5	⬤ ⬤ ◯	The Ultimate St. Clement's/Grouville	St.C./Gr	1 hour 45 mins
6	⬤ ⬤ ◯	Byways of St. Saviour and Trinity	St.S./Tr	2 hours 45 mins
7	⬤ ⬤ ◯	Byways, Tracks and Paths - St. Saviour and Grouville	St.S./Gr	1 hour 50 mins
10	⬤ ⬤ ◯	Sights and Sounds of Water	St. Lawrence	2 hours 20 mins
13	⬤ ⬤ ◯	St. Aubin to Noirmont and return	St. Brelade	2 hours 10 mins
17	⬤ ⬤ ◯	The Ultimate St. Brelade's	St. Brelade	2 hours 50 mins
19	⬤ ⬤ ◯	Byways and Tracks - St. Ouen	St. Ouen	1 hour 30 mins

Walks by Degree of Difficulty

⬤⬤◯ SOME DIFFICULTY

Walk		Walk Name	Parish	Time
20	◯⬤◯	The Ultimate St. Ouen's	St. Ouen	2 hours 50 mins
21	⬤◯◯	Tracks and Paths over St. Ouen's Bay	St. Ouen	1 hour 15 mins
25	⬤◯◯	The Ultimate St. John's/St. Mary's	St.J./St.M	3 hours
29	⬤◯◯	Rozel Bay – Coast and Hinterland	Tr./St.M	2 hours

⬤⬤⬤ VERY HARD

Walk		Walk Name	Parish	Time
11	◯⬤◖	Two Valleys	St. Lawrence	2 hours 20 mins
24	◯⬤◯	The Soul of St Ouen	St. Ouen	3 hours 20 mins
26	◯⬤◯	Byways and Paths – St. John's	St. John	1 hour 30 mins
27	◯⬤◯	Égypte	Trinity	2 hours
28	◯⬤◯	The Alternative Boulay Bay Hill Climb	Trinity	2 hours 15 mins

Degree of Difficulty Key

⬤◯◯	**EASY**
⬤⬤◯	**SOME DIFFICULTY**
⬤⬤⬤	**VERY HARD**

Bibliography

Walks For Motorists (1979)	F de L Bois
Jersey Rambles – Coast and Country (1992; revised 1997)	John Le Dain
Official Leisure Map	States of Jersey
Jersey Telephone Directory (2011)	Jersey Telecom
Jersey Street Guide	Ocean Publishing Corporation
Rambling Around Jersey (1991; Addendum 1994)	Kit Paget-Tomlinson
Island Walks (1991)	Beth Lloyd, Sue Hardy and Mike Stentiford
Tracks and Tales – 21 Coastal Walks (1988)	Mary Phillips
Handbook, Other Literature and Web-site	The National Trust for Jersey
Ballentine's History of Jersey	Marguerite Syvret and Joan Stevens
Old Jersey Houses	Joan Stevens
Old Jersey Houses – Volume 2	Joan Stevens
A Brief History of Jersey	Peter Hunt
The Sea was their Fortune	Roy McLoughlin
The Town of St. Helier	Edmund Toulmin Nicolle
Jersey Through the Lens	Richard Mayne and Joan Stevens
Portrait of the Channel Islands	Raoul Lempriere
The Bailiwick of Jersey	Jacquetta Hawks
Jersey Folk Lore	John H. L'Amy
Jersey - Witches, Ghosts and Traditions	Sonia Hillsdon
German Fortifications in Jersey	Michael Ginns and Peter Bryans
History of The Channel Islands	Raoul Lempriere
Jersey Evening Post (Various)	Jersey Evening Post
St Helier - A History and Celebration	Arthur Lamy
Grouville – The History of a Country Parish	Parish of Grouville, Edited by Rowland Anthony

Bibliography

St. Lawrence Jersey	Parish of St. Lawrence. Edited by Henry and Sheila Coutanche and Suzanne Le Feuvre
Jersey Long Ago – Book Three	Sonia Hillsdon and Geraint Jennings
The Boomer Legacy (La Moye Golf Club)	Peter E. Firth
A History of St. Ouen's Church (1993)	John Wileman
A Short History of the Church of St. Clement	Church Information Sheet
Parish Church of St. Brelade and the Fishermen's Chapel	Jarrold Publishing
Jersey's German Bunkers – Archive Book 9	Channel Islands Occupation Society (Jersey)
Batterie Lothringen – Archive Book 10	Channel Islands Occupation Society (Jersey)
4 Great Walks For You and Your Dog	JSPCA Animals Shelter
Pamphlets and Leaflets	Channel Islands Occupation Society (Jersey)
Pamphlets and Leaflets	The Jersey Heritage Trust
Pamphlets and Leaflets	The States of Jersey Planning and Environment Department
Booklets, Pamphlets and Leaflets	Jersey Tourism
Leaflets	The St. Martin Conservation Trust
Jersey Zoo	Durrell Wildlife Conservation Trust
Public Plaques and Information Boards en route	Various
Notes and background information	La Mare Vineyards and Distillery

Walkers' Notes

Walkers' Notes

Walkers' Notes